W9-BXC-687

DISCARD

JAMES LONGSTREET

Photograph by Cook Studio, Richmond

JAMES LONGSTREET

JAMES LONGSTREET

LEE'S WAR HORSE

BY

H. J. ECKENRODE

AND

BRYAN CONRAD

FOREWORD BY

GARY W. GALLAGHER

The University of North Carolina Press

Chapel Hill and London

To
DOUGLAS SOUTHALL FREEMAN
HISTORIAN, JOURNALIST, PUBLICIST

© 1936, 1986 The University of North Carolina Press
All rights reserved
Manufactured in the United States of America
99 98 97 96 95   8 7 6 5 4
Library of Congress Cataloging-in-Publication Data

Eckenrode, H. J. (Hamilton James), 1881–
James Longstreet: Lee's war horse.

Includes bibliographies and index.
1. Longstreet, James, 1821–1904. 2. Generals—
United States—Biography. 3. United States—Army—
Biography. 4. Confederate States of America. Army—
Biography. 5. United States—History—Civil War,
1861–1865—Campaigns. I. Conrad, Bryan. II. Title.
E467.1.L55E4   1986   973.7′3′0924   [B]   85-21000

ISBN 0-8078-1690-6

AUSTIN COMMUNITY COLLEGE
LEARNING RESOURCE SERVICES

CONTENTS

LIST OF MAPS

FOREWORD

JAMES LONGSTREET stood with Robert E. Lee and Stonewall Jackson in the great triumvirate of the Army of Northern Virginia. The title of his memoir, *From Manassas to Appomattox*, indicates the span of his service in the war. He commanded the First Corps of Lee's army from its creation in 1862 to the surrender in April 1865, and critical roles were his at Second Manassas, Fredericksburg, Gettysburg, Chickamauga, and the Wilderness. His magnificent conduct at Sharpsburg won him a sobriquet from Lee, who, when Longstreet reached headquarters late in the evening of that long and bloody day, grasped his lieutenant by the shoulders and said warmly, "Ah! here is Longstreet; here is my old *warhorse!*"[1] A stout fighter who took good care of his men, Longstreet was popular among soldiers in the ranks, who knew him affectionately as "Old Pete." He was Lee's most trusted subordinate after Jackson's death, on the battlefield a calm presence who, in the words a member of his staff, "was like a rock in steadiness when sometimes . . . the world seemed flying to pieces."[2] Combative to the end, he was with Lee at Appomattox when a Union officer approached bearing a message from Grant. "General," said Longstreet to his chief, "unless he offers us honorable terms, come back and let us fight it out."[3]

1. William Miller Owen, *In Camp and Battle with the Washington Artillery of New Orleans* (Boston, 1885; reprint ed., Gaithersburg, Md., n.d. [1982]), p. 157.
2. Gilbert Moxley Sorrel, *Recollections of a Confederate Staff Officer* (New York, 1905; reprint ed., Jackson, Tenn., 1958), p. 26.
3. Edward Porter Alexander, *Military Memoirs of a Confederate* (New York, 1907; reprint ed., Bloomington, Ind., 1962), p. 609.

Longstreet's record should have secured for him a position of honor beside Lee and Jackson in the postwar Confederate pantheon, but he became instead a beleaguered figure around whom political controversy swirled. His troubles began in 1867 in New Orleans, where he had settled after the war. Asked by a newspaper to give his views on continuing tensions between North and South, he urged southerners to accept their defeat on the battlefield and attempt to reconcile with the North. The day after the newspaper reported his response, Longstreet was startled to find that "old comrades passed me on the street without speaking." Much of the southern press quickly turned on him as a "deserter of my friends!" and a traitor guilty "of joining the enemy!" Clients withdrew from his previously successful cotton brokerage, and, unable to make a living in New Orleans, he eventually turned to General Grant and other northern friends, became a Republican, and accepted appointment to a succession of federal offices.[4]

Further injuring Longstreet's standing among many ex-Confederates was his candid view—first expressed publicly to a northern journalist in late 1865—that Lee had committed several blunders during the Gettysburg campaign.[5] The canonization of Lee was well under way by the early 1870s, and its orchestrators, men such as William Nelson Pendleton, Jubal A. Early, and J. William Jones, felt compelled to absolve him of all responsibility for the defeat at Gettysburg. Episcopal Bishop Pendleton, Lee's former chief of artillery, fixed the blame on Longstreet in an address at the 1873 dedication of the Lee Chapel in Lexington, Virginia.[6] Later

4. James Longstreet, *From Manassas to Appomattox* (Philadelphia, 1896; reprint ed., Bloomington, Ind., 1960), pp. xviii–xix, 635–38 (quotations on page 637).

5. The journalist was William Swinton, who cited Longstreet in his *Campaigns of the Army of the Potomac* (New York, 1866).

6. For a discussion of Longstreet's problems with the promulgators of the Lee cult, see Thomas L. Connelly and Barbara L. Bellows, *God*

attacks questioned Longstreet's performance on other fields
as well and suggested that Lee had thought little of his
abilities. Typical was an article in which Early pronounced it
a "fact well known in the whole army that General Longstreet was very slow in his movements on all occasions."
Dragging his feet as usual on both the second and third days
at Gettysburg, he had frittered away any chance for southern
success. Longstreet's "overweening vanity and egotism" prevented his shouldering any responsibility, concluded Early,
and prompted him to claim "the highest honors of that and
all other campaigns of the Army of Northern Virginia, by
depreciating its commander."[7]

Stung by these assaults on his reputation, Longstreet answered in newspapers, magazines, and his memoir of 1896.[8]
Always he made clear that he had "the greatest affection for
General Lee and the greatest reverence for his memory."
Their relations had been "affectionate, confidential, and
even tender"; only with "a reluctant spirit" did he offer his
judgment that at Gettysburg Lee "lost the matchless equi-
poise that usually characterized him." Thrown from balance

---

and *General Longstreet: The Lost Cause and the Southern Mind* (Baton
Rouge, La., 1982). Pendleton's speech, which he repeated many times
thoughout the South, was published in the *Southern Magazine* 15 (December 1874). Jubal Early had made substantially the same arguments against
Longstreet a year earlier at Lexington in a less publicized address. Susan P.
Lee, *Memoirs of William Nelson Pendleton* (Philadelphia, 1893), pp. 285–
86.

7. Jubal A. Early, "Reply to General Longstreet's Second Paper," in
Southern Historical Society Papers, ed. by J. William Jones et al., 52 vols.
and 2 vol. index (1876–1959; reprint ed., New York, 1977–80), 5: 275,
287. Many of the participants in the Gettysburg controversy aired their
views in the *Southern Historical Society Papers*.

8. Longstreet's writings include *From Manassas to Appomattox*, two
articles in the *Philadelphia Weekly Times* (reprinted by that newspaper in
The Annals of the War, Written by Leading Participants North and South
[Philadelphia, 1879] and in vol. 5 of the *Southern Historical Society
Papers*), and several pieces in *Battles and Leaders of the Civil War* (ed. by
Robert Underwood Johnson and Clarence Clough Buel, 4 vols. [New York,
1887]).

by "too great confidence in the prowess of his troops and . . . by the deplorable absence of General Stuart," Lee performed in a manner that betrayed "a great mind disturbed by unparalleled conditions."[9] Manfully, for he knew to do so would stir a hornet's nest, Longstreet asserted in each of his publications that Lee should have accepted his plan to take the tactical defensive in Pennsylvania.

The debate raged for years. Most former members of the First Corps agreed with Major Thomas Goree, who wrote Longstreet that "Pendleton has presumed upon your present unpopularity to make charges he otherwise would not have dared to utter." "Although we may differ in our political opinions," Goree added, "it has made no difference in my kindly feelings towards you personally, and I trust that it never will." Such sentiments from those who had served under him deeply touched Longstreet, who thanked Goree for the "tender feeling of friendship that you express and cherish. . . . 'Twould be strange indeed if the bonds of four years of severe service in a common cause . . . could be severed by time or trials." A private in Hood's Texas Brigade, speaking for many an old First Corps infantryman, observed: "I have heard since the war some censure cast at General Longstreet for Lee's defeat at Gettysburg, but heard nothing of the kind from the battling soldier who was a participant in the great struggle."[10]

9. James Longstreet, "Lee in Pennsylvania," in *Annals of the War*, p. 433.

10. Goree to Longstreet, 17 May 1875, and Longstreet to Goree, 21 May 1875, in Langston James Goree, V, ed., *The Thomas Jewett Goree Letters: Volume I, The Civil War Correspondence* (Bryan, Tex., 1981), pp. 285–89; William Andrew Fletcher, *Rebel Private Front and Rear* (Beaumont, Tex., 1908; reprint ed., Austin, Tex., 1954), p. 63. Goree had been on Longstreet's staff. For other friendly estimates by members of the First Corps, see Alexander, *Military Memoirs of a Confederate*; Sorrel, *Recollections of a Confederate Staff Officer*; Owen, *In Camp and Battle with the Washington Artillery*; and John Cheves Haskell, *The Haskell Memoirs* (ed. by Gilbert E. Govan and James W. Livingood [New York, 1960]).

Southern veterans in general found it difficult to criticize Lee, however, and the written consensus ran strongly against Longstreet. Fitzhugh Lee, Richard Taylor, and other respected officers added their voices to the chorus begun by Pendleton and Early.[11] A devastating blow came just months before Longstreet's death in the form of General John B. Gordon's reminiscences. An immensely popular figure who had commanded Lee's Second Corps in the latter stages of the war, Gordon averred that "impartial military critics" thought Longstreet's slowness in executing Lee's orders had brought defeat at Gettysburg. Gordon's most damning passage stated that "General Lee died believing (the testimony on this point is overwhelming) that he lost Gettysburg at last by Longstreet's disobedience of orders."[12]

The bitter controversy made Longstreet a lonely figure for much of his later life, "surrounded by a few of my old friends, and in occasional appreciative touch with others, North and South."[13] Social invitations were rare, and the United Confederate Veterans, dominated by John B. Gordon and Fitzhugh Lee, did not invite him to their grand reunions. "Everywhere except in the South," Longstreet wrote in 1894, "soldiers are accepted as comrades upon equal terms without regard to their political affiliations." But the U.C.V. had been "started for political purposes" and was not a proper veterans organization. Finding grim humor in a situation that barred him—the most famous living Confederate general—from the leading association of ex-Confederates, Longstreet remarked that he "had come to regard it as a high compliment to be excluded from the U.C.V., as my absence becomes more conspicuous than would my presence."[14] Longstreet

11. For the views of Lee and Taylor, see their articles in vol. 5 of the *Southern Historical Society Papers.*

12. John B. Gordon, *Reminiscences of the Civil War* (New York, 1903), pp. 160–61.

13. Longstreet, *Manassas to Appomattox*, p. 638.

14. Longstreet to Goree, 7 July 1894, *Goree Letters*, pp. 329–30. The

died in January 1904, a grizzled warrior estranged from much of his native South.

Before a year had passed, Helen D. Longstreet published *Lee and Longstreet at High Tide: Gettysburg in the Light of the Official Records*. Completed before Longstreet's death, this passionate defense specifically refuted Pendleton and Gordon's versions of Gettysburg and emphasized the closeness of Lee and Longstreet. Citing letters from Lee that gave ample evidence of affection, Mrs. Longstreet stressed that her husband bore "for General Lee the most profound love and respect." As a professional soldier, she went on, Longstreet discerned both strengths and weaknesses in Lee: he was brilliant in strategical movements and "absolutely perfect" as a defensive fighter but possessed a "headlong combativeness" that hampered his performance in offensive combat. "At Gettysburg," Mrs. Longstreet quoted her husband as saying, "all the vast interests at stake and the improbability of success would not deter him. In the immediate presence of the enemy General Lee's mind, at all other times calm and clear, became excited."[15] Significantly, the introduction for Mrs. Longstreet's book came not from the pen of a former Confederate but from that of Major General Daniel E. Sickles, the Union officer who had opposed Longstreet on July 2 at Gettysburg. It is doubtful that her labor of love changed many minds in the South, where neither statues nor a biography honored her husband.

Sons of Confederate Veterans proved equally hostile to Longstreet; not until 1961, "eighty-three years and 1246 camps after the first SCV camp was founded," did a group in Richmond take the name James Longstreet Camp. John C. Stinson (one of the camp's founders) to the author, 29 June 1985.

15. Helen D. Longstreet, *Lee and Longstreet at High Tide: Gettysburg in Light of the Official Records* (Gainesville, Ga., 1904), pp. 82–84. Forty-two years younger than Longstreet, Helen Dortch married the widowed general in 1897. She lived until 1962, defending her husband's name to the end. See *Newsweek*, 29 January 1962, p. 22.

In 1933, three decades after Longstreet's death, Hamilton J. Eckenrode decided the time had come for his biography. Trained in history at Johns Hopkins University, Eckenrode was historian of the Virginia Commission on Conservation and Development and the author of books on Rutherford B. Hayes, Jefferson Davis, Nathan Bedford Forrest, and various aspects of Virginia history. In December 1933, he wrote William T. Couch of the University of North Carolina Press that he had "learned a great deal" about Longstreet in studying the Virginia battlefields and thought a book about him "would be timely." Between G. F. R. Henderson's magisterial study of Jackson and Douglas Southall Freeman's forthcoming multivolume biography of Lee, justice had been done to those two Confederate giants, leaving Longstreet, in Eckenrode's view, "the only notable figure of the Civil War who has not yet been covered." "I should be glad to enter into a contract with you to write this biography," Eckenrode told Couch in closing, "if you care to undertake it." Four months later Couch answered in the affirmative.[16]

By the time he received Couch's reply, Eckenrode had decided to bring in as collaborator Colonel Bryan Conrad, his assistant at the Commission on Conservation and Development. Both men were Virginians. Conrad had served thirty years in the army and seen action during the Spanish-American War, along the Mexican border under General John J. Pershing, and in Europe during World War I. He had a profound knowledge of Civil War battlegrounds, especially around Richmond, and an admiration for Stonewall Jackson amounting to worship. Eckenrode hoped Couch would "see

16. Eckenrode to Couch, 22 December 1933; Couch to Eckenrode, 23 April 1934; biographical sketch of Eckenrode; University of North Carolina Press Records, University Archives, Wilson Library, University of North Carolina at Chapel Hill (cited hereafter as UNCPR). See also the obituary for Eckenrode in the Fredericksburg, Virginia, *Free Lance–Star*, 29 September 1952, p. 2.

the great importance of having a trained soldier associated with the writing of a military biography."[17]

Working against an initial deadline of December 1934, Eckenrode and Conrad at first proceeded swiftly. Eckenrode informed Couch that he expected the book to be "a revelation to students of the Civil War, as Longstreet's career has never been presented before, and it is an extremely important part of the war." Later in the year Eckenrode's administrative duties and an illness that struck Conrad slowed progress, however, and Couch began to worry. In February 1935, he wrote Eckenrode that "another manuscript on Longstreet—one that we are told is excellent—is now floating around looking for a publisher." The Press would not consider it, he added, unless Eckenrode and Conrad had abandoned their project. Doubtless spurred on by the appearance of a rival, Eckenrode promised the manuscript by April; it was almost finished, but before sending it to Chapel Hill he and Conrad wanted "the best military experts in the country" to review it. Agreeing that experts should go over the text, Couch emphasized how little time remained if the book were to be out in time to get a share of the Christmas trade. [18]

The manuscript arrived in May. Couch liked it and immediately sought confirmation of his judgment from the logical person, Douglas Southall Freeman, whose recently published *R. E. Lee* had won great acclaim. Freeman declined to read the manuscript, but did offer advice: "If I were you, I would not bother to get anyone to read a biography of Longstreet coming from Dr. Eckenrode and Colonel Conrad. They are both thoroughly competent students and . . . you may assume the manuscript is wholly satisfactory from a historical

17. Eckenrode to Couch, 24 April 1934, UNCPR; obituaries for Conrad in the Richmond *Times-Dispatch*, 22 June 1953, p. 19, and the Hampden-Sydney Alumni Association *Record*, October 1953, pp. 11–12.

18. Eckenrode to Couch, 17 May 1934, 1 March 1935, 1 April 1935; Couch to Eckenrode, 27 February 1935, 5 April 1935; UNCPR.

point of view." Couch informed Eckenrode near the end of June that, although he had been unable to find a qualified reader, the book would be out in the fall. Late revisions pushed back the date of publication to early 1936.[19]

Critical reaction to *James Longstreet: Lee's War Horse* demonstrated that opinion about the general remained sharply divided. Many reviewers took time to plead cases for or against Longstreet. The scholars who evaluated it for two leading American historical journals were Thomas Robson Hay and Donald B. Sanger, both, as it happened, strong partisans of Longstreet and the eventual authors of another biography of him. Writing in the *American Historical Review*, Hay called *Lee's War Horse* "the most sweeping indictment of the man and his methods yet published." Its emphasis upon Longstreet's ambition and extreme self-confidence, and upon his concern for his own advancement above all else, was "neither fair to Longstreet nor to the cause he served." Hay also deplored the absence of full documentation and a bibliography.[20]

Sanger's dissertation was the Longstreet manuscript that Couch had mentioned to Eckenrode in January 1935. In the *Mississippi Valley Historical Review*, he accused the authors of bias against their subject and unwillingness to grant General Longstreet a fair hearing. By limiting their citations and forgoing a bibliography, they obscured the sources upon which they based their slanted account. "The authors do not know General Longstreet," Sanger concluded. "The world must wait patiently for a scholarly and just assessment of the life, character, and services of Lee's 'War Horse.'"[21]

Other scholars did not think the book unfair to Longstreet. Robert D. Meade, later the biographer of Judah P.

19. Couch to Freeman, 30 May 1935; Couch to Eckenrode, 27 June 1935; Freeman to Couch, 31 May 1935; UNCPR.
20. *American Historical Review* 42 (January 1937): 368–69.
21. *Mississippi Valley Historical Review* 23 (September 1936): 276–78.

Benjamin, commended Eckenrode and Conrad for "the real-
istic treatment of their subject." They had employed careful
research and committed "only a few errors." Meade thought
their handling of Longstreet at Gettysburg was, if anything,
too kind: "Although the authors are free to admit his failings
in most cases, they feel that he was given too much blame for
the results of this battle. They shift more of the responsibility
here to Lee than do many critics." Alone among the scholarly
reviewers, Meade applauded the decision to avoid lengthy
footnotes that might intimidate general readers. The opinion
of Haywood Pearce, Jr., of Emory University, was that the
book recognized Longstreet's "rugged strength and military
abilities" but did not "hesitate to lay bare the faults of his
character." The authors' conclusions might be harsh, but
their product for the most part was "a very clear, though
sometimes sketchy and foreshortened, exposition of the salient features of terrain, strategic objectives, and tactical
movements involved in the various campaigns and battles in
which Longstreet figured."[22]

In addition to the learned journals, many popular magazines, influenced presumably by a surge of interest in the
Civil War following Freeman's *R. E. Lee* and Margaret
Mitchell's *Gone With the Wind*, also carried reviews of Eckenrode and Conrad's *Longstreet*. These typically summarized
the book with little if any analysis of its merits and weaknesses. The review in *Time* was representative, concentrating
on Gettysburg and postwar difficulties, the two aspects of
Longstreet's story best known to the public.[23]

Over the years, *James Longstreet: Lee's War Horse* increasingly came to be viewed as a severely critical treatment.
One reason for this was that it contrasted sharply with the

22. *North Carolina Historical Review* 14 (January 1937): 92–95; *Jour-
nal of Southern History* 2 (November 1936): 544–45.

23. *Time*, 30 March 1936, pp. 92–94. For another review of this type,
see *Harper's*, May 1936.

two subsequent biographies of Longstreet. Sanger and Hay's study, published by Louisiana State University Press in 1952, was, in the words of a prominent student of Lee's army, "sympathetic to the point of being eulogistic."[24] According to Sanger, who wrote the chapters on the war, Longstreet was the "best fighting general in the armies of the Confederacy and the best corps commander, North or South." Dismissing Eckenrode and Conrad's work by implication, Sanger stated confidently that his was "the first extended critical study of General Longstreet."[25]

Twenty-seven years later there appeared a third biography, Wilbur Thomas's *General James "Pete" Longstreet, Lee's "Old War Horse," Scapegoat for Gettysburg.* Thomas undertook to defend Longstreet, mounting in the process a shrill attack on Eckenrode and Conrad. Their apparent purpose, he said, had been "to destroy beyond redemption in the minds of his people one of the South's greatest soldiers." Their work amounted to nothing more than "groundless villification [*sic*]" made up of "insinuations, innuendoes, and assumptions often bordering on if not actually crossing the line of libel."[26]

Analysis of *James Longstreet: Lee's War Horse* would be out of place here—readers will no doubt prefer to draw their own conclusions. But some attention to the question of Eckenrode and Conrad's purported vilification of Longstreet is in order. The authors certainly saw serious defects in his

24. James I. Robertson, Jr., in his introduction to a reprint edition of Longstreet's *From Manassas to Appomattox* (Bloomington, Ind., 1960), p. xxiv.

25. Donald Bridgman Sanger and Thomas Robson Hay, *James Longstreet: I. Soldier, II. Politician, Officeholder, and Writer* (Baton Route, La., 1952), p. 3. This is not a true collaborative work. Sanger died before he could carry Longstreet's story beyond Appomattox; LSU Press commissioned Hay to write the postwar chapters.

26. Wilbur Thomas, *General James "Pete" Longstreet, Lee's "Old War Horse," Scapegoat for Gettysburg* (Parson, W. Va.: McClain Printing Company, 1979), p. xiv.

personality, most notably unbridled ambition, extreme self-confidence, and stubbornness. They ascribe to him a desire, usually successful, to impose his will upon fellow Confederates, often to the detriment of the southern cause. He was a poor subordinate, they argue, who sulked and dragged his feet when his counsel went unheeded. This behavior marred Longstreet's performances at Seven Pines, South Mountain, and elsewhere. "If he could have forgotten himself," they suggest, "he would have risen to great heights. But he never forgot himself—or very rarely—and so only a few times he reached the summits where the lofty dwell."[27]

This sense of wasted potential is central to most of the authors' critical judgments. In the heat of combat, where there was no time to think of himself, they see Longstreet at his best. Possessed of "great physical and moral courage" and the "perfect natural equipment for a soldier," he was a brilliant tactician whose imperturbable demeanor on the battlefield exerted a "marvelous influence over men." Amid crises at Sharpsburg, Chickamauga, and the Wilderness, Longstreet displayed gifts that gave evidence of vast capabilities. Sadly, he usually succumbed to a "thirst and hunger for fame and high position."[28]

The last word on James Longstreet is yet to appear. Meanwhile, he has continued to inspire able supporters and antagonists. Michael Shaara's Pulitzer Prize-winning novel *The Killer Angels* offers an engrossing and sympathetic portrait of Longstreet during the Gettysburg campaign. Tom Wicker's equally powerful *Unto This Hour*, which centers on the battle of Second Manassas, manages to argue both cases through the respective eyes of Longstreet's and Stonewall Jackson's soldiers. Thomas L. Connelly's explorations of the cult of the Lost Cause cast Longstreet in a favorable light. In

27. The quotation is on page 370.
28. The quotations are on pages 365–67.

contrast, Robert K. Krick has presented a most unflattering estimate of his actions on the second day at Gettysburg.[29] And so the literature grows. For those who would understand that literature, *James Longstreet: Lee's War Horse* is an interesting and necessary stopping place.

Several friends helped in the preparation of this short introduction. Barnes F. Lathrop, Michael Parrish, and Stephen Rowe took time from their own work to give it a critical reading, as did Allan Purcell, who also made available many volumes from his fine personal library. Pamela Upton of the editorial department at the University of North Carolina Press provided copies of the Couch-Eckenrode correspondence and other materials relating to the production of *Lee's War Horse*. Waverly Winfree of the Virginia Historical Society supplied information on Bryan Conrad. Their contributions strengthened the introduction—and also made working on it more enjoyable.

GARY W. GALLAGHER

Austin, Texas
July 1985

---

29. Michael Shaara, *The Killer Angels* (New York, 1974); Tom Wicker, *Unto This Hour* (New York, 1984); Connelly and Bellows, *God and General Longstreet*; Robert K. Krick, "'I Consider Him A Humbug' —McLaws, on Longstreet at Gettysburg," *The Maryland Line* 5 (May 1985): 8–10.

PREFACE

THIS VOLUME is an attempt to solve the great problem of the War of Secession, which is the relation between Lee and his corps commander, James Longstreet. The South's chance of winning the war rested mainly with Lee, or, rather, with the Lee-Jackson combination, which far outshone any combination on the other side. But the combination was, in reality, Lee-Jackson-Longstreet. The question as to how far Lee's strategy and the fate of the Confederacy were influenced by Longstreet is highly important, for it is certain that both were so influenced.

The matter has been dealt with at some length by Dr. Douglas Southall Freeman in his recent life of Lee, but more remains to be said, particularly on Longstreet's side. The present book discusses the relations of Longstreet to both his commanders, Joseph E. Johnston and Robert E. Lee, in considerable detail. It also gives possibly the first inclusive and detailed account of the Battle of Seven Pines and the most carefully worked out story of the Seven Days battles around Richmond in 1862, both accounts having been prepared by the authors after a most extended examination of the ground.

Longstreet's great influence in the Sharpsburg and Chancellorsville campaigns is pointed out, and the account of Gettysburg, which so deeply concerns Longstreet, has been prepared with the greatest care. The same thing is true of Chickamauga and the East Tennessee campaign. Then the story goes on to the Wilderness and to the end of the war.

Prepared by the authors from the official records, after a

careful examination of the ground around Richmond and at Manassas and Fredericksburg, as well as around Sharpsburg and Gettysburg, it offers new points of view on the Civil War and adds new material. Unnecessary technical detail is avoided, however, and every effort is made to make the story clear to the lay reader.

The book is essentially a military narrative, though Longstreet's career both before and after the war of 1861–1865 is related. A very careful analysis is made of the character and qualities of one of the leading commanders in American history, one whose life story, curiously enough, is now written for the first time. The Lee literature fills shelves in a library. This is the pioneer work on the career of James Longstreet.

H. J. ECKENRODE
BRYAN CONRAD

Richmond, 1936

JAMES LONGSTREET

CHAPTER I

BEGINNINGS AND START IN LIFE

JAMES LONGSTREET is one of the truly controversial characters in American history; in view of this fact it is singular that more has not been written about him. Although he was one of the leading soldiers of the South in the War between the States, a member of the trinity of Lee, Jackson, and Longstreet, a large literature has not gathered about him as it has about the others. The scribbling of biographies of Lee seems to be a favorite amusement of life-writers, and recently one of the finest works in American military history has been based on his character and deeds. But Longstreet has not been so honored, although the history of the War between the States cannot be understood without a knowledge of his career.

The man about whom one of the main controversies in American history has raged, and still rages, was born in Edgefield District, South Carolina, on January 8, 1821. But although Longstreet came from the Southern South, was the son of a planter, and was thus thoroughly Southern in environment and rearing, there was something curiously un-Southern about him. He was serious and stolid, not romantic as proper Southerners of that age were, more materialistic than idealistic. Perhaps ancestry had something to do with it, as Gamaliel Bradford has suggested, for some of his ancestors were from New Jersey and were Dutch in blood. Langestraat is the name originally, and there is something Dutch-like in Longstreet's physical massiveness and excessive stubbornness.

3

Longstreet spent his early years in the country, where he acquired his exceptional physical strength and endurance. Southern life in that period gave an unrivaled opportunity for physical development to those who chose to make use of it, in the sport life of the people, who put their children on steeds as soon as they were weaned, and taught them the use of firearms from the time that they were able to raise a gun.

The Longstreets were leading people in the lower South, and James Longstreet was connected with well-known families, such as the Randolphs and Marshalls of Virginia, and the Dents, who, his widow tells us, could trace their ancestry back to William the Conqueror, from whom it is possible James Longstreet fancied he inherited his military talent. The Dent relationship was important, because Longstreet's mother was Mary Ann Dent, closely akin to the lady who became the wife of U. S. Grant. Because of this connection, Longstreet and Grant knew each other well, and the latter, when president of the United States, befriended the former when he was only a poor ex-Confederate.

Longstreet was named for his father, James Longstreet. The latter's father was William Longstreet, one of the numerous inventors of the steamboat. He constructed a craft that ran for some miles on the Savannah River near the end of the eighteenth century. But he did not have means enough to develop the idea, and the Georgia authorities, to whom he applied, would give him no aid. So he suffered the fate of Fitch and Rumsey, and Robert Fulton carried off the prize.[1]

When Longstreet was twelve years old, his father died,

---

[1] Helen D. Longstreet, *Lee and Longstreet at High Tide; Gettysburg in the Light of the Official Records* (Gainesville, Ga., published by the author, 1905, [c. 1904]), p 97. Hereafter cited as *Lee and Longstreet*.

and this event caused a radical change in his life. His mother went to live in Augusta, Georgia, and then in Alabama. James Longstreet was reared by his uncle, Judge A. B. Longstreet, one of the leading Southerners of the time. President of Emory College, at Oxford, Georgia (quite a place in that time of modest schools), he was also a lawyer and judge. More than all that, he was a writer, a humorist. His *Georgia Scenes* is one of the most notable books produced in the South before the War between the States and is readable today.

A cousin in Alabama, who happened to be a member of Congress, determined the fate of James Longstreet by obtaining for him an appointment to the United States Military Academy at West Point. He was just sixteen years old, an early age to enter the military academy. In later years he recalled his experiences, typical of a green country boy, on what was then a long and perilous journey, from Georgia to West Point, New York. In passing through New York City, he had the customary adventure of those times with youthful "bunco steerers," as they used to be called in the good old days. A kind policeman rescued him and sent him on his way.

When he reached the decidedly primitive military academy of those days, which did not even have bathing facilities for the cadets, he was disillusioned to find that he would have to keep his own room and black his boots. There were no smiling ebony faces there such as he was accustomed to. All was hard, stern, cold.

At West Point, Longstreet did everything well that called for physical exertion. His widow, with pardonable idealization of a man she had not known in his youth, says that "He was very large, very strong, well proportioned. He had dark-brown hair, blue eyes, features that might have served for a Grecian model. He was six feet two inches tall, of soldierly bearing, and was voted the handsomest cadet at West Point." [2] As for his handsome features, one must have taken them on faith in middle life, for he had one of the largest, bushiest, most luxuriant beards in North America.

As a student he did not do well. His singularly perfect physical being seems to have overshadowed his mentality. In his third year he failed in mechanics but succeeded in making the class on a second trial. At that time he must have been near dismissal for lack of application. He was always near the foot of the class and was graduated little higher than his friend, Ulysses S. Grant. But successful soldiers are usually physical men, first and foremost, and both Longstreet and Grant were destined to surpass in rank and fame the other men of their class, the mental lights, the good boys, the pride of their parents. One conjectures that Longstreet was not a very good boy, that he was given to pranks, and that he might have told a fine tale of schoolboy escapades if he had so chosen.

After he was graduated, in the class of 1842, Longstreet was assigned to the Fourth Infantry and sent to Jefferson Barracks near St. Louis, then a famous Western military post. With him was his schoolmate and friend, Ulysses S. Grant, of the class of 1843. Much hinged on this fact. Longstreet had a fair cousin living near by, Julia Dent. It was Longstreet who conducted Lieutenant Grant to the Dent home and introduced him to Julia. Five years later Julia Dent and Grant were married.

In May, 1844, the young lieutenant, who had been enjoying life at Jefferson Barracks, was sent to Louisiana near Fort Jessup. There was organized "The Army of Observation" under that notable old Indian fighter, General Zachary

2 *Lee and Longstreet,* p. 100.

Taylor. In March, 1845, Longstreet was assigned to the Eighth Infantry, which he joined at St. Augustine. The Mexican War was then near the point of breaking out.

"The Army of Observation" was sent to Corpus Christi, Texas, when the Lone Star republic became a part of the United States. By mid-October, 1845, a little force of about four thousand men had gathered. Many of the leading army officers were there, including Taylor, Worth, and Twiggs; and Longstreet found life in that region, with its admirable opportunities for outdoor sport, much to his liking.

In March, 1846, Taylor was ordered to the Rio Grande at Matamoras. Across the wild and fenceless plains of Texas the column moved, with wild horses, deer, and antelope scampering in the distance. It was a life full of color and vividness for an adventurous young man. At a place called Arroyo Colorado, Mexican lancers blocked the way and forbade further advance, but retreated when Taylor brought up his batteries and threatened to open on them.

Things were anything but quiet in the American camp on the Rio Grande. Sentries and single soldiers were constantly being murdered by Mexicans, until presently small skirmishes began to take place between American dragoons and Mexicans. Then followed the engagement of Palo Alto, at which Longstreet was present but in which he does not seem to have taken part, as it was more of a contest between batteries of artillery than a battle. Finding the body of a woman after the action, Longstreet, young and impressionable, began to moralize on the horrors of war but was too healthy-minded to dwell long on such scenes.

At Resaca de la Palma, the infantry was seriously engaged, and the Eighth lost several officers killed and wounded, one of them a classmate of Longstreet's. Taylor sent the dragoons against the Mexican guns and there was a splendid charge in the good old romantic style. The infantry had to wade a lagoon. Passing the stream, the soldiers took the chance to drink but Longstreet tells us that he utilized the moment's pause to think of the girl he left behind him. "I drew her daguerreotype from my breast-pocket, had a glint of her charming smile, and with quickened spirit mounted the bank in time to send some of the mixed infantry troops to relieve May of his charge of the captive knight." [3] One feels that Longstreet did not linger over the photograph long. He paid his tribute to a romantic age and then went back to the practical details of war, for such was his nature.

Longstreet accompanied Scott's army in its invasion of Mexico. The army landed at Vera Cruz in March, 1847, and took that town after a siege. Then Scott advanced across the mountains on the city of Mexico. Longstreet went through all of this brilliant campaign. At Churubusco, on August 19-20, 1847, the Eighth Infantry made a name for itself, capturing prisoners and guns. At a moment of crisis, Longstreet carried the regimental colors.

Molino del Rey and Chapultepec followed in September. The first affair was a hard-fought battle in which the Americans suffered considerable loss. Longstreet's regiment was engaged and he went through a hot action without a scratch.

He was not so fortunate at Chapultepec, which was stormed on September 13. Longstreet's regiment was in the charge, but Longstreet himself was shot through the thigh while carrying the regimental flag. Pickett, afterwards famous, picked up the flag and bore it to victory.

Longstreet was given quarters in a native home in Mex-

<hr />

[3] James Longstreet, *From Manassas to Appomattox; Memoirs of the Civil War in America* (Philadelphia, J. B. Lippincott Company, c. 1895), p. 28. Hereafter cited as *M. to A.* The quotations from this book are made by permission of the publishers, J. B. Lippincott Company, Philadelphia, Penna.

ico City. There he received kind attention from his enemies, and by December 1, 1847, had sufficiently recovered to travel. Always he had enormous recuperative powers. He returned home with a month's leave and immediately set about the serious business of getting married. On March 8, 1848, he wedded Marie Louise Garland, daughter of his former brigade commander, Colonel John Garland. The ceremony took place at Lynchburg, Virginia. The marriage seems to have been a happy one and was certainly fruitful, for ten children were born to it.

By the autumn of 1848, Longstreet found himself back in the Jefferson Barracks. He remained with his regiment for some years, serving in the Indian campaigns in the West, of which he might have left a vivid account but did not. In fact, his early career is singularly little known. In 1855 he left the line and became a major in the paymaster department.

One would like to know more of this step. Apparently, it was taken because Longstreet despaired of preferment in the line. He says himself that his early ambitions had left him, though they were, in fact, only quiescent. But the better pay, essential for the head of a growing family, must have been alluring to the poor army officer, with no outside means. At all events, he bade farewell to arms and took up the prosaic task of making and paying accounts, wholly ignorant of the future in store for him. He had bade farewell to arms? Beyond doubt he thought he had. Living at Albuquerque, New Mexico, with a congenial if small society and with good opportunities for sport, Longstreet passed a quiet and not unpleasant interval before the resumption of his active military career.

CHAPTER II

THE GREAT ADVENTURE

LONGSTREET had renounced ambition, given up all hope of military fame, solacing himself with the irresponsible and pleasant life as an army paymaster stationed in the interesting and always picturesque New Mexico of that day. Unimaginative and rather buoyant by temperament, enjoying hugely the physical side of life, with an enviable capacity for food and drink, Longstreet was not apprehensive as the war clouds mounted in the sky at the beginning of 1861. The officers at Albuquerque, a congenial group amidst an alien population, half Northerners, half Southerners, hoped against hope that there would be no separation and no civil war, that the politicians would rig up some sort of compromise that would tide over the crisis, as they had done so often in the past. But this time the politicians' magic failed and, one day, the anxious watchers on the flat roof of a fort building saw a mail coach come dashing up in a cloud of dust. The coach stopped, the mailbags were taken out, and presently the consternation-struck officers were reading the dread news of the bombardment of Fort Sumter. War! The President of the United States calling for volunteers! The President of the Confederate States making proclamations! It had come at last.

Brother officers sought to prevail on Longstreet not to give up his comfortable berth, to remain in the United States army. But Longstreet met them with the argument, "What would you do if your state seceded?" and that silenced them.[1] No thought of the Union's being greater than the states seems to have entered the minds of the officers at Albuquerque. The war was simply that of one group of states against another.

Longstreet sent in his resignation from his office as major, with its salary, and—the future utterly unknown—departed from Albuquerque, accompanied by some of his friends, who rode a distance with him and with sorrow saw him disappear. Longstreet nearly always had friends, many friends. His self-assertiveness, his abounding health and virility drew people to him.

Passing by Fort Craig, on the opposite side of the Rio Grande, he stayed a night at Fort Fillmore, busy telling friends good-by. "How long will the war last?" some one asked him.

"At least three years," Longstreet answered, "and if it holds out for five years you may begin to look for a dictator."

To this Lieutenant Ryan, of the Seventh Infantry, responded, "If we are to have a dictator, I hope you may be the man."

It is characteristic of Longstreet that he tells this story quite complacently. Longstreet, too, thought that he would make a good dictator if dictators should come in season.

On his way, Longstreet, who seems to have been dubious as to the reception of his resignation in Washington, was relieved by getting word that it had been accepted and would take effect on the first of June. On that day he would be separated from Uncle Sam's payroll, a sad necessity. Already Longstreet was planning to become a paymaster of the new Confederate government. He seems to have had no thought of becoming an officer of the line and winning

[1] *M. to A.*, p. 29.

glory. Though, who knows? Perhaps even then, as he bumped along in the stagecoach over the sage fields, he was seeing the smoke of battles, seeing himself saluted by cheering men.

At all events his pulse quickened when he came to El Paso and passed into Texas and the territory of the new republic. At El Paso everything was excitement and enthusiasm. There Longstreet heard for the first time the strains of "Dixie" and the "Bonnie Blue Flag," tunes that were to stick in his ears for four years, and indeed until the end of life. There his regrets began to pass away as he came into the full current of a great national movement.

At El Paso Longstreet parted from his wife and family, whom he was not to see again for some time. The family went on to San Antonio by train while he chose the shorter route by stagecoach. On this journey Longstreet characteristically took under his wing two young Northern laborers on their way home, guaranteeing to see them through the Confederate lines. At Galveston they all shipped for New Orleans, where the Northerners found means to reach Union territory. Longstreet himself took the train for Richmond.

The nearer the train got to Virginia, the greater the excitement. Longstreet says, "At every station old men, women, and children assembled, clapping hands and waving handkerchiefs to cheer the passengers on to Richmond. On crossing the Virginia line, the feeling seemed to culminate. The windows and doors of every farmhouse and hamlet were occupied, and from them came hearty salutations that cheered us on to Richmond. The spirit electrified the air, and the laborers of the fields, white and black, stopped their ploughs to lift their hats and wave us on to speedy travel. At stations where meals were served, the proprietors, in response to offers to settle, said, 'Meals for those going on to join Jeff Davis are paid.' " [2]

Arriving in Richmond on June 29, 1861, Longstreet found himself in the center of the whirlpool. The city was crowded with soldiers and politicians and office seekers and speculators and every other human species, its hotel capacity so swamped that sleeping quarters were hard to find. Longstreet, reporting at once to the War Department, presided over by L. Q. Walker, had asked to be assigned to the pay department. With him, ambition was over. At least he fancied it was over, that bitterly ambitious heart! "I had given up all aspirations of military honor," he says, "and thought to settle down into more peaceful pursuits."

Shortly Longstreet discovered that West Point graduates were considered to be too precious to be squandered on dishing out the monthly dole to privates. They were needed to command the herds of soldiers who, in every uniform under the sun and in no uniform, thronged the streets of the Southern capital. On July 1, our unambitious seeker of peaceful pursuits must have felt his heart leap within him when he was given a commission as brigadier general and assigned to Beauregard at Manassas Station. What luck! Given a brigadier's commission and shipped off to the front, the best front! One wonders how Longstreet, late paymaster, obtained a brigadier's commission. No doubt his military record was well known to Jefferson Davis. Probably, too, something of Longstreet's solidity, his bigness, his calm self-assurance in that boiling human cauldron inspired confidence. Anyway he was boosted to high honors at once. Many well-known men were colonels while he was a brigadier general.

Taking the train Longstreet reached Manassas on July 2.

[2] *M. to A.*, p. 32.

Beauregard, glad to welcome a graduate of West Point, at once gave him a brigade composed of the First, Eleventh, and Seventeenth Virginia regiments, stationed at Manassas. Longstreet never had a kind word for Virginia or Virginians, but they were his first soldiers in the war. He at once set to work drilling his rather raw men. By July 6, he was drawing out his regiments in brigade evolutions. The military situation in Virginia was this: A Union army lay in front of Alexandria with another army west of the Blue Ridge near Winchester. Facing them were Southern forces, one under Joseph E. Johnston in the Shenandoah Valley, the other under Beauregard at Manassas.

The sad-faced Louisiana creole had decided to stand behind Bull Run, selecting with his admirable engineering skill the best position between the Potomac and the Rapidan. Along this stream, called a run but actually a small river that grows to the east into the Occoquan, which flows into the Potomac not far from Washington's Mount Vernon, the Confederates were strung out for miles, a curious congeries of raw recruits called from home to defend the native soil. A brigade under R. S. Ewell, afterwards noted, held Union Mills on the Confederate right; next was D. R. Jones at McLean's Ford; South Carolina Bonham watched Mitchell's Ford, while P. St. George Cocke guarded the fords between Mitchell's Ford and the Stone Bridge, later so famous. Between Mitchell's Ford and McLean's Ford, half a mile from each, is Blackburn's Ford, where Longstreet's Virginia brigade was stationed.

The ford lies in a bend of Bull Run. The north bank is a bluff, while the opposite south bank is a sandy shelf. For two days Longstreet's unaccustomed soldiers labored to erect defenses on the north bank of the stream before Beauregard transferred them to the south side.

Irvin McDowell, a good soldier, was in command of the Union army, now near Centreville. With a raw force but compelled to begin the campaign, McDowell advanced

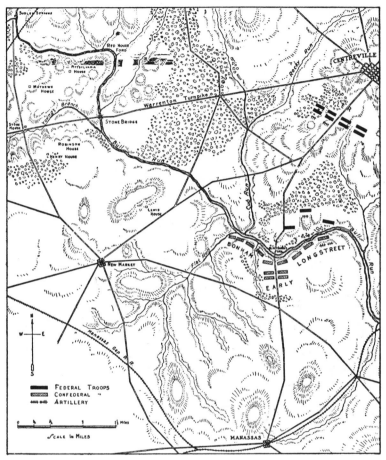

FIRST MANASSAS (BULL RUN), BLACKBURN'S FORD, JULY 18, 1861

southward on July 16. He had about thirty-five thousand men, many more than Beauregard, but except for some regulars his troops were even more untrained and untried than the Confederates. Two armed mobs were to try conclusions. It was McDowell's hard fate to command the mob that was most mob-like. When the battle finally came, on July 21, the Confederates numbered about thirty thousand in all, so that the odds were fairly even, except that the Union artillery was incomparably better. The Confederates dragged into the battle venerable cannon that had seen service in the War of 1812.

On July 16, the Confederates, well informed of everything going on, received word that McDowell would move against them the next day. The Union commander intended to move on Manassas, an important railroad junction. The road from Centreville to Manassas crossed Bull Run at Mitchell's Ford. The turnpike from Centreville to Warrenton passed over the Stone Bridge. McDowell considered three possible moves: first, turning the Confederate right; second, moving directly on Manassas through the Confederate center; third, turning the left above the Stone Bridge. After reflection, he determined to make a reconnaissance in force to try out the possibilities of the direct move on Manassas. Examination had shown him that turning the Confederate right would be difficult because of the broken and wooded nature of the country.

The Union division commander, Tyler, observing, saw artillery behind the ford; and in the woods the gleam of muskets told of troops. He decided to test the position. Artillery opened, and the Union infantry advanced. Across the stream both sides kept up a hot musketry fire.[3] The Union forces, under Tyler, advanced to Blackburn's Ford. Longstreet's troops received a baptism of fire when rifle balls and shell fragments began to fly amongst them. The men were startled and unnerved. War, glorious war, was becoming a

[3] Robert Matteson Johnston, *Bull Run; Its Strategy and Tactics* (Boston and New York, Houghton Mifflin Company, 1913), p. 134.

grim reality. But Longstreet was quite unaffected; danger had no effect on those iron nerves except to soothe them.

"Part of my line broke and started at a run," he says. "To stop the alarm I rode with sabre in hand for the leading files, determined to give them all that was in the sword and my horse's heels, or stop the break." [4]

Fortunately, he was not called on to murder any of his own men. The Confederates had recoiled, naturally enough, because they were on the low south bank of the stream, exposed, while the Northerners were comparatively protected by the high opposing bank. Opening the action with artillery, the Unionists advanced in line of battle to Bull Run and sought to cross it. Longstreet's twelve hundred men, after their first panic, stood their ground well and repelled the Unionists. A second attempt to cross the stream likewise failed.

But the Unionists were in some force, and Longstreet now called on Early, near by, for help. Help came, for Beauregard, anticipating the need, had already ordered Early forward. The latter's men came on the field just as the Unionists advanced a third time. Early's men opened fire so recklessly that Longstreet had to jump off his horse and lie on the ground to avoid being shot. By this time Confederate batteries were opening on the Unionists, who, facing a musketry and artillery fire, hesitated and finally withdrew entirely. The attempt to force a passage at Blackburn's Ford thus failed. While this little action was going on, the Unionists felt out the position at Mitchell's Ford, but were met by such a storm of shot and shell that they retired. The engagement ended as the Unionists learned what they had sought to know, that the line of Bull Run was strongly held and could be forced only with difficulty.

[4] *M. to A.*, p. 39.

This slight action, in which the Union loss was greater than the Confederate, though neither side lost more than a handful, greatly encouraged the Confederates, who had stood in some awe of the United States army before. The war was new then, and a skirmish in which many shots were fired, if ineffectively, was quite an event. Beauregard even wrote a report about it. "Brigadier-General Longstreet," he says, "who commanded immediately the troops engaged at Blackburn's Ford, on the 18th, equaled my confident expectations, and I may fitly say that by his presence at the right place at the right moment among his men, by the exhibition of characteristic coolness, and by his words of encouragement to the men of his command, he infused a confidence and spirit that contributed largely to the success of our arms on that day." [5]

Allowing for the exuberance of a new commander in a new war, Longstreet had done well. Indeed he had exhibited what was his greatest quality, his talent for defensive tactics. For resourcefulness in holding a position and making the most of the ground Longstreet has been seldom surpassed.

McDowell had now examined the Confederate right and tried the center and found them both unpromising; by the process of elimination nothing remained to try but the left. He decided to move around the Confederate left above Stone Bridge while making a demonstration in force at the latter point. Part of his army was to move down the Centreville-Warrenton turnpike to Stone Bridge, as if seeking to force a crossing there, while the major portion crossed Bull Run some distance above and took the Confederates in flank

---

[5] *The War of the Rebellion: A Compilation of the Official Records of the Union and Confederate Armies.* 130 vols. (Washington, Government Printing Office, 1880-1901), ser. I, vol. II, pp. 444-45. Hereafter cited as *O. R.*

and rear. It was a sound soldierly plan and might have resulted in victory if McDowell's troops had been more trustworthy.

The Confederates, confronted by McDowell, were concentrating behind Bull Run. Johnston, slipping away from the Union army in the Shenandoah Valley, crossed the Blue Ridge and reinforced Beauregard on July 20 with the brigades of Bee, Bartow, and Jackson (who was to become Stonewall the next day). While McDowell was preparing to turn the Confederate left on Bull Run, Beauregard was planning for his part to attack McDowell's left near Centreville. Fortunately for the Confederates, they were thrown on the defensive by the prior development of the Union offensive.

Evans, the officer commanding the Confederate force at the Stone Bridge, about eight o'clock in the morning of July 21 saw clouds of dust to the north and realized that some large troop movement was in progress. Convinced that the Union troops immediately in his front did not intend to attack, Evans left a small covering force at the Stone Bridge and moved to an eminence, known as Matthews Hill, a mile to the northwest. There he took up his position and awaited attack. The Unionists, crossing Bull Run several miles above the Stone Bridge, came down the stream and found Evans across their path at Matthews Hill. Bee, coming up about this time, assisted Evans in checking the Union advance. The Confederate commanders, Beauregard and Johnston, warned by the firing to the north, quickly changed their plan from an offensive battle at Centreville to a defensive stand on Henry Hill, a little south of Matthews Hill and near the Warrenton turnpike.

Jackson had moved up and taken position on Henry Hill, refusing to participate in the action going on on Matthews

Hill. There the superior numbers of the Unionists began to tell. Evans, Bee, and Bartow, driven from Matthews Hill, fell back on Henry Hill, on the crest of which Jackson's line of battle stood. It was then that Bee rallied his men with the cry, "See, there is Jackson standing like a stone wall!"

McDowell, bringing up his powerful artillery, opened on the Confederates on Henry Hill by way of prelude to a charge. In spite of Jackson's professional calm, which he had succeeded in conveying to his men, the Confederate outlook was very dubious. But Beauregard and Johnston were busying themselves in getting troops up to the danger point. Johnston recalled from the lower fords the brigades which had been directed to cross and advance on Centreville. Once more Longstreet recrossed Bull Run. He later declared that he crossed and recrossed the stream six times that day.

About this time new Confederate reinforcements—the brigades of Elzey and Kirby Smith—came on the field and attacked the Union batteries in the rear while the Confederate line stood firm on the hill. The Unionists were still superior in numbers and had not suffered heavy casualties, but at that moment they were seized by one of those panics to which raw troops are so liable. Almost in an instant the Union army, which up to a short time before had seemed on the point of winning the battle, suddenly went to pieces. Great masses of men, turning their backs on Henry Hill, began to retire toward Stone Bridge and Centreville. The Confederates had, to their own surprise, won a victory, and a complete victory.

Longstreet, who all this time had been chafing at his enforced reaction, received orders to advance and put guns in position to open fire on the retreating Unionists. But he did not open, for an officer rode up at that moment and forbade it. Longstreet at once demanded his authority for the order; and the officer, who belonged to Johnston's staff, had to admit that it was on his own initiative. Longstreet insisted on opening fire and was about to do so, when Bonham, coming up, directed him to desist. He then reluctantly gave up the idea of punishing the fleeing foe.

The battle was much more of a victory than the Confederate commanders, who had feared defeat, were aware of; they could not understand that the Union army, which a little while before had seemed so formidable, had dissolved into a mob of fugitives. Consequently, Beauregard and Johnston, both highly prudent men who did not believe in tempting fortune (and who therefore never won Fortune's smiles again, for Fortune is a woman and likes to be tempted), made no other use of the victory than to pick up a few prisoners and reap the harvest of abandoned cannon, muskets, wagons, sutler's stores, and other fruits of victory. Beyond advancing to the vicinity of Alexandria, they took no offensive step.

Beauregard, reporting on the battle, says: "Longstreet's brigade, pursuant to orders prescribing his part of the operations of the center and right wing, was thrown across Bull Run early in the morning, and under a severe fire of artillery was skillfully disposed for assault of the enemy's batteries in that quarter, but was withdrawn subsequently, in consequence of the change of plan already mentioned and explained." [6]

Longstreet must have been disappointed at his inaction in the great victory. He had been there on the field, ready for anything, and opportunity had come not to him but to Jackson, who had won instant fame. Never again were the

[6] *O. R.*, ser. I, vol. II, p. 498.

Confederates to have such a chance. For in July, 1861, the war was still a pageant, not a reality. Never again was the world to witness a similar mad flight to the rear, that singular jumble of soldiers and officers, sutlers, clerks, reporters, politicians, and harlots that made Bull Run a byword and a reproach for a long time. Before the Unionists took the field again in eastern Virginia they would be turned into a real army by that most scientific of American soldiers, George B. McClellan, who has never received the credit he deserves from the country he served so well.

CHAPTER III

THE WINTER OF OUR DISCONTENT

AUGUST, 1861, found the South all agog with enthusiasm, thousands of men swarming to the recruiting stations, begging to be taken, and, in most cases, being refused for lack of arms. For the South had gone to war with an improvidence and unpreparedness truly American. Richmond witnessed innumerable parades of organizations hastening to the front, with brass bands blaring out the national airs of the embattled South. Women tore up old silk dresses, in lieu of other materials, to make the new flag designed by Beauregard, the Starry Cross, which was thereafter to be the banner of the South.

The army, now stationed near Centreville, pined with the desire to go forward and win more victories, for the army did not doubt that victory would perch on its banners—if only it was led across that inviting Potomac just to the north. But the unenterprising Johnston and Beauregard could not persuade President Davis, who now expected foreign intervention, that temerity was safer than timidity, that audacity was the better course. Men not audacious were urging audacity, and their pleading was not convincing. The army continued to eat its heart out near Centreville, doing nothing more exciting than drill and erect earthworks—to repel attack! For inevitably Johnston and Beaureguard resumed the defensive. They could do nothing else, with Davis disinclined to action. Sit down and wait for the enemy to come on—then drive him back. And insensibly the impressionable Longstreet began to become defensive, too. It

23

seemed safer to wait in some strong position for attack rather than to attack.

At the beginning of September, the army was at Fairfax Courthouse, with outposts at Munson's Hill. Longstreet's force of character, his self-confidence had told on Beauregard and Johnston, both men lacking in self-confidence. There was something in his physical bigness and soundness, his calm assurance that affected men with weaker nerves. By September Longstreet was commanding the "Advanced Forces," a rather vague term for a mixed body of infantry and cavalry thrown ahead of the Confederate position at Fairfax to observe the enemy. It was on September 11, 1861, that Colonel J. E. B. Stuart, the ambitious young cavalryman who had won the confidence of his superiors by his enterprise, started out from Munson's Hill to make a raid on a Union force that had advanced to Lewinsville. Longstreet, in command, was prepared to move an infantry force by night to cut off the Unionists in conjunction with the cavalry, but Stuart either did not receive, or did not obey, Longstreet's instructions. Without waiting for the infantry, he attacked the Unionists, driving them back to their defenses.[1]

Longstreet, however, did not become angry over this misadventure. He explained in his report that it rained so hard in the night that he could not have moved his infantry. (Later it would take more than rain to halt a movement.) He even recommended Stuart for promotion to the grade of brigadier general. Thus the first suggestion for Stuart's elevation came from Longstreet, who had his report endorsed by Johnston and Beauregard. Stuart received the commission.

In the subsequent battle of Ball's Bluff, fought in Octo-

[1] *O. R.*, ser. I, vol. V, p. 182.

ber, Longstreet seems to have had no part. This rather brilliant little action confirmed the Confederates in the belief that they were superior to the Unionists, a belief that was somewhat shaken when in another engagement the enemy had rather the better of it.

In all this time from July to October, 1861, Longstreet had not done more than other brigadier generals—not so much as some of them. But in this world results depend much less on performance than on the impression one makes on superiors, and the impression that Longstreet made on his superiors was usually striking. It was the effect that self-confidence nearly always has, and Longstreet had unlimited self-confidence. If he had been called on to be the head of an army or of a government, he would have accepted the commission in the full assurance that he was capable of discharging the task better than anybody else. That assurance of his was at once his strength and his weakness, for it helped to bring him forward and, at the same time, it entirely prevented him from realizing his limitations.

All of this is by way of prelude to the fact that in October, 1861, the grade of major general was established in the Confederate army, and that the first five major generals were, respectively, Polk, Bragg, G. W. Smith, Huger, and Longstreet. Thus Longstreet preceded Jackson (who was not commissioned until later, not being so self-confident as Longstreet) and was preceded by G. W. Smith and Huger, on which latter fact tragedy was to rest. Laymen cannot conceive the bitterness of jealousy awakened in the military heart by gradations of rank that seem trivial to the lay mind. But these gradations are not trivial at all, since command and power and fame result from them. Huger and Longstreet were commissioned on the same day, with Huger preceding. Later other major generals were created, among them Jackson, who was thus junior to Longstreet, though his reputation was far greater.

On October 12, 1861, Major General James Longstreet was assigned to duty with the First Corps of the Army of the Potomac (for the Confederates first used that term) under Beauregard, while Major General T. J. Jackson was put in the Second Corps under G. W. Smith.[2] Longstreet was thus relieved of the command of the "Advanced Forces" by Stuart, and was given a division composed of his old brigade (later led by A. P. Hill), a Virginia brigade commanded by P. St. George Cocke, and a South Carolina brigade led by D. R. Jones. Longstreet, becoming dissatisfied with Jones, intrigued with a South Carolina congressman to get him transferred to another command and succeeded.[3] Jones was replaced by George E. Pickett, destined to so unique a fame. The remaining divisions were commanded by G. W. Smith (also a corps commander), E. Kirby Smith, and Earl Van Dorn. The two latter officers were soon sent West.

A fine autumn, which invited military operations but which was not utilized by the Confederates, was succeeded by a hard winter. The army suffered terribly. Beauregard was sent West, leaving Johnston in undisputed command. The unseasoned troops, living mainly in tents instead of in huts and as poorly provisioned as later in the war, were scourged by disease. Hundreds of homesick boys from the sunny South fell ill and died of measles and other complaints, dangerous in the cold of a northern Virginia winter. Furthermore, months of drill, drill, nothing but drill, unrelieved by action, of restraint and hardship and rough food, chilled the military ardor of the Southern people, which

[2] O. R., ser. I, vol. V, p. 896.
[3] Ibid., pp. 1001-2.

had been so high after Manassas. Furloughed and invalided men had tales to tell of the cold and sickness and mud of the camps at Centreville that made the stay-at-homes cling to their creature comforts. Volunteers came infrequently now, in fact hardly at all. Alarm filled the Confederate leaders, who saw their own army declining while the rival Union army was growing in numbers and discipline day by day. A glowing autumn had turned into a threatening spring.

Once more the Confederates were on the defensive as the vast efforts put forth by the Union became evident. In the West, U. S. Grant captured Fort Henry and Fort Donelson, thereby expelling the Confederates from western Tennessee. In the East, McClellan was preparing to move into Virginia with the great army he had created and trained, an army far superior in numbers, discipline, and equipment to any force the South could bring into the field.

McClellan considered three possible lines of advance. One was to move forward directly on Manassas, which Lincoln dearly desired to obtain in order to wipe out the humiliation of the previous year. But as this involved an attack on Johnston's heavy fortifications near Centreville, the cautious McClellan did not care for it. He prepared to draw the Confederates away from their defenses and he proposed either to move on Richmond from the lower Rappahannock or from the mouth of the James. The latter plan recommended itself to him particularly, since it would involve a shorter land passage and fewer streams to cross, but it did not meet with the approval of Lincoln, who viewed with concern the fact that the removal of the Union army to Hampton would leave Washington open to attack by the Confederates. Consequently, he agreed to McClellan's plan reluctantly and with the provision that Washington should be sufficiently guarded. And on the rock of this provision the campaign foundered.

Since it had become evident that the Union campaign would not be directed against Manassas and since the Confederate position in that vicinity was too advanced to impede Union army movements in eastern Virginia, Johnston prepared to fall back to the Rapidan River. There he would be in condition to move quickly if the Unionists should decide to come down the line of central Virginia to Culpeper, or to repair to the defense of Richmond if the capital were threatened from the east.

On March 9, 1862, Johnston began his withdrawal from Centreville, leaving large quantities of stores behind for lack of transportation. Longstreet's division, with Stuart's cavalry, brought up the rear of the retiring army. Stoneman's cavalry, following cautiously, fired a few shots at Stuart's troopers, but that was all. The Unionists made no attempt to interfere with the retreat.[4]

In the night of March 9, G. W. Smith informed D. H. Hill that the latter was temporarily assigned to Longstreet, who, Smith thought, was then on the Warrenton turnpike near Broad Run. Smith wrote next day, "I am fairly launched on a sea of mud." On March 11, four brigades crossed the Rappahannock River. Smith crossed that day on the Warrenton turnpike. "Longstreet," Johnston wrote, "is looking for better roads farther west, or perhaps a smaller stream." By the middle of March, Johnston's army was safely behind the Rapidan River. On March 13, 1862, Adjutant General Cooper issued an order assigning Robert E. Lee to duty at Richmond as army director under the President. That was the beginning of better times for the Confederacy. The first phase of the war in Virginia had ended.

---

[4] *Southern Historical Society Papers*, IX, 516.

CHAPTER IV

REAR GUARD AT WILLIAMSBURG

LONGSTREET's strong personality was more and more asserting itself and Johnston was leaning on him. When near the end of March, Johnston and G. W. Smith were called to Richmond to consult with President Davis, Longstreet remained on the Rapidan in command of the army. It was at this time that Stonewall Jackson, in the Shenandoah Valley, was preparing for his immortal Valley Campaign. Reporting the advance of the Unionists near Woodstock, Jackson asked for reinforcements. Longstreet answered that Jackson would have to come nearer the Rapidan position to make the sending of troops to him practicable. Johnston, appealed to, agreed that two days' march from his army was the limit for a detachment.[1] What really happened was that Longstreet was willing to bring, not send, the troops, provided that Jackson would recognize his seniority and give him the command. "I explained," said Longstreet, "that the responsibility of the move could not be taken unless I was with the detachment to give it vigor and action to meet my views, or give time to get back behind the Rapidan in case the authorities discovered the move and ordered its recall."[2] What sublime gall Longstreet had! Kindly offering to give vigor to Stonewall Jackson! Attempting to take the command from an officer whose reputation surpassed his own!

Jackson remained cold to the proposal. "As the com-

[1] *O. R.*, ser. I, vol. XI, pt. III, p. 419.
[2] *M. to A.*, p. 65.

mander of the district [Jackson] did not care to have an officer there of higher rank," Longstreet adds, "the subject was discontinued." [3]

This is a good illustration of the way in which Longstreet seeks to put others in the wrong. Jackson, he intimates, was ungenerous in not wishing to be superseded in command. He does not seem to have reflected on his own ungenerosity in seeking to take Jackson's command from him. It was all right, of course, to push Longstreet ahead anywhere; the wrong was in opposing his aspirations. It is hardly conceivable that the Valley Campaign would have been an improvement if conducted by Longstreet instead of by Jackson.

The incident is extremely significant and even sinister. It shows Longstreet, in the early part of the war, attempting to get the command of an army. Even then he was dissatisfied with a subordinate position, longing for complete authority. That longing was to grow with time and become one of the elements in the failure of the Southern cause.

By this time, April, 1862, the campaign was shaping itself. The Confederacy seemed on the point of collapse everywhere. The defeat at Shiloh in Tennessee and the fall of New Orleans were almost simultaneous. At the same time McClellan had transferred his great army to Hampton at the mouth of the James River and was preparing to launch his Peninsular Campaign for the capture of Richmond.

Always cautious, McClellan was held up for a time on the lower James-York Peninsula by J. Bankhead Magruder, master of deception, who confronted the Union host with a few thousand men skillfully displayed to the best advantage. His demonstration enabled the Confederate government to prepare to transfer Johnston's army to the Peninsula to reinforce him.

[3] *Ibid.*

This complete change of plan caused President Davis to ask for a conference with Johnston. The latter took with him G. W. Smith and Longstreet. Robert E. Lee and Secretary of War Thomas Jefferson Randolph were present at this historic council of war. Differences came to light, with Davis and Lee of one opinion and Johnston and his subordinates of another.

"I had nothing to say till called on," Longstreet says. "The views intended to be offered were prefaced by saying that I knew General McClellan; that he was a military engineer, and would move his army by careful measurement and preparation; that he would not be ready to advance before the first of May. The President interrupted and spoke of McClellan's high attainments and capacity in a style indicating that he did not care to hear any one talk who did not have the same appreciation of our great adversary. McClellan had been a special favorite with Mr. Davis when he was Secretary of War in the Pierce administration, and he seemed to take such reflections upon his favorites as somewhat personal." [4]

What was important in this consultation seems to be the fact that Longstreet, rebuked by the sharp-speaking Davis for expressing disrespectful opinions about McClellan, took a dislike to the President that he never entirely got over. Later he was in cordial relations with Davis, but the incident had something to do with the final alienation of the two men. The story is that Davis resented Longstreet's criticism of Albert Sydney Johnston, his friend.

Longstreet states that he intended to propose to the council that McClellan be left to Magruder while Johnston

---

[4] *M. to A.*, p. 66; Gustavus Woodson Smith, *Confederate War Papers. Fairfax Court House, New Orleans, Seven Pines, Richmond and North Carolina* (New York, Atlantic Publishing and Engraving Company, 1884), pp. 41-45.

combined with Jackson for a movement against Washington.

Magruder was facing McClellan's hundred thousand men with ten thousand and carrying off the affair with superb sangfroid. Now Johnston's army, consisting of the divisions of G. W. Smith, D. H. Hill, and Longstreet, with Stuart's cavalry, joined the thin gray line on the Peninsula near Yorktown. Thus a Confederate army of fifty thousand confronted the Union hundred thousand.

Magruder's defensive line ran across the James-York Peninsula from the Warwick, a confluent of the James, dammed up so as to overflow the surrounding low country. The left was at Yorktown, which was defended by earthworks and water batteries. At Norfolk on the south side of the James was Benjamin Huger with perhaps ten thousand men.

Johnston, now commanding on the Peninsula, made his assignments on April 18, 1862.[5] Magruder held the right of the line on the James River, D. H. Hill the left at Yorktown. Longstreet was in the middle. G. W. Smith commanded the reserve.

McClellan, delayed by many things, including bad weather, bottomless roads, and overflowed lands, slowly advanced to the Confederate position. He brought up heavy naval guns, which were put in position opposite the Confederate works at Yorktown. It was his intention to blow those defenses into pieces when all the preparations were made. Then he would advance on Richmond.

Johnston did not wait to be blown to pieces. Realizing what Lee and the Confederate authorities did not, that the army was in danger of having either flank turned by troops landed from the York or the James, he could see nothing to

[5] *O. R.*, ser. I, vol. XI, pt. III, p. 448.

do but retreat; but with his uncanny instinct for such matters he waited to the last possible moment for withdrawal. On the night of May 3, 1862, abandoning his elaborate defenses, he began to retire up the James. Longstreet had been entirely right in his prediction that McClellan would do nothing before the first of May.

The divisions of G. W. Smith and D. H. Hill were sent up the Yorktown-Williamsburg road; those of Longstreet and Magruder on the Hampton-Lee's Mill road, with Stuart covering both routes. Longstreet found himself in the rear of the retreat.

In the most disheartening circumstances, with incessant rain turning the roads into bogs and the camps into quagmires, the Confederates moved westward, followed slowly by the Unionists, who were contending with the same disadvantages. The Confederate column was held back by the wagon trains, which moved only at snail's pace and with the utmost difficulty through mud that constantly stalled the laboring teams. The result was that the wagons were not out of the way when, in the afternoon of May 4, the Union advance drew near Williamsburg, the ancient capital of Virginia. It thus became necessary for Longstreet to halt and hold off the pursuers until that groaning, creaking, mud-covered caravan of farm wagons conveying the Confederate stores was out of danger.

Anticipating just such a possibility, Magruder had thrown up a rear line of fortifications about two miles east of Williamsburg. The key to the line was Fort Magruder, which had redoubts stretching out from it toward the James and York rivers. The Peninsula is eight miles wide here but the ground near the York is very broken; thus the actual defensive line was not so wide as might be supposed.

The Union cavalry under Stoneman led the advance.

Hooker's division moved on the Yorktown-Williamsburg road, W. F. Smith's on the Hampton road, followed by Kearny, Couch, Casey, and Sumner. Near Williamsburg the two main roads leading westward converged, not far from Fort Magruder, which covered the junction. There Longstreet had taken up his position to protect the wagon trains.

About 4:00 P.M. on May 4, Union troops appeared in the open ground in front of Fort Magruder. Johnston, who was near by, hurried troops into the line of redoubts. There was heavy skirmishing until nightfall, but the Unionists did not press forward in force. It was a bad day for battle, with the rain falling in sheets. The corps commanders, Sumner, Heintzelman, and Keyes, conferred with Stoneman but came to no definite conclusion.

The Confederates prepared to resume their retreat. At 2:00 A.M. of May 5, Magruder began his march, with D. R. Jones's and McLaws's divisions, followed by Smith's and Hill's divisions. But that night the heavens had opened as in the aboriginal Flood and the wagons stuck in the mud and could not be moved. Longstreet, assigned the duty of covering the march, had been ordered to send troops to relieve the force in the fieldworks, and he sent two brigades.

R. H. Anderson was in immediate command at Fort Magruder. Expecting an early march and finding it difficult to make a reconnaissance in the falling darkness, Anderson put out pickets but did nothing more. At daylight he occupied Fort Magruder and the redoubts on the right of it, besides two on the left. Several other redoubts on the left were not seen, or at least were not occupied. The ground in front of Fort Magruder and to the right of it was open, but to the left it was heavily wooded and swampy.

At 7:00 A.M., Hooker's division emerged in the open ground on the Hampton road and began to skirmish with the

Confederates. Hooker occupied the fields in front of Fort
Magruder, with Smith on his right. Behind them Kearny,
Casey, and Couch were fighting their way forward through
the bottomless mud.[6] Hooker made some little progress in
front of Fort Magruder, succeeding in making connection

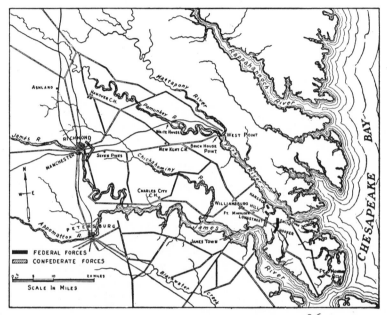

THE PENINSULAR CAMPAIGN, MAY 5, 1862

with the Union troops on the Yorktown road. Anderson began to be pressed by the Union line of battle, calling up Wilcox's brigade to support his right and, presently, A. P. Hill's
and Pickett's brigades.

It was at this moment that Longstreet, hearing the rising
tide of battle, rode to the front and viewed the scene.[7] Be-

[6] *Battles and Leaders of the Civil War; being for the most part contributions by Union and Confederate officers. Based upon "The Century War
Series."* 4 vols. Edited by Robert Underwood Johnson and Clarence Clough
Buel (New York, The Century Company [1887-88]), II, 195. Hereafter cited
as *B. & L.*

[7] *M. to A.*, p. 74.

fore him stretched heavy masses of blue-coated troops slowly deploying across the open spaces. While Fort Magruder and the redoubts were being held by a mere rearguard, the greater part of the Union army was coming up prepared for battle.

Seeing instantly the danger of the situation, Longstreet sent back for D. H. Hill's division, the march of which had been delayed by the wagons. Hill sent Jubal A. Early, with a couple of brigades. Posting Early in rear of the Confederate left, Longstreet asked for the rest of Hill's division, as the Union line of battle was pressing forward and the fighting was becoming general. Hooker, advancing against the Confederate right, met with fierce resistance, and, after a conflict of some time, recoiled in confusion. Just then Stuart, riding up with his cavalry, thought that the moment had come for pursuit and prematurely advanced. "As he did not recognize authority except of the commander-in-chief," Longstreet says, "he was only cautioned that the break was only of the enemy's front, that he would find reinforcements coming up, and this he began to realize by the clearer ring of their muskets." Johnston, coming forward, left the conduct of the engagement in Longstreet's hands, probably realizing that his lieutenant was a better tactician than himself.

About 3:00 p. m. Kearny came up on the Union side, and the rest of D. H. Hill's division on the Confederate. On the right the Unionists had been so badly punished that they did nothing more of consequence that day. It was different on the left.

On the Confederate left, reaching toward the York River, Hancock had advanced. Crossing a mill dam, he found and occupied several redoubts on the extreme left, which the Confederates had neglected to garrison. While Hancock was moving into the redoubts, officers reported to D. H. Hill that the former could be attacked to advantage.

Hill came up to Johnston and Longstreet, who were watching the conflict near Fort Magruder, and asked to be allowed to send Early against Hancock. Johnston referred the request to Longstreet, who demurred, explaining to Hill that the Confederates were merely fighting to gain time and would make a mistake in being drawn into a general engagement. But on Hill's insisting Longstreet gave consent.

"The brigade you propose to use is not in safe hands," Longstreet said to him. "If you will go with it, and see that the troops are properly handled, you can make the attack, but don't involve us so as to delay the march after night." [8]

This is Longstreet's characteristic way of slapping at an adversary, in this case Jubal A. Early, between whom and himself the bitterest feeling existed in later years.

The Confederates, under Hill and Early, made the mistake of advancing too soon from the cover of the woods into the open ground. There they came under the fire of the Union artillery and Hancock's infantry and suffered terribly. Raw, half drilled, exposed to a perfect tempest of canister and bullets, they were cut to pieces. The Fifth North Carolina regiment was almost annihilated. In few subsequent battles were the regimental losses severer than at Williamsburg. There was nothing for the Confederates to do but to withdraw, which they did. With the repulse of their attack, the battle gradually wore itself out. It had been a fierce combat, as rearguard actions are likely to be. Longstreet estimates the Union casualties at 2,288 and the Confederate at 1,565, figures that are probably about right. That night

[8] *M. to A.*, p. 78.

Johnston's army continued its crawling retreat untroubled by the Union cavalry, which could hardly move in the mud.[9]

Johnston accomplished his purpose, which was to rescue his imperiled wagon trains, and was indignant when McClellan claimed a victory. As the Confederates withdrew after the battle, it was quite natural for the Unionists to think they had gained a success; as the Confederates continued their retreat unimpeded, they imagined they had won the battle. On the whole, the advantage lay with them, inasmuch as their fierce resistance imposed caution on the Union commanders at a time when audacity might have accomplished much. Franklin's division, sent to the head of the York to intercept the retreat, let itself be pushed back by Hood's brigade, on May 7, in the action known as the battle of West Point or Eltham Landing. If Franklin had been in a mood for real work he might have cut into the Confederate wagon trains, still plowing through the mud, and forced Johnston to make a stand at a disadvantage. After passing Franklin, Johnston was safe and continued his withdrawal to the vicinity of Richmond without further annoyance.

On May 9, Johnston wrote Lee, the chief of staff, from New Kent Courthouse that he had divided his army into two parts. One part, under Smith, was moving on the New Kent road; the other, under Longstreet, on the road to the south, probably the Williamsburg road. Longstreet reached the vicinity of Long Bridge on the Chickahominy on the same day that Smith moved to Baltimore Crossroads.

The Union fleet, as well as the army, was moving up the James. On May 15, the gunboats attempted to run the gauntlet of the batteries on Drewry's Bluff, a few miles below Richmond, but were driven back after a spirited can-

---

[9] For Longstreet's report of the battle, see *O. R.*, ser. I, vol. XI, pt. I, p. 564.

nonade. This event alarmed Johnston for the safety of Richmond, and he was prone enough to retreat in any case. Nor was there any good position for a stand east of the Chickahominy. The result was that his army crossed the river, one wing at Bottom's Bridge, the other wing, including Longstreet, at Long Bridge. Johnston took position from Drewry's Bluff, south of the James River, to the Mechanicsville turnpike running northeast from Richmond. The right wing commanded by Longstreet, and including his own and D. H. Hill's divisions, extended from Drewry's Bluff to White Oak Swamp; the left wing, under Smith, stretched from White Oak Swamp to the Mechanicsville road.

All of the Peninsula east of the Chickahominy River was now free of the presence of Confederate troops, and the Union commander advanced without opposition to the swamps that enclose that small but difficult river. He had succeeded to the extent that he was now but a few miles from the Southern capital and almost in a position to begin its siege. The omens were everywhere unfavorable to the South, and the authorities began to make some preparations for evacuating Richmond.

CHAPTER V

COMEDY OF SEVEN PINES

JEFFERSON DAVIS riding out with Lee one May day had suddenly found himself in the midst of moving troops. On inquiry the President had been astonished to find that the men were Johnston's and that, as we have seen, they were retreating on Richmond. The army, having crossed the Chickahominy River, was still falling back. Davis felt, in a sense, outraged, since Johnston had not notified him of army movements so essential to the welfare of the government. Johnston, harboring a sense of injustice because given rank a grade below Lee, and naturally secretive and jealous of authority, had not seen fit to inform Davis of his intentions. And here began the break between the two men that was to have such important consequences.

The Union army followed, slowly, cautiously, looking for traps. On May 20, McClellan crossed the Chickahominy at Bottom's Bridge, fourteen miles east of Richmond, thus passing the last natural obstacle between him and the goal of his ambition. And yet his position was perilous, because he stood astride the swampy Chickahominy, which was unfordable and swelling from spring rains. The Union base of supplies was on the Pamunkey River, northeast from the Chickahominy, and the supporting Union force under McDowell was at Fredericksburg, directly north. Thus McClellan was forced to divide his army by the Chickahominy, inviting attack by the Confederates on one wing or the other.

The extreme left of the Confederate army was in the vicinity of Hanover Courthouse, some miles to the north of Richmond and so between McClellan and McDowell. McClellan's right wing, north of the Chickahominy, was commanded by the able Fitz-John Porter. In order to clear the way for the junction between McDowell at Fredericksburg and McClellan at Richmond, Porter attacked the small Confederate force at Hanover and defeated it. There was, therefore, nothing between the union of McDowell's forty thousand men and McClellan's hundred thousand—nothing but Stonewall Jackson. That obstruction, as on former and later occasions, proved formidable.

McClellan remained quiescent, waiting for McDowell to join him, his left resting on the other end of White Oak Swamp from the Confederates, his center at Seven Pines and Fair Oaks, his right on the north side of the Chickahominy. Johnston had drawn back his army to the immediate vicinity of Richmond; some of the troops camped at the Fairfield Racecourse in that city.

Bitter disappointment was in store for George B. McClellan. On May 24, he received a telegram from Lincoln stating that McDowell would surely march on May 26. Later, on the same day, came another telegram saying that McDowell was held at Fredericksburg because of Stonewall Jackson's move down the Shenandoah Valley toward the Potomac. The authorities in Washington began to tremble for the safety of their capital. Jackson's campaign in the Shenandoah Valley, Lee's strategic conception, was magnificently carried out by the able and aggressive Stonewall. This was the first fruit of Davis's act in making Lee chief of staff.[1]

Meanwhile McClellan was busy building bridges over

---

[1] *B. & L.*, II, 175.

the river, for the treacherous stream had a habit of rising madly and sweeping everything away. On May 30, 1862, the corps of Heintzelman and Keyes were on the south side of the Chickahominy, while Porter and Franklin were on the north side. Sumner lay on the north side near Bottom's Bridge. All day and night of May 30, rain fell in torrents, causing the river to rise and endangering the bridges.

Johnston had to do something, for the Confederates daily expected to hear of McDowell's marching to join Mc-Clellan, a move that would have spelled the doom of Richmond. The Confederate commander, consulting Smith, first thought of assailing the Union force north of the Chickahominy, the plan afterward adopted by Lee. Orders were given for that purpose; A. P. Hill crossed the river to begin the attack. However, the news that McDowell, after advancing one day's march toward Richmond, had been ordered back to Fredericksburg relieved the fears of the Confederate leaders for that side of the river. Examination showed that the opportunity on the Richmond side of the stream was much the better.

On the night of May 28, Longstreet, always prone to push his views and encouraged by Johnston's deference to his opinions, suggested an attack the next morning on the Union center at Seven Pines and Fair Oaks. Johnston was not quite ready and did not issue orders for the movement until May 30; the attack was to be made the next morning. The delay worked in his favor, as the Chickahominy was fast becoming so high as to be believed impassable. As a matter of fact, a further delay of a day would have been still better because the river was still higher then. Anyway, it seemed a great opportunity. If the parts of the Union army were divided by an impassable torrent, one wing might be destroyed before aid could come from the other. The

Confederates, much inferior in the total to the Unionists, in this way had a chance to be superior in numbers at the point of contact.

The Confederate commander issued his orders, which were partly written and partly oral; this invited disaster. His plan of battle was excellent because it was so simple. It is strange that a scheme so simple and involving such few possibilities for confusion should have gone astray, but so it was.

The Union left was strongly posted on White Oak Swamp; the right was in a fortified position north of the Chickahominy. What may be called the center was concentrated at two points, Seven Pines on the Richmond-Williamsburg road and Fair Oaks, a mile north. The principal weakness of the Union position lay in the fact that between Fair Oaks and the Chickahominy, two miles away, there was a gap unoccupied by Union troops. If the Confederates intervened between the Chickahominy and Fair Oaks they would take the Union position in flank and rear and should win a great victory. Fair Oaks was the best point for the main attack, but as the plan worked out the main attack was to be made at Seven Pines by the right wing, which Johnston put under Longstreet.

Two roads running east from Richmond were available for Johnston's advance against the enemy. These two highways, the Nine-Mile road to the north and the Williamsburg road south of it, roughly paralleled each other for some miles until finally the Nine-Mile road, curving at Fair Oaks, joined the Williamsburg road at Seven Pines. The main Union position covered this strategical point where the two roads joined. Earthworks had been thrown up here, as well as some distance to the front and to the rear. Casey's division held them.

JAMES LONGSTREET

On the night of May 30, Longstreet's troops were so disposed that they could advance without trouble along the Nine-Mile road, the one nearer the Chickahominy. Three of his brigades were camped at the Fairfield Racecourse, near the junction of the Nine-Mile road with the Creighton

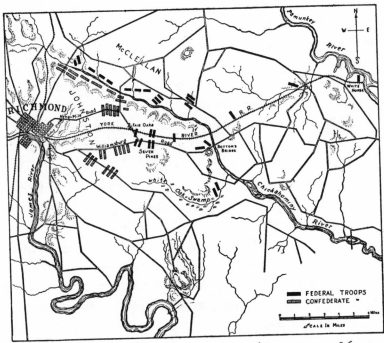

BATTLE OF SEVEN PINES (FAIR OAKS), MAY 31, 1862

road, while the other two brigades lay on the Nine-Mile road a mile or so to the east. Huger, who had crossed from the south side of the James, was at a point where the old Williamsburg road approached the city, near a small stream known as Gillis Creek. D. H. Hill was not far from him. G. W. Smith was camped near Meadow Bridge on the Chickahominy, with A. P. Hill near by.

The easiest method of handling these forces on the two roads would have been to send Smith, Longstreet, and A. P.

Hill on the Nine-Mile road, and Huger and D. H. Hill on the Williamsburg road, as in that case no transfers of troops would have been necessary. And this was Johnston's original intention, but it was not carried out. A curious change in dispositions was made, one that wrecked the Confederate hopes.

Human nature is the incomprehensible factor in military movements, as in all other events, that defies analysis and prevision. The Unionists were in a disadvantageous position, about to be attacked by a superior force of Confederates animated by the spirit that comes to all men who are fighting for hearth and home. Johnston was a skillful, if over-cautious, commander. All the odds at that moment favored the Southern chances of success. And there can be little doubt that the Confederates would have won a victory if Johnston's plan had been adhered to. But the deciding factor in the matter was not the ability of the commander or the number of the troops but the relative rank of Smith, Longstreet, and Huger. That seems to have been the rock on which the ship foundered.

The point was that Smith was the senior major general present, Johnston's second in command. He would be the ranking officer in any part of the field in which his troops were engaged, and Smith had been assigned the task of supervising the attack down the Nine-Mile road.[2] Thus Longstreet, if he operated on that road, would be, under Smith, a mere division commander.

There seems to have been a change of plan in the night of May 30-31, due possibly to Longstreet's representations. Longstreet was assigned the command of the right wing, which involved the transfer of his troops from the Nine-Mile road to the Williamsburg road, a change certain to

[2] *B. & L.*, II, 220-63.

cause confusion. Johnston states that he placed the right
wing under Longstreet on the understanding that when the
column neared Seven Pines the command would devolve
on himself. It never did.

On the morning of May 31, Longstreet, seeking Huger,
conferred with him on the question of seniority, claiming
it for himself. In reality Huger was senior, but he allowed
himself to be overslaughed by the positive Longstreet. Thus
the latter secured what he desired, the undisputed command of the Confederate right wing. And this fact, taken
in conjunction with the awkwardness of transferring troops
on the morning of battle from one road to another, wrecked
the Confederate plan.

Longstreet's rear brigades, marching from the racecourse
on the Nine-Mile road to the Williamsburg road soon came
athwart Huger's column on the latter road at the crossing
of Gillis Creek. Huger had to wait for hours while Longstreet's column preceded him. Though the stream could be
forded, the infantry passed over a footbridge, one by one.
Johnston had given orders for an attack at daybreak of
May 31; hours after that time the troops were just getting
into position for the advance against the enemy.[3]

The new plan called for Smith and A. P. Hill to move
on the Nine-Mile road, Longstreet and D. H. Hill on the
Williamsburg road, and Huger on a third parallel road to
the south, the Charles City road. The main assault was not
to be made on the weak Union force at Fair Oaks but on
the fortified center of the line at Seven Pines. Longstreet
had now realized his ambition of being the commander at
the vital point. At a farmhouse, meeting Huger and D. H.

[3] G. W. Smith, *Confederate War Papers*, p. 104. Smith here states that Longstreet crossed Whiting's line of march. He may have crossed both Whiting's and
Huger's.

Hill, he had claimed seniority and had had his way. This weakness on Huger's part was to end in the ruin of his career.

It was not until afternoon that Longstreet, having settled the question of rank and put his own troops on the road leading directly to Seven Pines, moved to the attack. D. H. Hill preceded him, while Huger moved along the Charles City road. Hours had been lost when time was valuable.

At one o'clock the signal guns sent D. H. Hill off on the Williamsburg road, but he started alone. Longstreet was not yet ready; he claimed that he was delayed by Huger. If so, Huger was only paying him in his own coin. The Union force at Seven Pines was commanded by Major General Erasmus D. Keyes; his advance on the Williamsburg road was under that stout old soldier, Silas Casey. Hill, coming on this advance line, took it with a rush. Casey's force was thrown back on the main line at Seven Pines.

Hill, advancing to the Union defenses at Seven Pines, found them strongly held, and here the battle raged furiously. The ground, saturated with rain, was a swamp through which the soldiers forced their way with difficulty. Hill, unsupported as yet by Longstreet, was doing the fighting. The Confederates, with superior numbers at hand, were actually inferior at the point of contact, a situation which showed poor generalship. Indeed, mismanagement was wrecking Johnston's excellent plan. Reinforcements came up on both sides, but more numerously on the Northern. The fighting was fierce and close, with heavy casualties. The Confederates were driven back by force of numbers.

Huger's force was on the Charles City road, which bore away at a certain point from the Williamsburg road. Longstreet had sent three of his brigades on that road to support

Huger's attack on the extreme Union left, an attack never made. Of the thirteen brigades in the Confederate right wing, only five engaged that afternoon. But their fighting was superb. After being denied at Seven Pines for some time, and even driven back, they finally stormed Keyes's fortified position. Keyes, however, was only driven back, not crushed, and the Confederate losses were heavy.

Meanwhile another engagement was in progress at Fair Oaks, a mile away. There Whiting (commanding Smith's division), moving on the Nine-Mile road, had come into collision with the Union right south of the Chickahominy, just then being reinforced by Sumner's division from across the river. Although the bridges were swaying under the strain of the torrent, the Unionists crossed them, bringing succor to their comrades. But the Union troops at Fair Oaks, assailed themselves, could not lend aid to their comrades at Seven Pines.

For several hours the battle raged on a front of about two miles, from south of the Williamsburg road at Seven Pines to Fair Oaks. Through the flooded woods the Confederates advanced, exchanging deadly volleys with the protected Unionists and, finally, driving them from their defenses at Seven Pines. The bushes were everywhere full of the dead and wounded; some of the Confederate regiments were wrecked.

The crisis came at the end of the battle, a battle not especially favorable to the Confederates. About twilight, Johnston, who had been away from the field and along the Chickahominy most of the day, was badly wounded on the Nine-Mile road. His disablement removed a commander disinclined to great offensive movements in favor of one capable of anything. At the moment, however, there was consternation in the Confederate camps when the news came

that in addition to the thousands of casualties the chief himself had been laid low.

Johnston was immediately succeeded in command by Gustavus W. Smith, who was prostrated by the responsibility.
Johnston says in his book that he thinks he would have won
a great victory the next day if he had not been wounded
in the evening of May 31.[4] Smith, who did not win a victory the next day, does not share his opinion. He is probably right, for the Confederate army on the morning of
June 1, 1862, was hardly in condition to win a battle. It
had suffered severe losses and was much disorganized. The
Unionists, reinforced from the north side of the Chickahominy, were stronger than they had been at the beginning
of the engagement.

In this first great battle in the East the Confederate generalship had been poor. Johnston himself seems to have exercised no control over events, and Longstreet, who actually
conducted the battle so far as it was conducted by the Confederates, had done it badly, demonstrating the fact that
he was as unskillful at offensive tactics as he was skillful at
defensive. Indeed, he had illustrated the essentially defensive character of his military talent. On the Southern side,
the fighting of D. H. Hill was the outstanding feature. In
fact, Hill won the action at Seven Pines, where the Confederates would probably have been repulsed as they were
at Fair Oaks but for his fierce energy.

On the night of May 31, the Confederates were not prepared to withdraw from the battle, sadly as they had mis-
managed it. Longstreet, who had succeeded in getting into
action only a fraction of the force under him, was charged

---

[4] Joseph E. Johnston, *Narrative of Military Operations, Directed, during the
Late War between the States, by Joseph E. Johnston, General, C. S. A. . . .*
(New York, D. Appleton and Company, 1874), p. 141.

by Smith with the conduct of the action on the morning of June 1. The direction of the battle was now changed. The Unionists held position at Fair Oaks and along the railroad running through that point. The Confederates faced north, toward the railroad instead of toward the east as on the day before. They were still in somewhat superior force but the numbers were nearer equality than on May 31.

Smith ruined his battle by leaving it to Longstreet, but poor Smith was too nervous himself to have done anything. About 6:30 A. M. the sound of firing came to the waiting commander in such volume as to indicate that Longstreet was attacking in force. But it did not last long, and its recession told the harassed Smith that the Confederates were retiring, not advancing.

Longstreet, indeed, had spent all of his offensive energy the day before. He made what was a mere demonstration with a small part of his force and then fell back on the defensive, appealing to Smith for reinforcements and declaring that he was fighting the whole Union army. He had had enough of it and sought an excuse to break off the action. To D. H. Hill, his best fighter and one who could be counted on to go in with his coat off, Longstreet gave no orders at all, indicating that he was avoiding battle, not seeking it. About 11:00 A. M. the firing died out; the battle was over.

It was disheartening to the Confederates. Since they were successful at Seven Pines, they claimed the battle, calling it by that name, just as the Unionists, who were victorious at Fair Oaks, claimed the battle and called it by that name. Tactically it was a drawn battle, but strategically it was a Confederate defeat. With largely superior numbers they had failed to crush one wing of the Union army, failed lamentably. On June 1, President Davis called Lee to the command of the host, now known as the Army of Northern Virginia; and Lee, instead of going on cooling his heels as combined strategist and head office boy to Jefferson Davis, took the command of the army that was destined to gain immortal glory under him and almost to win the war.

CHAPTER VI

LONGSTREET IMPOSES HIS WILL ON JOHNSTON

THE battle of Seven Pines was a bloody fiasco. Bloody it was, since the two armies had lost about ten thousand men, nearly evenly divided. The confidence of the Unionists was raised by their successful resistance to what was a larger force, even if much of that force was not brought into play. The only units that entered the battle on the Confederate right, on May 31, were the four brigades of D. H. Hill's and one of Longstreet's. His other brigades and Huger's had not been engaged. With this considerable force, he had done nothing on June 1, calling instead for reinforcements.

Huger's reputation was ruined by his inaction, which was not his fault, as he was under Longstreet's command. His fault lay in submitting to Longstreet's claim of seniority, a claim that was not true. Both Johnston and Longstreet laid the blame on Huger for doing nothing on May 31, though Huger had been shunted off the Williamsburg road, where he belonged, to make way for Longstreet, and had, in addition, received no positive orders to engage. The bewildered and overslaughed Huger was made the scapegoat the leaders felt was needed. It is difficult to see what he could have done under the circumstances. Sent down the Charles City road by Longstreet, he was south of White Oak Swamp, on which the Union left wing rested. As the swamp was in flood and impassable, Huger could not cross it to attack the Union flank; if he had attempted to do so he would probably have been cut to pieces.

Singularly enough, the battle of Seven Pines, or Fair Oaks, has never been adequately studied by historians. Northern historians have seldom given the Union division commanders and Union troops credit for their valorous stand on May 31-June 1, 1862. Southern historians have usually taken Johnston's account as basic, and Johnston's account is practically worthless. Indeed Johnston himself hardly knew what was going on, because he had let Longstreet do what Lee was strong enough largely to resist— that is, he had allowed Longstreet to impose his will on him. Seven Pines is a classic example of the unwisdom of permitting a subordinate to change battle plans at the last moment.

From the disposition of the troops it is evident that Johnston first intended Smith and Longstreet to attack down the Nine-Mile road and to make the main assault on the unguarded Union right flank at Fair Oaks. That this was generally understood is evidenced by the fact that one of Johnston's staff officers going down the Nine-Mile road in search of Longstreet ran into the Union pickets and was captured.

Longstreet, however, with that burning ambition of his, was in no mood to play second fiddle to Gustavus W. Smith, and this would probably have been the case if he had gone along the Nine-Mile road. What seems to have happened is that Longstreet sought Johnston, some time in the evening of May 30, and persuaded the commander to let him transfer his own force from the Nine-Mile road to the Williamsburg road. Moreover, he induced Johnston to give him the command of the right wing, which the commander probably did on the assumption that Longstreet was next in grade to Smith and, consequently, the senior major general on that flank. When Longstreet at first broached to Huger

the subject of his command of the right wing, Huger demurred, possibly because the original arrangement had been
for him to command that wing. As we have seen, Huger
gave in to the stronger will and ruined himself by doing it.

The most curious feature of the whole affair is that Johnston never realized how he had been duped by Longstreet.
Writing years after the war and at a time when Longstreet
was generally most unpopular, he had no criticism to make
of that officer, though prone to harsh criticism. Perhaps his
partiality for Longstreet was due to the fact that both of
them had grievances and disliked Davis. Johnston, in fact,
never recovered from the wrong done him by Davis in
giving him a grade below Cooper, A. S. Johnston, and Lee,
all of whom had been colonels in the United States army
while he had been a brigadier general. The fact that A. S.
Johnston and Lee were line officers while he himself was
quartermaster general (probably the reason for Davis's
granting them a higher grade) made no difference to him.
Although he was given the command of the best army, and
thus had the best opportunity to win glory, while Lee had
no very definite place at all, he was dissatisfied. His superior
rank in the United States army was not recognized by the
Confederate States.

Yet he let Longstreet wreck his admirable plan of battle
at Seven Pines and turn a victory into a failure without resentment. The reason for this is that he never understood
that Longstreet's stronger will had imposed itself on him
and caused him to alter his plan in such a way as to intro-
duce confusion and lead to frustration. He probably imagined that the change of plan, by which Longstreet was
switched from the Nine-Mile road to the Williamsburg
road and put in charge of the attack at Seven Pines, was of
his own devising.

The truth is that the small, nervous Confederate commander, lacking in self-confidence, could not resist Longstreet's magnificent self-assurance and physical largeness. Six feet tall, broad as a door, hairy as a goat, there was something about Longstreet that would have inspired confidence even if his dogmatic utterances on all subjects had not done so. Longstreet was never at a loss, never hesitant (at least in appearance), never lacking in knowledge of what should be done in any given circumstances; and such a character was the wine of life to the rather backward Johnston. Indeed, if Johnston had continued in command of the army, Longstreet would have controlled him just as he attempted to control, and even to a certain extent succeeded in controlling Johnston's successor, Lee. It was hard to resist that viking, with his immense Lombard beard, his rugged power, and his invincible certainty.

At Seven Pines, Longstreet showed that he was not, naturally, a fighting general. Apparently appalled by the task he had intrigued to secure, he let a fighter do the fighting, standing aside himself. D. H. Hill fought his battle, not Longstreet. Faced with the responsibility of conducting the engagement on June 1, he opened the action with a feeble attack, which he dropped as soon as possible. It is true that he did not make a vital mistake in so doing, because the Confederates, disorganized as they were, were in no condition to fight an offensive battle, but a natural fighter would not have been convinced of the fact without a stouter test. It was not until late in the war that Longstreet, essentially a defensive soldier, developed offensive power. Then it was too late; the opportunities had passed.

Strangely enough (and yet not so strangely either) Longstreet, whose mismanagement was mainly responsible for the bloody failure, had his prestige increased by the battle, not diminished. Other leaders were ruined by the affair, among them Smith and Huger. Smith, suffering from nerves, was sidetracked in North Carolina. Huger never recovered from the slander, industriously promoted, of his inactivity at Seven Pines. A. P. Hill, later famous, had little part in the engagement. Whiting, actually in command at Fair Oaks, gained some applause, as did D. H. Hill; but the main glory, such as it was, went to Longstreet. He had been in command at Seven Pines, the point where the Confederate success was won, and consequently he was the hero of the battle. His fame spread overnight. His real failure was not understood then, as it is not understood now.

If there had been any students of character on the Confederate side they could have seen what were Longstreet's traits: overweening ambition, extreme self-confidence and willfulness, strangely balanced by lack of aggressiveness in action. His career was to bear out the developments of Seven Pines.

CHAPTER VII

DRAMA OF THE SEVEN DAYS

WHEN Lee succeeded Johnston in command of the army, on June 1, 1862, the prospects of the Confederacy were gloomy. The bright skies of 1861 had disappeared behind thick clouds. Not only had the Confederates in the West been defeated at Shiloh, had been driven back to Corinth, and had lost New Orleans, but the main army had entirely failed in its effort to crush a part of the opposing Army of the Potomac. At that moment it appeared probable that the Confederacy would lose Richmond as it had lost New Orleans.

The cause now rested on the shoulders of one man, and he was the single man in the country able to command victory, Robert E. Lee. With clear discernment of the need of the hour, Jefferson Davis had unhesitatingly named him to the post made vacant by the wounding of Johnston.

Lee faced the crisis without dismay. He had already been directing affairs to a certain extent for some time, and he was responsible for the idea of Jackson's Valley Campaign, so ably conducted by that redoubtable soldier. Jackson, as Lee viewed the situation, had made victory possible by scattering the Union forces in western Virginia and keeping McDowell inactive at Fredericksburg when he was so badly needed at Richmond. Lee realized the possibilities involved in concentrating the Confederate forces at Richmond against McClellan while the Union forces remained dispersed. It had been Johnston's idea simply to concentrate all available forces in the Confederacy at Richmond to meet a similar concentration of Union forces. With deeper strategic insight, Lee planned to divide the Unionists by Jackson's Valley Campaign, while preparing for the junction of the Confederate forces. And by carrying this plan into practice he changed the whole outlook of the war.

Lee took over a collection of commands rather than an army. The ordnance was antiquated while the infantry largely shouldered flintlock muskets, some of them dating from the eighteenth century. The staff was utterly inexperienced, being composed mainly of civilians, as the Confederates could not use their few West Point graduates for staff work. Although it had been evident for some time that Richmond would be the scene of serious fighting, no mapping had been done—in contradistinction to McClellan, who had had excellent maps made—and the high command was without adequate charts of the terrain of the campaign. Indeed, the Confederate ignorance of the country in the immediate vicinity of their capital is remarkable. These disadvantages —poor organization, lack of a staff and wretched maps— were to prevent the measure of success that might otherwise have been attained.

Besides, there was what may be called the element of luck, which was still, in certain important matters, running against the Confederates. Lee, engaged in reorganizing the army and drawing reinforcements to it from the South, naturally desired accurate information about the position of McClellan's army. It was then just the dawn of aerial observation, for at that very time Count Zeppelin was making ascensions in a captive balloon in the Union army. The Confederates were obliged to rely on *terra firma*, on the reports of spies and the findings of cavalry outposts.

It was in mid-June that Lee decided he must have more

accurate information and sent his young cavalry leader, Stuart, who had already made a name for himself, on an expedition to the rear of McClellan's right wing. Stuart, taking one thousand two hundred horsemen, got in McClellan's rear toward the Pamunkey River, but, instead of returning as he had gone out, decided on the bold measure of riding entirely around the Union army. This he succeeded in accomplishing without loss; the whole South rang with exultant laughter over the feat. The net result was, however, unfortunate. McClellan had been thinking for some days of changing his base of supplies from the Pamunkey River to the James, since it became increasingly evident that the Washington government was not going to let McDowell come to his aid. Stuart's raid seems to have brought to his attention the danger of his supply line from the Pamunkey River to Richmond and hastened his arrangements for the transfer. And this change was the principal factor of the campaign soon to begin. Stuart made his ride on June 15; on June 18, McClellan issued his first orders looking to the Change of Base, as it is known in history. At that very moment Lee was shaping his strategy to attack McClellan's line of supply and cut him off from his base—soon his old base—at the White House (scene of Washington's honeymoon) on the Pamunkey River.

As June deepened toward July, McClellan remained astride the Chickahominy as at the time of Seven Pines, while the Washington war lords wondered why he did nothing, for they underrated Lee's strength as much as McClellan overrated it. Porter, commanding the right wing, which was still north of the Chickahominy, occupied the hamlet of Mechanicsville, six miles northeast of Richmond. The river was now somewhat down, but it was still high and the swamp through which it runs was impassable without causeways. South of the Chickahominy the Union army stretched to White Oak Swamp, where the left rested. Lee's forces were south of the Chickahominy and Huger was south of James River.

From the nature of the country the Chickahominy River determined the movements of the armies. Of the country north of the stream the Confederates had only general ideas. They hardly knew that in the vicinity of Porter's position three creeks lead into the river, each running through a deep ravine with swampy bottom: Beaver Dam Creek, half a mile north and east of Mechanicsville; Powhite, three miles east of Beaver Dam; and Boatswain, a mile east of Powhite.

Beaver Dam Creek makes a wide bend around Mechanicsville and flows into the Chickahominy a mile and a half southeast of the hamlet. Powhite's upper tributaries, spreading out like a fan, concentrate in Gaines's Millpond, out of which the stream runs to join the river. Boatswain Creek flows through a deep and heavily wooded ravine with marshy bottom. These three ravines and hillsides offered excellent defensive positions for the tactics of that period and had not been overlooked by the accomplished engineers on McClellan's staff.

Porter had taken position on the high bank east of Beaver Dam Creek, having the stream between him and assailants from the south side of the river. It was a good position against a purely frontal assault but one easily turned from the right. Lee planned to turn it from the right and force its evacuation as a preliminary move in his attack on McClellan's line of communications, his main objective. He had some idea of the formidable nature of the Union position on Beaver Dam Creek, though it appears that his subordinates did not share his knowledge.

On June 11, Lee sent Jackson, who was still in the Shenandoah Valley, an outline of his plan of attack on McClellan —for Lee was already scheming to take the initiative—but sent it apparently with the idea that it might leak out, for he stated that he expected to attack the Unionists *south* of the Chickahominy. In reality, he had practically decided to attack them north of the river. At all events he drew Jackson down to Ashland, sixteen miles from Richmond, before the movement became known to the Union leaders. He had also brought up troops from the Far South. The result was that Lee succeeded in concentrating eighty thousand men in the vicinity of Richmond, a sufficient force with which to take the offensive.

On June 23, a council of war was held at Lee's headquarters, the Dabb house on the Nine-Mile road. Lee, Jackson, Longstreet, D. H. Hill, and A. P. Hill, already the most notable group of Southern leaders, were present. Then it was that Lee revealed his real plan of action. It was Jackson's part to get in the right and rear of Porter's position on Beaver Dam Creek, crush him, and cut the Union line of supply; he was to be supported by the divisions of D. H. Hill, A. P. Hill, and Longstreet. In other words, by far the greater part of the Confederate army was to be concentrated against Porter's single corps. While Jackson, who was north of the Chickahominy at Ashland, came up behind Porter, three other commands placed at bridges over the river were to cross to the north side and join, successively, in the operation. On the south side of the Chickahominy, Magruder was to hold the Union forces there by demonstrations.

The immediate object of the operation was to crush Porter's corps, destroy the railroad supplying McClellan's army, and cut him off from his base, and so force him to leave his trenches and fight. If the plan had worked as projected,

Porter would have been crushed and McClellan cut off, but the plan did not work and could not have done so, for the reason that McClellan was changing his base to the James River, and the railroad and the White House were no longer of value to him.

Longstreet's part in the plan was not without some importance. He states that early in June, Lee called a conference at his headquarters, which awakened in his mind misgivings, "as experience had told that secrecy in war was an essential element of success," but his apprehensions had been allayed when he discovered that Lee was sizing up his subordinates without giving away his ideas.

Longstreet says that on the day following this conference he rode over to headquarters and "renewed" his suggestions of an attack on McClellan's right flank. He probably means by this that he had first proposed the movement to Johnston.[1] He assured Lee that the Union position on Beaver Dam Creek could be easily turned and the force there dislodged. Lee heard without expressing approval or disapproval, but Longstreet thinks that his suggestion caused Lee to change his plan from an attack on the south side of the Chickahominy to one on the north side. That is as it may be.

Longstreet states that on June 16 he suggested to Lee that Jackson be brought down from the Valley to take position on the Confederate left, only to be told by Lee that an order had already been sent to that effect.[2] Then, according to Longstreet, Lee revealed his plan, which was for Jackson to attack Porter while he himself assailed the Union forces south of the Chickahominy. To this Longstreet demurred, thinking that Jackson might be cut off, and offered as a substitute the plan of a combined attack of the Confederates

[1] *M. to A.*, p. 114.
[2] *Ibid.*, p. 120.

on Porter with nothing but a demonstration on the south side of the river. At least that is Longstreet's account of it.

Then came the council of war on June 23, to which Jackson had come by hard riding. After a discussion Lee explained his plan and went out of the room, leaving the lieutenants to work out the details. Longstreet had questions to ask Jackson.

"You will have distance to overcome," he said, "and in all probability obstacles will be thrown in the way of your march by the enemy. As your move is the key of the campaign, you should appoint the hour at which the connection may be made coöperative."

"The morning of the twenty-fifth," Jackson promptly responded.

"You will encounter Federal cavalry and roads blocked by felled timber," Longstreet went on, "if nothing more formidable. Ought you not to give yourself more time?"

Then Jackson agreed to change the date to June 26. (The accounts by D. H. Hill and Longstreet [3] do not altogether agree, but this seems to be the substance of the conversation between Longstreet and Jackson.)

When Lee came back to the council chamber, he was told (probably by Longstreet) that the subordinates had worked out the plan and that Jackson had appointed the morning of June 26, "when he would lead the march," Longstreet says, whatever that means. Beyond doubt, Longstreet was right in thinking that Jackson needed more time for his movement; it would have been better, for certain reasons, if June 27 had been selected for the beginning of the attack instead of the afternoon of June 26. But here the time element enters, for the Confederate leaders knew that McClellan could not be kept much longer in ignorance of Jackson's

[3] *Ibid.*, p. 121; *B. & L.*, II, 347.

coming down from the Valley. In fact, a deserter had already informed McClellan, who did not credit the report.

By the plan, Jackson was to leave Ashland on June 25 and camp that night near Slash Church, some miles nearer the scene of action. At 3:00 A. M. on the morning of June 26, he was to cross the railroad (now C. & O.) at Ashcake Station and *turn* Beaver Dam Creek, taking the direction toward Cold Harbor. Stuart, with his horsemen, was to join Jackson at Slash Church and cover his advance. It is to be noted that Jackson was ordered to go around Beaver Dam Creek. If he had moved as ordered, he would have gone around Porter's position on Beaver Dam Creek and struck his rear.

Jackson was delayed in starting from Ashland. On June 25, he sent Lee a message stating that because of rain and the condition of the roads he would be late. Thus it seems that rain made the first hitch in the plan. After an early start, he struggled all the morning of June 26 along narrow, winding, deeply-rutted roads, set in dense woods, which were in places obstructed by trees cut down across them and sometimes occupied in front by skirmishing enemies. His men, accustomed to the open country and the good roads of the Valley, seem to have been exhausted by the heavy mud and the intense heat. At all events, Jackson went into camp at Hundley's Corner, three miles away, at 3:30 P. M. He went into camp while the three commands that were to coöperate with him in the movement strained their ears for the sound of his opening guns. At least that is the picture painted by the historians. In fact, it seems that Jackson had done about all that he could that day. The other generals should have awaited his initiative and the high command kept contact.

The other commands were arrayed at various bridges over the Chickahominy: Branch, farthest north at Winston's

Bridge, would first cross on Jackson's approach; then A. P. Hill, at the next lowest bridge, Meadow, would begin to move on Jackson's and Branch's approach; finally, D. H. Hill and Longstreet, at the Mechanicsville bridge, would join in when the approach of Branch and A. P. Hill dislodged Porter's outposts from Mechanicsville. D. H. Hill was to move behind A. P. Hill to the support of Jackson, Longstreet to follow and support A. P. Hill. It was a cumbersome scheme, full of chances of misadventure; Lee would have done better to have drawn a simpler plan.

It was now 4:00 P. M. of June 26; even the long June day was wearing away without fighting. A. P. Hill was not the man to be defrauded of a chance for action. Determined to attack whether Jackson came up or not, fearing that disaster would follow delay, he crossed the Chickahominy and moved down the left bank to Mechanicsville. It is obvious that Lee had no intention of fighting at Mechanicsville, desiring to maneuver Porter from it by the threat of Jackson's approach; and it seems that as the afternoon waned without word of Jackson, he sent a dispatch to A. P. Hill to postpone the advance. If the order was sent, Hill either did not receive it or disregarded it, for he committed the army to battle. He was given to acting rather than to thinking; his corps, it will be observed, precipitated the battle of Gettysburg.

A. P. Hill's men, brushing aside the Union pickets at Mechanicsville, advanced easterly to Beaver Dam Creek. The whole line was halted by the fire from Porter's position on the east side of the creek. The Confederates, coming to Ellerson's Mills, made a fierce frontal assault on Porter, whose infantry rested behind breastworks while his artillery crowned the hill behind. The Confederates, rushing down the hillside toward the creek, came under a frightful fire of musketry and artillery, beneath which whole regiments melted away. Hill brought up other troops and did not desist from his hopeless effort until he had lost about two thousand men; the Unionists, well protected, suffered little.

A disheartening situation faced Lee on the night of June 26, 1862. His first essay in command of an army had not prospered; the combination had not worked. Jackson had not come up as expected, and A. P. Hill had attacked prematurely, with the result that the army had suffered heavy loss and was discouraged. It is probable that the new commander slept little that night, considering how he might repair the errors of the day.

Lee's strategy, however, was already bearing fruit. McClellan, at last aware of Jackson's proximity, in the night of June 26 gave orders for Porter's withdrawal from the position on Beaver Dam Creek he had defended so well. A little after daylight on June 27, Porter began to retire along the road leading east, in order to take his stand at the next and much stronger prepared position. Lee must have been cheered when the pickets reported that the Unionists were retreating from his front. A. P. Hill's men pushed on cautiously in pursuit. Lee, following them, came to Walnut Grove Church, a mile or so beyond Beaver Dam Creek, where, hearing that Jackson was near, he awaited his lieutenant's approach.

On this day, as on the day before, matters were becoming badly mixed. Although Lee had sent a staff officer in the early morning, presumably to guide Jackson around the head of Beaver Dam Creek, the officer conducted Jackson's column to Walnut Grove Church, west of the millpond at Gaines's Mill, instead of taking it to the north. D. H. Hill, who was to support Jackson, had crossed the latter's line of march and was taking the route assigned to Jackson.

Whether Lee changed Jackson's route or whether, as is more probable, the staff officer took the wrong road cannot now be told. At all events, Jackson and D. H. Hill were across each other's line of march.

Soon Jackson came up to Lee waiting at Walnut Grove Church, and the two generals had their first field conference. At that place Jackson was set right by Lee and followed D. H. Hill on the indicated road. It was the part of these two commands, in Lee's plan, to cut McClellan's supply line; the march would have brought Jackson to the supply railway if there had been no contact with the enemy.

The confusion caused by the staff officer's mistake (or a change of orders) was unfortunate since it caused Jackson's delay. When the error was corrected, A. P. Hill pushed on past Walnut Grove Church and came on the Union rearguard at Gaines's Mill, where the fighting which has given its name to the battle of June 27 began, though it did not culminate there. The delay enabled Porter to get under cover at his new position, which was not on Powhite Creek, as the Confederate leaders thought, but a mile east of it on Boatswain Creek.

It was about 1:30 p. m. when A. P. Hill's skirmishers, coming to Powhite Creek at Gaines's Mill, found Porter's rearguard on the opposite side of the stream. Forcing a passage, Hill followed the retreating rearguard across the fields and down another hill to the deep ravine of Boatswain Creek, on the other side of which he discovered the Union line in position. With his usual impetuosity, Hill sent his troops down the hillside and up the slope beyond the run, only to have them repulsed with heavy loss by the infantry along the hillside and the artillery on the crest. In fact, he was now assailing an even stronger position than the one at Beaver Dam Creek. A. P. Hill then appealed for aid to Lee, who was at New Cold Harbor, a little distance in his rear.

Meanwhile Jackson, following D. H. Hill, came to Old Cold Harbor, about a mile east of New Cold Harbor. Hill was advancing southward to the McGee house, by which route he would have struck the extreme right of the Union

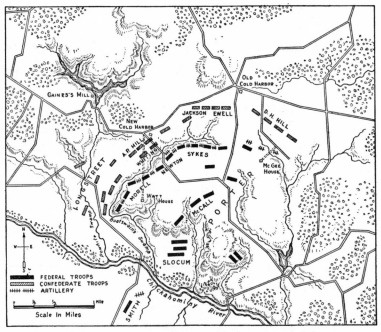

BATTLE OF GAINES'S MILL, JUNE 27, 1862

position; but when the sound of battle came from Powhite Creek, Jackson withdrew Hill to the cover of the woods, leaving a wide open space in front, across which he expected Porter to be driven by A. P. Hill and Longstreet. Whether or not Lee had planned it, Jackson saw the opportunity for a pincer movement by enclosing Porter between A. P. Hill and Longstreet on one side and D. H. Hill and himself on the other.

McClellan's skilled engineers had selected a good position overlooking the ravine of Boatswain Creek, which at this point takes the form of a horseshoe, with the toe about the place where still stands the Watt house; the right side extended northeast, the left side southeast. A. P. Hill struck the toe near the Watt house and began the attack.

Porter's position had one weak spot, and the acute D. H. Hill at length discovered it. The right end was in the air where the ravine of Boatswain Creek no longer protected it. In other words, the Confederates had only to move around Porter's right to force him to evacuate his position on Boatswain Creek just as he had evacuated that at Beaver Dam Creek. But the discovery was made too late to utilize, for by the time Jackson and D. H. Hill learned of it the right wing of Lee's army was engaged in a desperate frontal assault on the left of Porter's position. From left to right the Confederates' commands ran: D. H. Hill, Jackson, A. P. Hill, Longstreet.

When A. P. Hill failed in his attack and called for help, Lee sent in Longstreet, who came on Hill's right not far from the river. Longstreet had no more success than A. P. Hill, and Lee suddenly realized that the situation was growing critical. It was late afternoon; and so far from Porter's being driven from his position, he was holding his own and wrecking whole Confederate brigades. With a valor seldom surpassed the Southern infantry crossed the marshy stream, through the dense thickets, to breast the opposite hillside and be mowed down by hundreds by the protected Union infantry and the Union artillery, placed gun against gun along the crest.

Jackson was called on for aid and sent troops, which A. P. Hill and Longstreet put into the attacks they were still making. Lee grew desperate. The sun was setting, not on a victory as he had expected but on what looked, every minute, more and more like defeat. If he were forced to fall back on Richmond, defeated, the situation would be almost hopeless. More justly perhaps than any other battle of the war, Gaines's Mill may be called critical, for if the Confederates had lost it the fall of Richmond and the end of the new government would probably have followed speedily.

Lee finally succeeded, however, in his aim, which was to make a combined attack on the Union position. All along the line, from D. H. Hill on the extreme left to Longstreet on the right, the Confederate infantry, following their red flags and disregarding the awful hail of bullets and canister that swept their ranks, rushed up the hillside, poured over the breastworks, and carried the position at the bayonet's point. Longstreet claims that his men made the break. On few battlefields in history has a finer charge been made than by the Confederates at Gaines's Mill. The Unionists, fewer in number and resisting with desperate gallantry, were over-powered. As night fell they made for the bridges over the Chickahominy, to find safety by joining the main army on the south side. Jackson's men had in their front Sykes's regulars, who as steady as on parade and disdainful to the last, fell back in good order before the surrounding swarm of Southerners.

Just here McClellan had the chance of his life. Lee had lost eight thousand men, Porter six thousand. Only by the most desperate efforts and by the self-sacrifice of the company officers, who led their men with absolute disregard of life, had the Confederates been able to carry the Union position at all. McClellan had sent Porter aid most sparingly; if he had given him one more division it is probable that the night of June 27, 1862, would have witnessed the precipitate retreat of Lee into the Richmond defenses. The tragedy of it, from McClellan's standpoint, was that many divisions stood in line on the south side of the Chickahominy River without firing a shot. As it was, the Confederates had won a costly victory.

The point is that they had won. Lee had gained his first battle and would now go on to victory after victory. It is curious to consider how near his career came to ending on the field of Gaines's Mill, on June 27, 1862. A little more courage and energy on McClellan's part and that would have happened.

Heavy as his losses were, Lee had carried out a part of his plan, for he had defeated Porter if not crushed him. He was now on McClellan's supply line and believed, for the moment, that he had cut the Unionists off from their base. He calculated that McClellan would have to cross the river and attack him in order to regain his supply line or make a disastrous retreat to Hampton. Yet he must have been puzzled when he learned that Porter's troops had re-treated across the Chickahominy instead of toward the Pa-munkey and the White House. His puzzlement grew the next day, June 28, when he found that the Unionists were making no move in the direction of the White House. Late in the day he grasped the situation when Stuart's cavalry reported that masses of supplies were burning at the White House, indicating that McClellan had changed his base. Lee, studying the reports, understood that the Union army was probably making for the James River and a new base of operations. Thus his fine stroke at McClellan's supply line failed through no fault of his own.

With his strategic acuteness, Lee now made preparations to cut McClellan off before he could reach the James, if indeed he was moving in that direction and not down the Peninsula toward Hampton. Lee's orders for June 29, how-ever, were somewhat unfortunate. In the first place, he seems not to have known that the Unionists had destroyed their bridges over the Chickahominy when they retreated, particularly the bridge, or series of bridges, known as the Grapevine Bridge, with its long causeway through the swamp. Unaware of this, Lee directed Jackson to cross at Grapevine Bridge and pursue the Unionists. Magruder, who was south of the river, was to join Jackson in an attack on the Union rearguard, while Longstreet and A. P. Hill crossed the Chickahominy by the upper bridges and pushed around the Union army toward the James. With Jackson and Magruder holding McClellan, and Longstreet and A. P. Hill taking him in flank, Lee hoped to destroy him.

It should be noted that Magruder had, in reality, played a deciding part in the battle of June 27, though historians have overlooked it. Left south of the Chickahominy with a small force and directly facing the main Union army, the great master of camouflage had made such a demonstration that the Union corps commanders had been smitten with fear. Two Alabama regiments had emerged from the defenses and actually initiated an attack on the Unionists at Golding's Farm. The result was that when the cautious McClellan asked his corps commanders if they could spare troops they all answered in the negative, and Porter was left to his fate.

Now, on the morning of June 29, Magruder pursued the retreating Unionists southward, expecting to be joined by Jackson. But the latter was halted by having to reconstruct the bridges and causeway at Grapevine Bridge. Longstreet, in his book, states that Jackson could have forded the Chickahominy, but the statement is absurd. Even if the infantry had managed to get across the again-swollen river, no artillery or wagons could have been taken. In fact, Jackson should be praised for the rapidity with which his skilled engineering force replaced the bridges that had taken the Unionists weeks to construct. By midnight of June 29, he was ready to cross, and did so.

Magruder, having only a few weak brigades and being behind the greater part of the Union army, fought an action

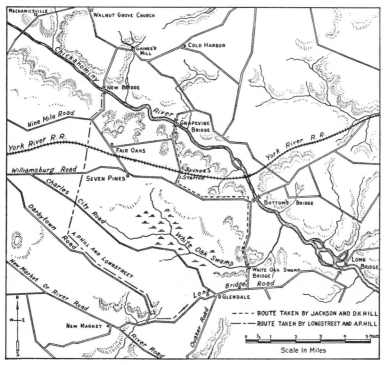

CONFEDERATE MOVEMENTS, JUNE 29-30, 1862

in the morning of June 29 at Allen's Farm and late in the afternoon came on the Union position at Savage's Station on the supply railroad. It was Lee's expectation that Magruder would be supported by Jackson from the north and Huger from the south, but neither of the supports appeared. Consequently, Magruder found himself unable to fulfill his task of holding the Union army at bay while the other commands surrounded it. He did attack at Savage's Station in the late afternoon of June 29, fighting a brisk action in which about one thousand men were killed and wounded on both sides. Then, discovering that he was attacking the greater part of the Union army, crowded together in the vicinity of Savage's Station, he wisely hauled off before his weak force was annihilated. For this he was somewhat blamed by Lee, who did not understand the situation. Magruder could not have held fifty thousand men with five thousand and he did well to escape disaster.

If Lee had directed his columns toward James River with the distinct purpose of heading off McClellan he might have succeeded, and this indeed seems to have been his plan; but the plan was so elaborate and so involved with coöperations that, in the absence of good staff work, it had little chance of success.

The main roads running eastward from Richmond between the Chickahominy and James rivers are as follows from north to south: Nine-Mile road; Williamsburg road; Charles City road; Darbytown road; and the River road. The location of these roads may be described as having the general relation of fingers to a hand. Lee's plan was to send Jackson in immediate pursuit of the retiring Unionists to attack them, and also probably to prevent their doubling back toward the north in the event of being cut off from the James. Huger was to follow the Charles City road, A. P. Hill and Longstreet the Darbytown road, and Theophilus Holmes the River road. This last force was scheduled to capture Malvern Hill, an eminence of great strength not far from the James, toward which in the course of events McClellan would bend his steps. It seems probable that Lee intended to hold McClellan between Holmes at Malvern Hill and Jackson and Huger at White Oak Swamp while A. P. Hill and Longstreet attacked him in the flank. If this plan could be carried out, the destruction of the Army of the Potomac was well-nigh certain.

The plan was not carried out, owing to several circumstances. In the early morning of June 30, Lee had a long conference at Savage's Station with Jackson, who by this time had crossed the Chickahominy and was following on McClellan's trail. No doubt Jackson received his instructions, of which nothing is known. He took up his march for White Oak Swamp, which he reached about noon. The artillery was placed on the heights north of the stream and opened fire on the opposing artillery south of it. Jackson himself spent a considerable time in examining the various crossings of White Oak Swamp, finally coming to the conclusion that the passage of the stream in the face of strong opposition was impracticable. He has been greatly blamed for this decision, for which, nevertheless, he had reason.

White Oak Swamp is a narrow but rather deep stream with a bad bottom, meandering through a swamp of formidable character in that it is covered with a dense and almost impenetrable jungle. The crossings were few and the fords very bad, for which reason the Unionists had built several bridges, which they destroyed in the morning of June 30 after they had completed the passage of their wagon trains. It was possible for infantry to get across the stream but impossible for wagons and artillery. If Jackson had forced a passage he must have done so along narrow roads exposed to artillery fire, and his losses would have been great.

It is likely that if he had forced a passage, as he has been so much censured for not doing, his command would have been too disorganized to take an active part in the battle of Glendale near by. Besides, there is the possibility that Jackson was where he was in order to block any movement of McClellan's down the Peninsula. Although not so stated in his report, Lee's plan seems to have been another attempt of the pincer movement essayed before at Gaines's Mill. Jackson could not have forced a passage of White Oak Swamp without heavy loss, but he could have moved around the head of the swamp and debouched on the Charles City road where Huger was. In that case, however, McClellan would have had a free passage of White Oak Swamp in case he turned back from the James River. At all events, Jackson remained inactive all day of June 30, 1862, though the battle of Glendale was raging only a mile and a half away. Lee himself was at Glendale, and if he was dissatisfied with Jackson's passivity he could easily have sent him an order to act. That Lee made no such move would seem to indicate that he saw nothing censurable in Jackson's conduct, and it strengthens the belief that Lee was again trying the pincer operation.

From White Oak Swamp a highway runs south to Malvern Hill, known as the Quaker road or the Willis Church road. As there was another Quaker road, confusion was caused by this duplication of terms, for Magruder, ordered to follow the Quaker road, took the wrong highway of that name. All through the night of June 29 and the forenoon of June 30, the Union wagon trains rumbled south toward Malvern Hill and, by another road east of the Quaker road, to Haxall's Landing on the James River. The troops followed the Quaker road; by midday part of the Union army had passed a certain point called Glendale, where the Charles City and the Long Bridge roads came into the Quaker road, the pivotal point.

Unfortunately, the Confederates let the Unionists establish themselves on Malvern Hill. Holmes, old and deaf, was quite inadequate for his part of the task, the hardest part. He tried to seize the elevation but allowed himself to be pushed off by Union troops and scared away by the firing of gunboats in the river. Longstreet himself might have reached Malvern Hill in the night of June 29 or the early morning of June 30, in which case a fierce conflict would have occurred there, with chances favoring the Confederates, who were not encumbered with wagon trains like the Unionists. But Longstreet did not go to Malvern Hill.

The Darbytown road, making a great curve to the south, came into the Long Bridge road, running northeast, not far from Malvern Hill; and Longstreet reached this point in the evening of June 29. The Long Bridge road paralleled the Quaker road, from which it was not far distant.

Longstreet, arriving at this junction, camped there, and A. P. Hill on Newmarket Heights. If, instead of stopping, Longstreet had pushed across the Long Bridge road, he would have come into the Quaker road not far from Malvern Hill; and, in the evening of June 29, he could have taken that position, since then only a small part of the Union army had arrived there. Even on the morning of June 30, he could have reached Malvern Hill in time to cut McClellan's column in half and throw it into confusion. Instead of doing this, he turned northeast on the Long Bridge road and was followed by A. P. Hill, whom he now commanded. The result was that in the forenoon of June 30, while McClellan's troops and wagons were proceeding south to Malvern Hill, Longstreet and Hill were marching north on the Long Bridge road, the two forces moving in opposite directions and almost in sight of each other.

When Longstreet reached the vicinity of the junction of the Long Bridge road and the Quaker road, known as Glendale, in the early afternoon of June 30, all of the Union army had passed that point except the strong rearguard detailed to hold off Jackson at White Oak Swamp and Longstreet at Glendale. It thus follows that the battle of Glendale, or Frayser's Farm (to give it two of its seven names) was a rearguard action in no way involving the safety of the Union army as a whole. The Northern writers appreciate this fact, which has been apparent to no other historians. Glendale is usually represented as the crux of the Seven Days (which it was not in any sense), and a flank attack on McClellan's moving army. It is true that Longstreet and A. P. Hill should have headed McClellan off from Malvern Hill or attacked him in the flank but, instead, they attempted to crush his rearguard. Consequently, if Jackson had managed to cross White Oak Swamp, pushing the force there before him, he might have reached Glendale in time to enable the Confederates to smash the rearguard instead of fighting a drawn battle as actually occurred. But it does not appear that his presence would have had any other effect, and his losses would probably have offset the Union losses. Glendale has been misunderstood. Represented as Lee's great opportunity in the Seven Days, it was nothing like as good a chance as July 1 or July 2.

Late in the afternoon Longstreet deployed his troops across the Long Bridge road to the Charles City road, near the point where those thoroughfares meet the Quaker road. Here were fields mingled with dense woods. Davis and Lee were there to witness what all hoped would be a great victory, because they did not know that McClellan had already crossed the Confederate front and was safe on Malvern Hill. The Union line ran immediately in front of the Quaker road, so essential to hold, for about two miles. Kearny was on the right, McCall in the center, Hooker on the left, with Sedgwick in reserve behind McCall, on whom the brunt of the attack fell.

The Confederates, advancing through the woods and

across the open spaces, speedily came to grips with the Unionists, who because of the forest could not use their artillery to much advantage. Longstreet's men swept forward until the lines of blue and gray intermingled, and there followed a fierce mêlée with bayonets and gun butts. Longstreet was thrown back with heavy loss and called for help. At that time only A. P. Hill was at hand. Jackson was held up at the crossings of White Oak Swamp; Huger was on the Charles City road not far away, but the road was so obstructed by felled timber that his progress was slow. Holmes was doing nothing on the River road; Magruder was being kept marching from place to place by contradictory orders.

Longstreet now put A. P. Hill into the fray. Thus a Confederate force of twenty thousand men was assailing the Union rearguard of perhaps the same numbers. As the shadows lengthened Longstreet reinforced his own worn troops, thinned by fighting for several hours, with Hill's fresh men. Presently Hooker, advancing from his position, came into contact with Longstreet's right, and another terrible struggle followed. Hooker was finally repulsed, while, on the Confederate left, Hill's troops drove back McCall, who held the center of the Union line. As night thickened the Unionists began to withdraw, leaving McCall a prisoner within the Confederate lines. About twelve thousand men had fallen on both sides, but McClellan's retreat was not blocked. The rearguard, shattered by its losses, fell back rather precipitately on Malvern Hill, but the Confederates were in no condition to pursue.

McClellan was now ensconced on Malvern Hill, and the opinion prevails that he was safe there. This was by no means the case; he was still some distance from the river and was, in reality, in a perilous position. The Union corps commanders in the morning of July 1 made strenuous preparations for the desperate struggle they expected and about which they felt anything but confident. The guns, of which McClellan had a great number, were arranged in rows, hub against hub, and behind them the infantry stood in line of battle.

The morning of July 1 found Lee endeavoring to get his army together for pursuit. Longstreet and A. P. Hill were too broken by Glendale to do much, but Jackson, Huger, and Magruder came up, giving Lee a large force to use in his final effort to crush the foe. The two armies were now concentrated and facing each other, not far apart.

Lee held a council of war. He was eager to attack, for he feared that McClellan was about to escape, while the signs of haste evidenced by the arms and equipment thrown away by the retreating rearguard the night before led him to believe that the Union army was demoralized, which was far from being the case.

There was no need to blunder head on against Malvern Hill, a most formidable position. A road to the east led to Haxall's Landing and to Lamptie Hill, two miles from Malvern Hill, an admirable position for artillery. If the Confederates moved around McClellan and seized this hill, the latter would be in a most perilous position. And at the council Jackson advised Lee to move by the left, which would have completely flanked Malvern Hill. But Longstreet gave the counter advice to make a frontal assault on Malvern Hill, and his counsel prevailed. D. H. Hill had warned Lee of the strength of the position, whereupon Longstreet, laughing, said, "Don't get scared, now that we have got him licked." [4]

It is hard to understand why Lee made this unfortunate

[4] *B. & L.*, II, 391.

decision.[5] Perhaps Jackson's stock had fallen since he had not taken part in the battle of June 30; perhaps Longstreet's had risen because he had directed it. Probably Lee's blood was up and he preferred fighting to maneuvering. He wished to strike the Union army before it recovered its morale—only the Union morale was still good.

There is so much confusion in the accounts of the battle of Malvern Hill that a satisfactory narrative cannot be reconstructed. It was by far the worst engagement Lee ever conducted, if he can be said to have conducted it. In the first place, the Confederates had to approach Malvern Hill through a swampy jungle that made the proper deployment of troops impossible. In the second place, it was found impracticable to employ artillery, and that fact alone should have caused a change of plan. Because of the dense forest, the Confederates were able to find ground for only a few guns, which were blown to pieces the moment they opened fire on the massed Union batteries on the hill.

Lee, having accepted Longstreet's advice to make a frontal assault, asked him to find a position for artillery. Longstreet reported that he knew of a space for sixty guns, with chances of an enfilading fire on the Union position. This was on the extreme right of the Confederate line, but there was no room for sixty guns. The few guns that were brought up were speedily silenced.

It followed from this that the Confederate infantry was called on to assault massed batteries supported by an infantry line of battle while having no artillery support itself. And presently the Confederate commanders found the difficulties of forming a line of battle almost insuperable.

Malvern Hill on its northern slope is a long and gradual

[5] G. F. R. Henderson, *Stonewall Jackson and the American Civil War*, 2 vols. (New York, Longmans, Green and Company, 1898), II, 74.

incline, affording an ideal field of fire for a force holding it. On its southern face it rises abruptly from the plain, allowing a view for miles. At its northern foot is a stretch of tangled, marshy woods in which the Confederates were obliged to form for the assault. The troops lined up as best they could in the dense undergrowth.

Meanwhile the ruin of the Confederate batteries that had opened fire brought Lee to the realization of the situation and he began to consider taking Jackson's advice. He sent for Longstreet to ride with him to the left in order to find a way to turn the Union position.[6] After a short survey Lee concluded that the movement was practicable and gave orders to that effect. But it seems he failed to cancel his previous order for the frontal attack, for which the line of battle had formed. The charge was to be made when one of the commands raised a shout and went forward. It reveals the poverty of Confederate resources and the quality of the staff work that the signal for opening the battle was to be a shout.

Presently some body of men shouted and troops on the Confederate right moved forward out of the shelter of the woods. From right to left the Confederates swept forward against the hill, defended by scores of cannon and a line of battle of many thousands of men. Magruder on the right conducted the attack as much as anybody did; the commands seem to have been independent of control, and certainly Lee was able to exercise none. Driven back by the awful artillery fire, the Southerners went forward again and again with superb self-devotion, only to be mowed down by hundreds. Yet so splendid was their ill-directed valor that the battle was by no means one-sided; if the Confederates could have attacked in unison instead of by brigades, as they did, they

[6] *M. to A.*, p. 144.

would probably have stormed the Union position in spite of everything.

At length Magruder, whose command had been cut to pieces, called for reinforcements, and Jackson sent troops into the fray. But before the attack was renewed, night fell on the scene and closed the battle.

In this engagement, besides attempting a general control of the field, in which he failed, Longstreet did little. Late in the day he sent A. P. Hill to Magruder's aid and brought up his own division as a support for the extreme Confederate right.

In some places the Confederates approached the Union line, and squads of them, where the ground was favorable, clung to the positions they had reached; but the major part of the field was so swept by an annihilating artillery and infantry fire that nothing could stand before it. In this unnecessary engagement, poorly planned and badly executed, the Confederates lost about five thousand men and the Unionists perhaps two thousand.

McClellan was beaten, however, if his army was not. In the night of July 1 he abandoned the field and continued his retreat to Harrison's Landing on the James River. If he had stood his ground and renewed the conflict the next day, there is no telling the result. The Confederate army, worn out with constant fighting and shattered by its terrible losses, was in no condition for battle; if McClellan had advanced on the morning of July 2, he would probably have won a decisive victory. Some of the Southern leaders were afraid that he would hold his ground, but not Jackson; he had measured McClellan. "No, he will clear out," Jackson said, and it turned out that way. As the sun rose on the morning of July 2 and the Confederate pickets discovered that the enemy had withdrawn, the army felt that it had won a victory, as in a sense it had. It had gained the field at least, if not the prize of the hostile host.

Now comes the last and, in some respects, the greatest opportunity of all presented to the Confederates in the Seven Days. McClellan, on reaching the low ground at Harrison's Landing, felt that he was safe at last; the wearied and bleeding army relaxed its vigilance. And then Stuart made a blunder that recalled it to its still dangerous position.

Stuart, who had done little of consequence in the Seven Days, had been recalled to the army from the north side of the Chickahominy on June 30; he reached Jackson's left in the night of July 1. It was his business now to cover the Confederate advance.

The morning of July 2, 1862, was cloudy and oppressive. The enemy was gone and it was necessary to follow. Jackson, being on the Confederate left, was directed to begin the pursuit. Magruder and Huger were to follow Jackson. Lee went with them. D. H. Hill's division remained on Malvern Hill. The reserve divisions were sent by another way, the Charles City road. Heavy rain now came on, retarding all movements.

Stuart, riding in advance, in the evening of July 2 came on Evlington Heights overlooking the low ground around Harrison's Landing. By some oversight the heights were not occupied by the enemy and afforded a perfect position for shelling the Union camp, with perhaps important results. It appears that Stuart reported his findings to Lee and Jackson in the night of July 2. If so, nothing was done about it at the time.

In the morning of July 3, Stuart himself, with a small force of cavalry, occupied Evlington Heights and opened on the host below him with a tiny howitzer. His popgun could have no effect but that of arousing the Union leaders to their imminent danger. Infantry was directed against Evlington Heights and Stuart was driven away. Then the Union engineer corps began to work like mad throwing up a heavy line of fortifications that remains until this day.

On the morning of July 4, the main Confederate army came up. Longstreet rode to the front and, as he says, "ordered General Jackson to drive in the enemy's skirmishers and prepare to attack." If he thus ordered Jackson, who was not under his command, he must have considered himself just then in charge of the army. Jones's division, coming up, was put on Jackson's left and A. P. Hill on his right. Longstreet's own division was in reserve.[7]

Jackson pushed back the pickets in front of the Union position on Evlington Heights and then, Longstreet asserts, "reported his troops not in condition for the work, and asked a delay until the commanding general was up." If this is true, Jackson probably preferred to be commanded by Lee rather than by Longstreet, who was pushing himself into the control of the army.

A note was sent to Lee, who arrived in about half an hour. He and Jackson examined the Union position and found it too strong to assault, as it was. The pursuit was over. McClellan was left to refresh his exhausted army on the banks of the James while Lee withdrew his own equally worn-out force to points nearer Richmond.

Lee had failed in his effort to destroy McClellan and he had suffered considerably heavier losses than the enemy. At the same time he had completely frustrated the campaign against Richmond, which was perfectly safe for the time. In one week he had risen from comparative obscurity to fame; the world was ringing with his name. The Confederacy, responding to the victory, began to revive. It was seen

[7] *M. to A.*, p. 146.

that the war, far from being nearly over, as had been supposed by many, was actually only beginning.

Next to Lee, Longstreet had garnered the greatest fame. The reason for this was that he had conducted the battle of Glendale, which gave him the reputation of being a "fighting general." At Mechanicsville and Gaines's Mill he had done nothing more than others; at Malvern Hill he had not distinguished himself; but he had been in command at Glendale and that had made his name.

Jackson's reputation had fallen somewhat. Looked on as a superman after the Valley Campaign, he was expected to accomplish great things. These he had not done. He had come up slowly at Mechanicsville and had been delayed by the Chickahominy River and the White Oak Swamp. He had not been at Glendale at all and had done little at Malvern Hill. If it had not been for his early fame, he might have been shipped off to remote provinces, as were Magruder, Huger, and Holmes, but he was too great a personage for such treatment. The historians, even to this day, have not realized the difficulties with which he contended, for few of them have been over the ground concerned. Almost none of them has realized that the greatest lost opportunity of the Seven Days was Longstreet's failure to take Malvern Hill instead of marching north to Glendale and fighting a rearguard action.

Nevertheless, Longstreet showed great improvement in the Seven Days. His offensive tactics at Seven Pines had been wretched. At Gaines's Mill he had handled his men to far better effect, and at Glendale he had conducted a severe offensive action with considerable success. But it still remained true of him that he was essentially a defensive fighter, not offensive, and he was to continue thus to the end of the war. It would appear that the futility of Malvern

Hill, the heavy losses of the attacking Confederates, and the lighter losses of the defending Unionists won him completely to the defensive view. To him, thereafter, successful war consisted in holding a strong position against an enemy fully exposed by assaulting it.

CHAPTER VIII

APEX AT MANASSAS

AFTER McClellan had established himself at Harrison's Landing on the James River, with fortifications that are still massive in places, there came a lull in the war. McClellan had to reorganize before he could resume the offensive, and the same condition confronted Lee, whose army had lost heavily and was much disorganized. The month of July was spent by both sides in making ready for the next campaign.

Now that the Confederates at Richmond had a breathing spell, they began to fight the Seven Days' battles over again, especially in the newspapers. Longstreet had basked in the light of glory for some days, when an article appeared in the *Richmond Examiner* attributing much credit for the victory to A. P. Hill. As Hill was under Longstreet, the latter's jealous nature flared up at once. He had a reply published in the *Richmond Whig* that was uncomplimentary to Hill. The latter thereupon refused to have anything to do with Longstreet. Longstreet put him under arrest, and Hill asked to be assigned to another command. The knot was finally cut by transferring Hill, but the incident was not a promising one and reflected no credit on Longstreet, who appeared in the light of a superior resenting glory given a subordinate.

As August came on, the new campaign began to take form. The Union government, out of patience with McClellan for a failure due as much to the government itself as to any other factor, was looking for a new commander.

The considerable bodies of Union troops which had been kept scattered over northern and western Virginia by the Confederate strategy were consolidated in the Army of Virginia (Banks, Frémont, and McDowell), commanded by John Pope, who had met with some success on the Mississippi and who was a man of great self-confidence. Halleck was brought East and made commander-in-chief, and he prepared to direct the strategy of the Union forces in Virginia from his office in Washington. Burnside came up from North Carolina with his troops, touching at Hampton Roads and later going on to Aquia Creek. A great army was in process of formation in northern Virginia; if McClellan should be added to it, Lee would be faced by an overwhelming concentration, a situation worse than the one that had met him when he assumed command of the army on June 1.

The Army of Virginia, of which Schenck's and Banks's divisions were at Front Royal, Ricketts's at Warrenton, and King's at Fredericksburg, received word from Pope, on July 10, to be ready to march at any moment. On July 12, Lee in Richmond was startled by the news that Pope had reached Culpeper Courthouse that morning. Culpeper, a station on the Orange and Alexandria Railroad (now Southern) was an important point, and not far from the Virginia Central Railroad, Richmond's connection with the Shenandoah Valley and the West.

To meet this threat Jackson was ordered, on July 13, to move with his own and Ewell's divisions to Gordonsville. Although McClellan's unweakened host was still at Harrison's Landing, Lee was forced to take the risk of detaching troops from his own army to oppose Pope. If he did not take such a step, he would be in danger of being caught between McClellan on one side and Pope, coming from the north, on the other.

Pope was a very different personage from the gentle-
manly McClellan. His small successes in the West had made
him confident, and he was of a hard and self-assertive nature. Noncombatants began to suffer in Virginia as they had
not done before, for property was destroyed and people
were put under arrest. Pope's former comrades serving in
the Confederate army began to recall the stories about him,
as soldiers will, particularly of his attempts to find artesian
water in the desert of Texas. They sang a little song current
years before in the army:

> Pope told a flattering tale,
>   Which proved to be bravado,
> About the streams which spout like ale
>   On the Llano Estacado.[1]

Jackson reached Gordonsville on July 19 and began to
take stock of the situation. Meanwhile Lee was considering
the sending of sufficient troops to him to enable him to defeat Pope while the commander himself watched McClellan.
Then, with Pope defeated, Jackson would return to Richmond to take part in an offensive against McClellan.

Late in July, the Union commander at Harrison's Landing began to show signs of moving against Richmond. Longstreet busied himself with surveying the country north of
the James and, on July 22, ordered troops to occupy Newmarket Heights in order to block McClellan's route to Richmond.

Lee had now definitely decided to reinforce Jackson and
take the risk of being attacked by McClellan. A. P. Hill,
still under arrest and still eager to leave Longstreet, was

---

[1] E. P. Alexander, *Military Memoirs of a Confederate; a Critical Narrative*
(New York, Charles Scribner's Sons, 1907), p. 176.

ordered to Gordonsville. "I want Pope to be suppressed," Lee said.[2]

The risks were very great, but Lee was getting used to taking risks. The question was, Where would Burnside go? If he joined McClellan, Lee would be so outnumbered that Richmond would be in danger. On the other hand, if he reinforced Pope, Jackson, opposing the latter, would be greatly overmatched.

For a time it looked as if Lee had taken too great a chance in sending Hill to Jackson, for on August 5 McClellan advanced from his entrenchments as far as Malvern Hill, where he took position. The Confederates, coming up, confronted him in the same position they had occupied on July 1. Brisk skirmishing went on, but no battle was fought. Then, on August 7, the Confederate pickets discovered that the enemy had withdrawn; McClellan went back to Harrison's Landing. Evidently his movement was simply a demonstration. Things were beginning to take shape, for Lee had learned that Burnside was moving to Aquia Creek to join Pope. That was now the threat, not McClellan.

Jackson, reinforced by A. P. Hill, was ready for action. Advancing, he drove the Unionists from Orange Courthouse, ten miles north of Gordonsville. On August 8, Jackson, scattering the Union cavalry guarding the fords, crossed the Rapidan River and was now near Pope's advance.

Still moving, he crossed Robertson River, on August 9, and struck Banks's corps at Cedar Mountain, where a very sharp action took place. The Unionists put up a desperate fight and, though outnumbered, gave Jackson all he could do to defeat them. Defeat them he did in the end, driving them back to Culpeper. The next day, August 10, he found

---

[2] Douglas Southall Freeman, *R. E. Lee, A Biography*. 4 vols. (London and New York, Charles Scribner's Sons, 1934-35), II, 267.

that Pope's whole army was gathering in his front and he retired to Gordonsville. As he designed, his blow had drawn Pope toward him.

Cedar Mountain showed Lee that Jackson was too weak to defeat Pope; if that officer was to be disposed of, the whole army would be needed. He then and there made one of the greatest decisions of his career, one that demanded the utmost audacity. He determined to leave Richmond weakly garrisoned and to move with the rest of his army to join Jackson. On August 13, Longstreet received orders to proceed to Gordonsville.

Longstreet traveled to that town by the Virginia Central Railroad (C. & O.), taking ten brigades. Two others, Hood's and Whiting's, joined him a little later. After reaching Gordonsville and learning something of the situation, he wrote Lee suggesting a move amidst the foothills of the Blue Ridge against Pope's right wing.

Lee answered on August 14, "At this distance, without knowing the position or strength of the enemy, it is impossible for me to decide the question you propose. I incline, however, to the right flank movement. The easiest way of accomplishing that I should prefer. You, being on the spot, with all information before you and the benefit of consultation with officers acquainted with the ground and circumstances, must use your own judgment. . . .

"It is all important that our movement, in whatever direction it is determined, should be as quick as possible. I fear General Pope can be reënforced quicker than ourselves; prepare accordingly. Order transportation of the respective brigades to the point on the railroad you wish the troops to halt." [3]

It was just at this time that Lee learned that McClellan

[3] *O. R.*, ser. I, vol. LI, pt. III, p. 676.

was sending troops to Pope. That meant that Pope was to have the main Union army in Virginia and so was the principal threat. It meant also that Lee now had the opportunity to fight Pope without fear of McClellan, who would never dare to attack Richmond with a reduced force. Lee then decided to go to Gordonsville himself and take command. When he sent the dispatch to Longstreet, on August 14, he asked the latter to arrange a conference of the two lieutenants with himself as soon as he arrived.

Lee reached Gordonsville on August 15. He was now to operate in a very different region from the York-James Peninsula—the Virginia piedmont, a lovely blue-grass country (with forests but with wide open spaces between the forests), rolling up to the Blue Ridge Mountains, those lovely, gentle hills that form some of the most pleasing scenery in the United States. It was far easier to conduct marches and deploy troops in this region than in the tidewater, with its thick jungle and almost impenetrable swamps.

Lee, Longstreet, and Jackson held their conference on August 15, with a map provided by the topographically-minded Jackson. Before them was the Rappahannock-Rapidan line, which Lee studied with close attention. In the angle formed by the two rivers, Pope's army, which Jackson estimated as being fifty thousand strong originally, rested. Since then twenty thousand reinforcements had come to him, giving him perhaps seventy thousand men. Pope's front was to the Rapidan, his back to the Rappahannock. Thus situated, he fancied that he was secure, whereas, in reality, he was in imminent danger. If the Confederate cavalry could burn the bridges over the Rappahannock and the infantry be thrown across the Rapidan before Pope knew what was going on, the Union commander would be trapped between the rivers and might be destroyed.[4] It was the best opportunity Lee had yet had.

The time element, however, was all important. Troops were being sent from McClellan to Pope, Lee knew; he did not know that McClellan would follow. Given this reinforcement, Pope would have perhaps 110,000 men and would be too strong for Lee to assail with the troops he had at his command. In other words, Lee had to defeat Pope before the junction was made. If the two armies united, he would be forced to fall back on Richmond, which would be once more in grave danger.

The Confederate leaders agreed to attack, but did not agree immediately on the mode of attack. Longstreet supported the operation which he had been the first to suggest and which was ultimately adopted, a movement around Pope's right; this would put the Confederates among the foothills and would offer good defensive positions. But Lee thought it would be better to attack Pope's left wing, as in that way he would intervene between Pope and McClellan. When could the advance be made?

Jackson urged that the army cross the Rapidan on August 16 and fight the battle on the following day. Longstreet advocated delay in order to get supplies for his men. Jackson offered to lend him bread. However, as the cavalry could not be put in motion at once, it is not likely that Longstreet held up the operation, though some observers thought that he did. It was decided to make the movement on August 17 and to fight the battle on August 18.[5] Orders were issued on August 16, not much more than a day after Lee's arrival at Gordonsville.

Longstreet had accompanied Lee to the summit of

[4] Freeman, *op. cit.*, II, 280.
[5] *Ibid.*, p. 282.

Clark's Mountain, an isolated elevation near Orange Court-house. "There, between the two rivers," he says, "clustering around Culpeper Court House, and perhaps fifteen miles away, we saw the flags of Pope's army floating placidly above the tops of the trees. From the summit of the mountain we beheld the enemy occupying ground so weak as to invite attack." [6]

The advance was not made as directed. One division of troops was just arriving from Richmond. The cavalry was not in place and the commissaries did not have sufficient bread. Lee postponed the march until August 19.

It was not made then, because of the fact that Fitz Lee, whose cavalry was to lead the advance, had not received definite orders from Stuart, the cavalry commander. Lee was obliged to postpone the movement another day, until August 20. And now it was too late to catch Pope napping. For the Union commander, learning of the presence of Lee's army behind Clark's Mountain, began a hasty withdrawal from his perilous situation. Hearing of a stir in the Union camp, Lee rode again with Longstreet to the top of Clark's Mountain and once more surveyed the enemy camps. Lines of wagons, looking in the distance like ants, were in motion, followed presently by columns of dark figures, which the observers knew to be troops. It was with profound regret that Lee realized that Pope was escaping from the trap just before it closed on him. Never before or afterward did he have such an admirable opportunity to gain an annihilating victory.

Lee now altered his arrangements. He was to go in pur-suit of the retreating Unionists. Longstreet, commanding the right wing of the army, was to cross the Rapidan at Raccoon Ford (where eighty years before in the Revolution

[6] B. & L., II, 515.

Lafayette had been), while Jackson, with the left wing, should cross at Somerville Ford and follow.

In the morning of August 20, 1862, the two wings of the Army of Northern Virginia passed the Rapidan River. The infantry numbered about fifty thousand men, the total force about fifty-five thousand. D. H. Hill and McLaws, if not detained by the enemy in the vicinity of Richmond, would increase the army to sixty-seven thousand men. But they did not arrive for this campaign. That day Longstreet reached Kelly's Ford on the Rappahannock, while Jackson was at Stevensburg, with his advance at Brandy. Lee and Jackson bivouacked that night at the latter place.

Lee now learned that Pope's army was strung along the Rappahannock River, the fords of which were held in force. Longstreet and Jackson, advancing to the south bank of the river, began to come in contact with the Union pickets and artillery on the opposite shore.

Lee had decided to try a turning movement around the right flank of Pope's army, as originally suggested by Longstreet. His arrangements called for Stuart to go ahead and cover the march of the infantry. Jackson, moving upstream until he came to good fords, should cross, with Longstreet following. The trouble was that the Unionists, on the other side of the river, kept up with the Confederates on their westward slant. As a diversion Lee decided to try a cavalry raid against Pope's railroad communications and gave Stuart orders accordingly.

On August 22, Stuart started off on his ride; Jackson, finding the ford of the river at Fauquier White Sulphur Springs undefended, sent Early across. Just then there came a terrific rainstorm, which brought down such a flood of water that Early on the north bank of the stream was cut off from Jackson. Longstreet was on the river lower down.

In the morning of August 23, Longstreet opened fire with his batteries on the enemy across the river at Rappahannock Bridge. At the same time Jackson was endeavoring to re-build the bridge at the Sulphur Springs, in order to relieve Early from his awkward situation. Fortunately, the day wore away without an attack on Early. The cavalry raid was bearing fruit, for Stuart, striking the foe at Catlett's Station, had captured Pope's headquarters with all the papers. From them Lee learned that McClellan was moving to the junction with Pope and that what was to be done must be done quickly. In order to strike Pope before McClellan reached him, it would be necessary to draw the former away from the latter. Lee decided to strike at Pope's supply line, the Orange and Alexandria Railroad, hoping to put a part of his force between Pope and Washington, a maneuver that would alarm the Union authorities.

In the morning of August 24, Early succeeded in crossing to the south bank of the Rappahannock, just as the Unionists began concentrating against him. A. P. Hill's artillery, opening on them, dispersed them.

Meanwhile Lee was deciding on his plan. It was the greatest of his evolutions. Behind a cavalry screen, Jackson was to cross the river, move around Pope, cut his communications and, if possible, get between him and Washington. Pope would attack him, and it was Jackson's business to hold the former until Lee and Longstreet could come up with the rest of the army and finish him. This was the first great Napoleonic maneuver attempted by Lee, and he was, perhaps, unaware that he was reproducing the methods of the greatest of strategists, though Jackson, who had studied Napoleon's campaigns profoundly, probably had some inkling of it.

Jackson would have three divisions, Taliaferro, Ewell,

and A. P. Hill, twenty-three thousand men. That would leave Lee with thirty-two thousand men until reinforcements reached him from Richmond. He was taking the gravest of risks, but only by taking risks could he hope to win victories.

A. P. Hill continued his artillery firing until the night of August 24. Longstreet then came up, covering the river front as far west as Waterloo Bridge, four miles above the Sulphur Springs. Jackson, moving at dawn of August 25, crossed the river above Waterloo Bridge and began his famous march around Pope.

Through nearly the whole of August 25, Longstreet's artillery kept up a fire on the enemy on the opposite bank as if preparing to force a passage there, but there was no battle. Longstreet was merely demonstrating in order to keep the enemy from observing Jackson's operation.

In the morning of August 26, Lee, watching the enemy, discovered signs of stir among them. That might mean that the Unionists were turning against Jackson, and, in any event, they must soon learn of his movement. Lee then determined to follow Jackson without delay. Pope was extending his right wing, under Sigel, Banks, and Reno, up the river in search of Jackson, who meanwhile had bivouacked at Salem (now Marshall) on August 25. On August 26, Jackson passed through Thoroughfare Gap and reached Gainesville, where Stuart joined him with the horse. With a cavalry screen in front of him, Jackson then moved on Bristoe Station on the Orange and Alexandria Railroad, which he reached about nightfall after a march of thirty miles. Two trains were captured, with some prisoners.

In the night of August 26, Jackson sent a detachment from Bristoe Station to Manassas, seven miles ahead. These troops, coming on the station, dispersed the guard there and made immense captures of stores. Of all the events of the war this was the one that gave the Southern people the most satisfaction, this capture of Pope's supplies. The story was told for years, with gusto, of the half-starved and ragged Confederates coming upon a scene where tons of provisions were piled along the railway and where the stores of sutlers offered such a variety of viands and of beverages as the Southern countrymen had never dreamt of before; of how privates were to be seen drinking champagne and devouring canned lobster and caviare, of soldiers carrying off food, shoes, clothing, everything portable. After the soldiers had had their fill the torch was applied, and the whole mass of supplies and provisions went up in smoke. Soon messages came over the wires to the startled Pope, who suddenly discovered that the missing Jackson was in his rear and on his communications. Thereupon he turned, as was natural, in that direction—and rather away from McClellan. The first part of Lee's plan had worked like clockwork.

Pope concentrated his army in the vicinity of Warrenton. At Alexandria, waiting transportation, were Franklin's Sixth Corps, ten thousand strong; Sturgis's division, ten thousand, and Cox's seven thousand. If Pope could add to his army all these reinforcements, he would face Lee with overpowering strength.

When, in the afternoon of August 26, Pope's army turned away from the Rappahannock, Lee knew that the time had come to move. He asked Longstreet whether he preferred to force a passage of the river or to follow in Jackson's path.[7]

Longstreet, fearing that the road to Warrenton would be held by the Unionists in strength, told Lee he would follow Jackson by the roundabout route. That afternoon Longstreet's troops began their march, bivouacking at Orleans.

[7] *B. & L.*, II, 517.

In the morning of August 27, Longstreet, with Lee, moved on ten miles to Salem (now Marshall). Longstreet was slow in starting that morning, and Lee became impatient. Riding off toward Salem accompanied only by staff officers and orderlies, he suddenly came upon a squadron of Union cavalry in the road. The situation was critical, for Lee was at the mercy of the enemy. But the staff formed in line across the road like cavalry, and the blue horsemen, thinking they had come upon Longstreet's advance, retired. It was a close call for Lee.

The end of Jackson's second day of march had found him at Bristoe Station; the end of Longstreet's second day saw him at White Plains, many miles short of Jackson's effort. It was not until 3:00 P. M. on August 28 that Longstreet came to the northern end of Thoroughfare Gap. In forty-eight hours, Jackson had marched forty-six miles, Longstreet, twenty-eight. The latter, however, had been somewhat delayed by the appearance of Union cavalry, which had not annoyed Jackson.

Jackson was now where Lee wanted him, between Pope and Washington: Lee did not know that Pope was rapidly massing against his daring lieutenant, who was already in peril. He hoped to reunite the two wings of his army and face Pope somewhere in the vicinity of Manassas—with McClellan too far away to help. On the morning of August 28, if Jackson was still at Manassas, Lee and Longstreet were twenty-two miles from him, one long day's march. But Thoroughfare Gap had to be passed, and it remained to be seen if that was open. Couriers coming through the gap in the morning of August 28 brought Lee the news that Jackson had fallen back from Manassas to Groveton, which was only nineteen miles from where Lee then was. The reunion of the two wings of the army seemed about to be consummated speedily.

When Lee and Longstreet approached Thoroughfare Gap at 3:00 P. M., the former expected to give the weary men a long rest before completing the march. Thoroughfare Gap is a pass in the low and lovely Bull Run Mountains, a spur of the Blue Ridge—charming rolling country with

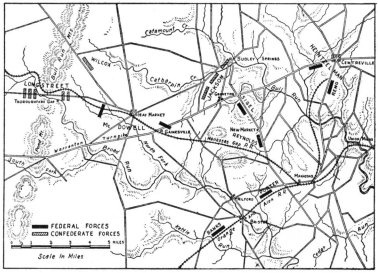

SECOND MANASSAS (BULL RUN), AUGUST 28, 1862

wide blue-grass fields and gentle, hazy mountains all along the horizon.

Although Thoroughfare Gap was reported to be open, Longstreet sent D. R. Jones's division ahead to seize the pass and cover the movement of the army. On coming to the gap, the advance found masses of bluecoats on the other side. They were men of Ricketts's division, sent there by McDowell. Thus in the afternoon of August 28, Lee seemed to be checkmated. If the gap was held in force, he must either fight a battle to get through or move around it to the north. In either event there would be a delay, and meanwhile Jackson, confronted by the greater part of Pope's army, might be destroyed.

At noon on that day Pope had reached Manassas in hot pursuit of Jackson. He ordered Reno's corps and Kearny's and Hooker's divisions of the Third Corps to Centreville in search of the elusive Jackson, who had left Manassas after completing the work of destruction. McDowell, having word of Longstreet's approach along Jackson's path, detached Ricketts to Thoroughfare Gap to hold him in check, a most timely move and one that might have changed the whole course of the campaign if it had been properly followed up.

Jones, finding the enemy in front, sent troops over the mountain by a path. They rushed ahead to gain the crest, while the enemy on the other side did likewise. The Confederate skirmishers, reaching the top first, opened fire on the clambering Unionists and drove them back. At the same time Hood's division crossed the mountain by a cattle trail, while Wilcox was sent to Hopewell Pass, north of Thoroughfare Gap. Seeing himself in danger of being surrounded, Ricketts withdrew to the east, leaving the gap open for the passage of Longstreet's force. But if he had been supported by another division, the movement of the Confederates would have been blocked, for a time at least.

Jackson, meanwhile, was having adventures. He was playing a game of hide-and-seek with Pope until Lee and Longstreet could join him. Not able to remain on Pope's railway line at Manassas and unable to go too far north for fear of being cut off from Longstreet, he had moved to Groveton near the old battlefield of Manassas. There on the Alexandria-Warrenton turnpike he took position, with whereabouts unknown to the mystified Unionists. He was there in the late afternoon of August 28 when King's division passed along the turnpike going to Centreville. It seemed to Jackson that Pope might be escaping, since his troops if they went on northward would soon come in contact with McClellan. Then there would happen just what Lee was intending to avoid, a concentration of the two Union forces against him.

Jackson decided to attack this division and thus draw on him the various units of Pope's army before it could be reinforced by McClellan. Advancing from his hidden position, he boldly assailed the passing column. The Unionists, forming line of battle, advanced in turn against him. The battle of Groveton which followed was one of the severest small engagements of the war. The Unionists fought with desperate gallantry, at times forcing back the Confederates and keeping the issue in doubt. Finally, Jackson threw in his reserves and succeeded in driving the enemy from the field, about nine o'clock at night. In this action, in which the casualties were unusually heavy for the numbers engaged, Ewell was badly wounded, losing a leg, and Taliaferro also.

The situation on the morning of August 29 was that Jackson had disclosed his position to Pope, who at once turned against him, while Lee and Longstreet had cleared Thoroughfare Gap and were moving to aid the bold Jackson. Fortunately, on this morning Stuart joined Lee, who thus had a cavalry screen for his march.

Longstreet followed the regular road east from the gap on August 29. "I marched at daylight," Longstreet says, "and filed to the left at Gainesville at nine o'clock. As the head of the column approached Gainesville the fire of artillery became more lively, and its volume swelled to proportions indicating near approach to battle. The men involuntarily quickened step, filed down the turnpike, and in twenty minutes came upon the battle as it began to press upon Jackson's right, their left battery partially turning his right." [8]

It was at Gainesville that Longstreet's troops, turning off, took the Warrenton turnpike, near which the Second Battle of Manassas (Bull Run) was already raging. For Jackson, having shown his whereabouts, had fallen back to the bed of an unfinished railroad, which gave his men some cover, and awaited the assaults he knew were coming. Kearny, Sigel, and Reynolds, from right to left, assailed him, though chiefly with artillery. There was some hesitation in throwing infantry against his partially protected troops.

About noon of August 29, Pope arrived on the field and took command. Heintzelman's corps (Hooker's and Kearny's divisions) held the Union right. Next to him was Sigel. The left wing was held by Reynolds. Reno, who had reached the field, was in reserve. Porter and McDowell, off to the left, had been ordered to come up. From 2:00 P. M. to 4:00 P. M. the battle raged furiously, and Sigel's corps was badly broken. Jackson, also, sustained severe losses.

The point was that Lee and Longstreet were now on Jackson's right and able to enter the conflict at any moment if they chose. That the right wing of the army held off for more than a day while the left wing was being pounded by the enemy is surely one of the strangest situations in military history. That this occurred was due to Longstreet's extreme reluctance to advance. He wanted to fight a defensive action.

Longstreet's troops were deployed for battle and ready. "When I reported my troops in order for battle, General Lee was inclined to engage as soon as practicable, but did not order. . . . I asked him to be allowed to make a reconnaissance of the enemy's ground, and along his left. After an hour's work, mounted and afoot, under the August

[8] *M. to A.*, p. 180.

sun, I returned and reported adversely to attack, especially in view of the easy approach of the troops reported at Manassas against my right in the event of severe contention." [9]

Meanwhile Jackson was hard pressed by numbers, while Longstreet was making his leisurely observation, surely a characteristic Longstreetian touch. At one time the Unionists broke through Jackson's left and reached the railroad cut, but were driven back. Lee, chafing at his inaction and unsatisfied by Longstreet's report, was preparing to send engineers off to the right when word came that a large force of the enemy was coming up. This was Porter's corps, followed by McDowell's. Porter, finding Confederate troops in his front, halted while McDowell pulled off from him and joined Pope's army in front of Jackson's position. Longstreet, seeing only Porter before him, reported to Lee that he did not think the enemy intended to attack at that point.

Lee now returned to his first idea of attacking down the turnpike and striking the left of Pope's army. But Longstreet again demurred. "Though more than anxious to meet his wishes, and anticipating his orders, I suggested, as the day was far spent, that a reconnaissance in force be made at nightfall to the immediate front of the enemy, and if an opening was found for an entering wedge, that we have all things in readiness at daylight for a good day's work. After a moment's hesitation he assented." [10]

Lee was now acting on Longstreet's initiative and against his own better judgment. If he had attacked early in the afternoon before Porter and McDowell arrived, he might have won a decisive victory, for Pope's army had been roughly handled by Jackson and some of the units were

[9] *Ibid.*, p. 181.
[10] *Ibid.*, p. 183.

becoming disorganized. But now action was postponed until
the morning of August 30. Up to this point the execution on
the Confederate side had been perfect, but from now on it
was wanting in the element of promptness, owing to Longstreet's reluctance to advance. He wanted to fight on the
defensive, to be attacked.

Wilcox and Hood were directed to examine the enemy's
position and report on the advisability of attacking at daylight. "They came to corps headquarters a little before
twelve o'clock," says Longstreet, "and made separate reports, both against attack, with minute items of their conclusions." [11]

Late in the afternoon Pope sent orders to Porter to
assault the Confederate right at dawn. The Union commander was still ignorant of Longstreet's arrival and, thinking that Jackson alone was in front of him, desired to crush
that wing of the Confederate army before the other could
come up. But Porter, knowing more of the condition of
affairs and aware that a large force was off to his left, did
not attack as ordered. If he had done so, he would have been
taken in flank and rear by Longstreet and crushed. However,
because of his failure to advance, he was blamed for the loss
of the battle and was court-martialed and cashiered from the
service, a most unjust decision. But then he was an intimate
friend of McClellan's.

Entirely unaware of the situation, Pope made ready to
destroy Jackson when dawn broke on August 30, 1862. As
Jackson had drawn back his infantry from the railroad embankment to the woods behind, leaving only a few skirmishers in front, Pope concluded he was retreating and prepared to pursue. But while there were only skirmishers in
Jackson's front, they did not retire as retreating troops would

[11] *Ibid.*, p. 184.

have done, and this fact should have given Pope matter for consideration.

At one o'clock the Union commander renewed the assaults on Jackson. Porter, supported by King, Heintzelman, and Reno, was to turn his left flank and sweep down his line. Then Pope had an unpleasant surprise. As the Unionists advanced to the attack, the notes of a bugle rang out clearly and a swarm of soldiers broke from the woods where they had been under cover and ran down to the embankment to take their places. Far from retreating, Jackson was prepared to give the foe a warm reception.

A fierce and bitter struggle followed. Jackson's men stood their ground, exchanging volleys with the advancing Unionists until the field was littered with the dead and wounded. The guns on both sides belched canister at the opposing masses. After several days of constant fighting Jackson's ammunition was running low. On one part of his line it gave out entirely, but his valiant men, undismayed, repelled an attack with stones. Assault after assault was made by the Unionists, who advanced most gallantly to the railroad embankment, came under the full fire of the Confederate infantry and artillery, and fell back, only to come on again. So the furious contest went on, and Jackson was pressed hard.

All of this time Longstreet's men, near by, had not pulled a trigger. Longstreet was still opposed to advancing and he was still controlling Lee. The commander was planning an attack but was not yet ready. "General Lee," says Longstreet, "had settled upon a move by Sudley Springs, to cross Bull Run during the night and try to again reach Pope's rear, this time with his army." [12] An excellent move but one

[12] *M. to A.,* p. 186.

that should have been made before. With Jackson in jeopardy there was no time for maneuver.

Longstreet fully approved of the new plan. "About three P. M.," he writes, "I rode to the front to prepare to make a diversion a little before dark, to cover the plan proposed for our night march. As I rode, batteries resting on the side of the turnpike thought that battle was at hand, and called their officers and men to stand to their guns and horses. Passing by and beyond my lines, a message came from General Jackson reporting his lines heavily pressed, and asking to be reinforced. Riding forward a few rods to an open, which gave a view of Jackson's field, I came in sight of Porter's battle, piling up against Jackson's right, center, and left. At the same time an order came from General Lee for a division to be sent General Jackson. Porter's masses were in almost direct line from the point at which I stood, and in enfilade fire. It was evident that they could not stand fifteen minutes under the fire of batteries planted at that point, while a division marching back and across the field to aid Jackson could not reach him in an hour. . . . So I called for my nearest batteries. Ready, anticipating call, they sprang to their places and drove at speed, saw the opportunity before it could be pointed out, and went into action." [13]

Canister, poured at short range into the flank of the charging Union masses, completed the discomfiture begun by Jackson's infantry. The Unionists halted, wavered, and began to fall back, unable to stand the awful enfilading hail of balls.

When he heard the sound of Longstreet's guns, Lee sent word to him that if he could see anything better to do than reinforcing Jackson to do it. Now close to the front, the

[13] *Ibid.*, p. 186.

commander was quick to observe the effect of Longstreet's artillery fire, under which the Union line was dissolving. The moment had come to throw the whole army on the Unionists. Without another moment's hesitation, he ordered Longstreet to attack.

Longstreet, too, had seen the opportunity and was ready to assail a faltering foe. "General Longstreet is advancing," Lee sent word to Jackson. "Look out for and protect his left flank." Longstreet's left would pass in front of Jackson's right unless the latter himself moved forward. Of Longstreet's force, Wilcox held the left end; Hood was next to him, and Kemper next to Hood, with Jones on the extreme right. Evans and R. H. Anderson were in support.

The charge was splendidly made, not this time by detachments, as in the Seven Days, but by the whole line. The Unionists did not give ground without a severe struggle, and Jackson's tired men failed to join speedily in the advance. Adjustments had to be made of the lines of Jackson and Longstreet, almost at right angles to each other. But Longstreet swept on, driving the foe before him, and presently Jackson's line also moved forward. It was a sublime scene. Out in the open fields the battle could be seen to advantage. Batteries flaming in every direction. Masses of bewildered Unionists, fired on in flank and front and yet reluctant to give way. Through the dense smoke haze the long, advancing lines of brown-coated men with their red flags showed vividly in the obscurity. Everything apparently confusion, but everything going well according to Lee's will. When he did attack, Longstreet was splendid.

Overwhelmed by surprise, Pope watched his fine army, attacked on two sides by the foe he had imagined to be retreating, break up except at points on his right wing, where knots of men continued to resist furiously. The afternoon was waning, a light rain began to fall, there was no hope of retrieving the battle. Nothing was left but retreat, if that could be effected, if escape was not cut off.

Longstreet pressed eastward along both sides of the Warrenton turnpike; Jackson was moving south to the turnpike. It seemed in the rout and confusion of the moment that the Confederates might make large captures. But some Union regiments held the strategic Henry Hill with magnificent courage, enabling the mass of the army to get across Stone Bridge and the fords of Bull Run.

Presently night fell on the field, and Lee had done all that could be done that day. Pope's army was in full flight for Alexandria. Unfortunately for the Southern cause, there were no impediments in the way. If Lee could have performed the maneuver on August 30 he designed for August 31, he would have been on the other side of Jackson with Longstreet, and half of his army would have held the crossings of Bull Run against the Unionists. Then Pope's army would have been lost indeed. Or, if the attack had been made early in the day, the Confederates would have had hours of daylight for pursuit.

Lee had won a great and startling victory, and just in the nick of time. Franklin's corps from Alexandria was almost on the field when the battle ended. If Pope, instead of seeking to crush Jackson, had fallen back to Centreville, he would have soon come into contact with McClellan and would have been in overwhelming force.

Longstreet's handling of the situation, when he at last elected to do something, was admirable; but his long delay had imperiled Jackson and caused the latter heavy losses. Also in waiting until the afternoon to move, he had lessened the chance of decisive victory, for it was one of the faults of

Confederate management that Confederate attacks were almost always made in the afternoon, sometimes in the late afternoon.

Lee showed a strange irresolution at Second Manassas. There can be no doubt that he thought of taking the offensive as soon as he came to the battlefield and found Jackson engaged. But he let Longstreet persuade him to wait and to wait again. It was only after Lee had practically determined not to fight in the Groveton vicinity but to cross Bull Run and intervene between Pope and Washington that he finally decided on immediate action. If, on arriving at Groveton, he had moved around to the other side of Jackson and had had Longstreet form the left wing of the army instead of the right, he would have made a masterly move and must have effected large captures in the event of success. But in that case Pope would have known of Longstreet's presence and would not have laid himself open to counter attack as he did. Considering all the circumstances, with Pope outnumbering Lee and with thirty thousand other Union troops close at hand, Second Manassas must ever stand as one of the most remarkable campaigns and battles of modern history. No campaign and battle ever fought on American soil were better conducted.

And yet Longstreet was dissatisfied, critical. In writing of it, he speaks of the "errors" of the Second Manassas, committed of course by Lee and Jackson, for Longstreet himself never committed errors. At least he admits none. Always in his book he is impeccable.

The outlook of the war had now changed startlingly. Not long before, Richmond had been in danger. With Pope defeated and McClellan discredited and out of favor, Washington was imperiled. And there can be no telling what the result might have been if the Confederate government, at this favorable juncture, had gambled and given Lee all the troops on the Atlantic seaboard. With a hundred thousand men Lee might have won the war after the Second Manassas.

CHAPTER IX

FAILURE IN MARYLAND

THE Second Manassas definitely put the North on the defensive instead of the South. Indeed, in the summer of 1862, the South enjoyed a surprising if brief renaissance of power. In Kentucky, Braxton Bragg and Kirby Smith, mediocre generals both, were approaching the Ohio River. In Virginia, Lee was threatening Washington itself. The fortunes of the Northern Union were at a low ebb.

The situation was due to the genius of Lee, ably seconded by Jackson; Lee's victory over McClellan in the Seven Days had saved Richmond; his victory over Pope at the Second Manassas endangered Washington. Thus one great man, with no increase of resources, had reversed the situation of June, 1862. Then the Confederacy was failing. Now, at the beginning of September, the Union seemed to be declining. Lincoln, chagrined by his experiment in putting Pope in command of the main field army, had recalled McClellan with speed and had given him more authority than he had enjoyed before. If Washington was to be saved, the government knew of no man who could do it better than McClellan. Nevertheless, he was in a false position. Fighting for the Union only, untouched by abolition fanaticism, unaffected by hatred of the South, he was out of place in a war that had turned to fanaticism as the surest weapon to secure victory. It might have been presaged then that he would be used by the Washington government only as long as danger was near, to be discharged at the first moment of relaxation.

The Confederate government had its highest hopes in September, 1862. The reason was that the alignment of states was not so definite then as it became a little later— in fact, in that same September. It was believed that Maryland had been coerced into remaining in the Union, that the presence of a Confederate army on its soil would be the signal for a general rising of the people against the oppressive central government in Washington. At least that was the hope of the Richmond authorities. Lee seems not to have expected so much. He thought that the passage of the Potomac by his army would be an excellent prelude to peace negotiations with the Washington government. He did not understand that the war was to the death and that the only peace would be one between the conquerors and the defeated. It was determined to invade Maryland.

There were drawbacks that made Lee hesitate. First, the size of his army, numbering only fifty thousand men; marching and disease and battle had taken a terrible toll of his host. Second, its condition. The army was worn out with marching and weakened by lack of proper food; more important, still, it lacked shoes, for perhaps half the men were barefooted or nearly barefooted. They could limp along the muddy roads of Virginia but would be spavined by the macadam turnpikes of Maryland. Third, there was lack of transportation. Lee would have to abandon railway connections and leave his base far behind when he entered Maryland. He would have to live on the country. The commander, dubiously consulting Longstreet on this point, was told that the soldiers could subsist for a while on fruit and "roasting ears." Longstreet adds that he urged Lee to keep the army undivided and to restore its strength by short marches. Lee proposed to send him to Harper's Ferry, the village where the Shenandoah joins the Potomac. There Halleck had a large force of troops, which he continued to keep in spite of McClellan's protest, thereby aiding the Union cause materially. Lee's misfortunes sprang in no small degree from this same Harper's Ferry. Longstreet did not like the task, and Lee, seeing his unwillingness, dropped the subject. The army had crossed the Potomac on September 5-6, 1862, and it was while Lee and Longstreet were riding together near Frederick that they heard the sound of distant firing and Lee suggested to Longstreet that he capture Harper's Ferry.[1]

Longstreet supposed that the subject was dismissed, since he had disapproved of it, and he was beginning to fancy that he inspired Lee's plans. What was his disagreeable surprise when, on going to Lee's tent in Frederick, he found the tent closed against all intrusion and the commander in close conference with Jackson!

"As I had not been called," says Longstreet, "I turned to go away when, General Lee, recognizing my voice, called me in. The plan had been arranged. Jackson, with his three divisions, was to recross the Potomac by the fords above Harper's Ferry . . . and occupy Loudoun Heights, those heights overlooking the positions of the garrison of Harper's Ferry. . . . I was to march over the mountain by Turner's Gap to Hagerstown."

Finding everything arranged, Longstreet offered no objection, though he was chagrined to see Jackson occupying so high a position in the chieftain's confidence. He was not yet Lee's mentor.

Lee changed the order to a certain extent, assigning Longstreet to Boonsboro instead of to Hagerstown and sending

[1] *M. to A.*, p. 201.

D. H. Hill's division with him. The divisions of Jackson, McLaws, and Walker were detached to surround Harper's Ferry and invest it, two of them from the Virginia side, McLaws from the Maryland. This disposition left McLaws in a dangerous place if the Union army should decide to move westward without delay. Later, probably on Longstreet's request, the order was changed again, assigning Longstreet to Hagerstown, twelve miles from Boonsboro. Only D. H. Hill was to remain at the latter place, guarding the important pass through South Mountain known as Turner's Gap. This new arrangement of forces lost the campaign. It lost the campaign because McClellan moved westward so rapidly that he forced the passes of South Mountain before Lee could hold them in sufficient force. But why did Lee not realize the vital importance of South Mountain, that continuation of the Blue Ridge crossing Maryland from south to north? It is difficult to say.

Counting on McClellan's slowness, Lee dispersed his army widely, offering wonderful opportunities to an alert opponent. Undoubtedly he supposed that the Army of the Potomac was much more disorganized by its defeat at Second Manassas than was the case. Besides, he did not realize McClellan's predicament. The latter was a general who had to fight, and that soon, in order to hold his job. And McClellan wished to hold his job.

In spite of their weariness, the Confederates showed energy. On September 10, Jackson began his march to Harper's Ferry. McLaws, by hurrying, beat Jackson to his destination and occupied Maryland Heights across from Harper's Ferry without opposition. Walker shortly appeared on the Shenandoah River side. The investment was thus complete and the garrison had no hope of relief unless McClellan should advance rapidly to its succor.

What were Lee's plans for the invasion? We have no information on the subject except from a single source, Major General John G. Walker, who discussed the campaign with Lee in Frederick.[2] Walker states that Lee expected to concentrate his army at Hagerstown after the fall of Harper's Ferry, destroy the B. & O. Railroad, and advance to Harrisburg. There he would demolish the Pennsylvania Railroad bridge over the Susquehanna. With both railway lines between Washington and the West cut, Lee would turn to Philadelphia, Baltimore, or Washington, as might be deemed best.

The statement does not sound like Lee. He was not prone to open his mind to subordinates and he usually did not so confidently count his chickens before they hatched. It may be doubted that Lee had any definite idea beyond winning a victory in Maryland that might enable his government to offer peace terms with a chance of acceptance. No doubt he wished to stay in Maryland as a conqueror and not a raider. Moreover, the tearing up of a few miles of railway and the burning of a bridge could not delay traffic very long, as Lee knew well.

He overlooked the most important feature in the strategical situation, South Mountain. If he had occupied its passes in force he would have put McClellan to great pains to dislodge him; he would have fought a defensive battle with large chances of success. Lee employed the Blue Ridge in Virginia to excellent effect; it is strange that he could make little use of its continuation in Maryland.

If he had held the gaps in South Mountain and planted his artillery, he would have fully protected the troops besieging Harper's Ferry and would have had his army in hand for any movement. McClellan would have had to do

2 *B. & L.*, II, 605.

one of two things: force the gaps, a dangerous process, or turn the enemy from the north, which would have uncovered Washington. Lee had the game in his hands, but for some reason he did not elect to play it. Yet he somewhat realized the importance of the South Mountain gaps, as is evidenced by the fact that he attempted to hasten Longstreet from Hagerstown to Turner's Gap as soon as he heard of McClellan's forward movement. And both D. H. Hill and Longstreet stopped on reaching Boonsboro, exactly the right thing to do.

Just then something happened that cost Lee the campaign. A report came to him that Union cavalry was moving on Hagerstown from the north. Instead of dispatching Stuart's cavalry to ascertain the truth of the rumor, Lee sent Longstreet with his infantry division, a bad error. He accompanied Longstreet to Hagerstown. Thus he was at some distance both from Boonsboro and Harper's Ferry, the critical points.

The army was now widely dispersed in the face of the enemy. Jackson, McLaws, and Walker were besieging Harper's Ferry; Hill was at Boonsboro, Longstreet at Hagerstown. Lee was deliberately leaving himself unguarded to the thrust of his opponent's rapier, trusting that the opponent would be too unenterprising to thrust. But nothing can be taken on credit in war. The unenterprising McClellan suddenly became imbued with sufficient energy and initiative greatly to endanger Lee and to ruin his campaign.

Sometime in the night of September 13, Lee received information that suddenly altered the whole outlook and turned complacency into anxiety. Stuart sent word that McClellan's army was at the foot of South Mountain. Stuart himself had been driven back on South Mountain by the host of Unionists advancing toward Crampton's Gap and

Turner's Gap, the two main passes of South Mountain. Harper's Ferry was still holding out, and McLaws on the northern side of the Potomac was in imminent danger of being cut off from Lee by the enemy occupation of Crampton's Gap.

This news caused Lee and Longstreet to hold a conference. "General Lee," Longstreet says, "ordered me to march back to the mountain early the next morning. I suggested that, instead of meeting McClellan there, we withdraw Hill and unite my forces and Hill's at Sharpsburg, at the same time explaining that Sharpsburg was a strong defensive position from which we could strike the flank or rear of any force that might be sent to the relief of Harper's Ferry. I endeavored to show him that by making a forced march to Hill my troops would be in an exhausted condition and could not make a proper battle. Lee listened patiently enough, but did not change his plans, and directed that I should go back the next day and make a stand at the mountain." Later Longstreet wrote Lee a note reiterating his objection to fighting at South Mountain.[3]

Longstreet was, as usual, attempting to guide Lee and showing his disrelish for fighting except on the defensive. The point was that Longstreet did not wish to fight, either at South Mountain or at Sharpsburg. What he really wanted was to retreat into Virginia without a battle. McClellan's unaccustomed aggressiveness had puzzled and discouraged him.

Lee was too good a general not to know that it would be better to fight at South Mountain than at Sharpsburg. Yet he seems to have let Longstreet instill in him some of the latter's slowness and inertia. It was strange for Longstreet to talk of twelve miles exhausting an army inured to marching.

[3] *B. & L.*, II, 665.

Lee undoubtedly let Longstreet's self-assertion impose on him.

The result of Longstreet's reluctance was that he did not get away from Hagerstown early in the morning of September 14, as Lee had directed. He speaks, it is true, of a hurried march to Boonsboro, but what sort of hurry was it that did not bring him over the twelve miles until 3:00 P. M.? As an excellent turnpike connects Boonsboro with Hagerstown, there was no difficulty in getting cannon and wagons over the road in good order. But Longstreet did not wish to fight at Boonsboro, and no power could make him do what he did not wish to do. It followed, from Longstreet's poor handling of the situation, that the Confederates suffered a severe reverse at Boonsboro, which should not have happened.

Why had the Union commander so suddenly come to life? Partly because he was fighting to hold his job. Partly, too, because fate, tired of playing into the hands of the Confederates, had turned again to the Union. An order of Lee's, outlining his troop movements, was picked up in the deserted Confederate camps at Frederick where some careless soul had left it, and brought to McClellan. The latter then knew Lee's dispositions for the campaign. Having learned so much, McClellan moved westward without waiting for further reinforcements or extra supplies. Yet Lee had the chance of occupying both Crampton's Gap and Turner's Gap before the Union army arrived and did not do so, apparently because Longstreet demurred. Longstreet's one thought was to get out of Maryland.

When Longstreet reached Boonsboro at 3:00 P. M., D. H. Hill was trying desperately to hold off a host of enemies bent on securing the pass. The Confederates were making a gallant stand but they were greatly outnumbered and had almost no artillery. Garland, one of their best brigadiers, had been killed, and their losses were out of proportion to their numbers. Two of Hill's brigades were attempting to hold off eight Union brigades.

Longstreet, joining Hill on the mountain, found the Confederate situation bad. What he might have done then if he had been aggressively inclined it is difficult to say; but the stand was made against his judgment, and Longstreet was never able to put his heart into anything in which his head did not concur.

"I discovered," he says, "that everything was in such disjointed condition that it would be impossible for my troops and Hill's to hold the mountain against such forces as McClellan had there, and wrote a note to General Lee in which I stated that fact, and cautioned him to make his arrangements to retire that night. We got as many troops up as we could, and by putting in detachments here and there managed to hold McClellan in check until night, when Lee ordered the withdrawal to Sharpsburg." [4]

The truth is that Longstreet did not wish to make a stand at South Mountain and did so only in a half-hearted way. Even granting the fact that he arrived on the scene tardily and after the Unionists had gained the crest of the mountain, there seems to be no reason why he should not have attempted to drive them off and hold the pass. Why Sharpsburg was a better place for a battle than South Mountain defies the imagination to conjecture. It was not a better place at all, but Longstreet was determined to fall back there, and, by the handling of his troops at South Mountain, which was mediocre, he imposed his will on Lee.

D. H. Hill was one of the fiercest fighters in the army, and if he had been effectively backed by Longstreet it seems

[4] *B. & L.,* II, 666.

that he would have had a chance of winning a victory. Hill
says that of Longstreet's nine brigades only four were seriously engaged, a commentary on the latter's zeal in this
action. Hill states further that at South Mountain nine
thousand men held off thirty thousand for hours, and those
figures probably represent the numbers heavily engaged.
Longstreet had many more troops at hand and could have
put them in the fight. He alleges, however, that his men
were so exhausted that numbers fell out of the column,
unable to keep up; and this is probably true, for the Confederates had been driven to the point of human endurance
by constant marching without regular rations and by being
forced to depend on what food they could snatch from the
fields in passing. Hooker was in command of the Unionists
at South Mountain, and he was greatly pleased with the
work of his troops; it was no mean feat for them to mount
the steep slopes of South Mountain and carry a position held
by a brave and determined force. South Mountain was a
confused fight amidst boulders and trees, in which the Union
commanders handled their men better than did the Confederate; it showed conclusively that the Union army had
recovered from the defeat of the Second Manassas and was
ready for aggressive action. When Turner's Gap was taken,
two other passes went with it, Crampton's Gap and Fox's
Gap, the three gateways of South Mountain.

The battle of South Mountain was important, inasmuch
as it marked the ruin of Lee's Maryland campaign. He
had lost the breastwork of the mountain and would be
forced to fight now, if he chose to fight, in a position where
he would have no advantages. His own miscalculation of
McClellan's activity, coupled with Longstreet's reluctance
to hold South Mountain, had cost him this reverse. If he
had been dreaming of the Susquehanna, as Walker states,

that dream now came to an end. The engagement had the further effect of heartening the Union army. Up to this moment Lee had towered above the Union commanders as a sort of superman, dreaded by foes as much as admired by friends, but now that he had been outmaneuvered and driven from a strong position the whole Union host experienced a return of confidence.

In the morning of September 15, Longstreet's and Hill's commands fell back from the vicinity of South Mountain, crossing Antietam Creek in the afternoon and taking position immediately in front of the little town of Sharpsburg, which is two miles north of the Potomac River at Shepherdstown. In determining to make his stand there, Lee was influenced by Longstreet, who had assured him of the excellence of the position without having much knowledge of it. Lee could not have been enthusiastic over the position when he examined it, for a poorer one, from his own point of view, could hardly have been found.

There are no natural features to give a defending force any advantages. It is a beautiful and open country, with wide and sweeping ridges, which afford admirable positions for artillery, by far the strongest Union arm. Since the soil is hard limestone, with outcroppings of boulders everywhere, and since there was little timber, the Confederates had no chance to construct fieldworks. In other words, they were exposed to artillery fire with little protection. The ridges east of the Antietam are as high as those west of it, which means that the Confederates had no commanding elevations, so important in that day of direct artillery fire. Lastly and most important, the Confederate army was backed against the Potomac River, wide and deep. Defeat would probably mean the loss of the army, something that Lee must have realized fully. And this was the position Longstreet says he recommended to Lee as being better than South Mountain!

What would Lee do in this difficult situation, to which daring generalship and McClellan's sudden energy had brought him? More than half of his army was still at Harper's Ferry, the rest in grave danger at Sharpsburg. Ninety thousand men were coming up against him. It was now that Longstreet showed his real mind by advising a withdrawal to Virginia. And Lee himself seems to have intended to retreat across the Potomac, until he learned, about noon on September 15, that Harper's Ferry had fallen and that Jackson could move that evening to join him. It was then that he decided to fight at Sharpsburg instead of falling back into Virginia. General Alexander thinks that the political situation had something to do with his determination, that he did not wish to retreat from Maryland so soon after entering it as a deliverer; and Alexander may be right. There seems to have been no other reason to fight a battle on the Antietam.

Longstreet explains why he advised Lee to make a stand at Sharpsburg and then urged him to retire from it. He says:

"As long as the armies were linked to Harper's Ferry, the heights in front of Sharpsburg offered a formidable defensive line, and in view of possible operations from Harper's Ferry, through the river pass, east of South Mountain, formed a beautiful point of strategic diversion. But when it transpired that Harper's Ferry was surrendered and the position was not to be utilized, that the troops there were to join us by a march on the south side, its charms were changed to perplexities. The threatening attitude towards the enemy's rear vanished, his line of communications was open and free of further care, and his army, relieved of entanglements, was at liberty to cross the Antietam by the upper fords and the bridges, and approach from vantage-ground General Lee's left. At the same time the Federal left was reasonably secured from aggression by cramped and rugged ground along the Confederate right. Thus the altered circumstances changed all the features of the position in favor of the Federals." [5]

The charms of Sharpsburg, whatever they may have been, were certainly changed to perplexities in Longstreet's view. But Lee was not disturbed, for Jackson came up the next day, September 16, and Lee now had the greater part of his army in hand. A. P. Hill remained at Harper's Ferry for the moment.

In the afternoon of September 16, the Unionists, pushing forward across Antietam Creek, fought a sharp action with the advanced troops on the Confederate left but did not bring on a general engagement. By the massing of troops against his left, Lee was apprised that the first blow would fall there the next morning. The left was held by Jackson, the center by D. H. Hill, the right by Longstreet. The Confederates faced east. Lee had not more than thirty thousand infantry on the field, to oppose perhaps seventy thousand of the enemy.

What had become of Lee's army? Ten thousand of his men were straggling, chiefly because of sore feet and lack of food. The weak were weeded out; those that now stood in line at Sharpsburg were, perhaps, the best men America has ever produced, tough, hardy, brave, competent. An observer in Shepherdstown gives the following view of Confederate stragglers as she saw them: "When I say that they were hungry, I convey no impression of the gaunt starvation that looked from their cavernous eyes. All day they crowded to

[5] *M. to A.,* p. 228.

the doors of our houses, with always the same drawling complaint, 'I've been a-marchin' an' a-fightin' for six weeks stiddy; and I ain't had n-a-r-thin' to eat 'cept green apples and green cawn, an' I wish you'd please to gimme a bite to eat.' . . . never before or after did I see anything comparable to the demoralized state of the Confederates at this time. Never were want and exhaustion more visibly put before my eyes, and that they could march or fight at all seemed incredible." [6]

The battle of Sharpsburg opened at daylight of September 17, 1862, one of the most terrible days in American history. The ridges behind the Union line of battle were packed with battery after battery of long-ranged artillery. Hooker was in command on the Union right, Sumner in the center, and Burnside on the left. A simultaneous attack all along the line would probably have resulted in a great Union victory, but McClellan was afraid to risk it. He developed his battle from right to left.

Jackson, on the Confederate left, felt the brunt of the first assault. Heavy masses of Unionists advanced against his position but were driven back with loss by the destructive fire of the Confederate infantry. The battle moved back and forth as Union reinforcements were thrown in on one side and as the Confederate defense stiffened on the other. The Southerners, veterans of the first order, won numerous temporary successes, but as soon as they advanced beyond their position they came under the full fire of the massed Union ordnance and were torn to pieces. On the other hand, Jackson could make little use of his artillery, because his guns were outranged and overmatched by the batteries on the eastern ridges. For more than an hour a terrible conflict raged on the Confederate left, in which Jackson's losses were

[6] *B. & L.*, II, 687-88.

severe but which ended with the wrecking of Mansfield's and Hooker's corps, so shattered as to become disorganized.

When the battle on the Confederate left had died out, McClellan launched an attack on the center, held by the redoubtable D. H. Hill. The latter fought with cold desperation, but the Union guns succeeded in getting an enfilading fire on his position with the result that a hedgerow along a lane held by the Confederates was piled with their dead and wounded for its whole extent. So great were the losses inflicted on Hill, particularly by the Union artillery, that at times the Confederate center was almost without troops.

But Lee, forgetting his curious whim that the army head should have nothing to do with tactics, was now in full command, and he showed on that day with what wonderful skill he could fight a defensive action. He used his reserves to the best possible advantage, with the result that the Unionists, no matter how much they shook his line, were unable to break it.

McLaws's and Walker's divisions were sent to Hill's relief, driving Sedgwick before them. But attack after attack was made by the Unionists, against which the Confederates had all they could do to stand up. The losses were so heavy that the field became a mixture of fragments of commands. At one time Hill seized a musket and rallied numbers of these disorganized men. It seemed time after time that the Confederate line would break, but the attacks grew weaker and weaker and finally ceased. The Union losses were terrible; many of their best officers, including some of high rank like Mansfield, were killed or wounded.

It was now about one o'clock, and the Union assaults on the Confederate left and center had failed; a breathing spell followed. Lee and Longstreet, riding behind D. H. Hill's line, were joined by him. Lee and Longstreet dismounted in

order to observe from the crest of the ridge; Hill remained
on his horse. Longstreet asked Hill to move aside, fearing
that a horseman seen there would draw the enemy's fire.
Just then, seeing a puff of smoke from a distant cannon, he
remarked, "There is a shot for General Hill." [7] And sure

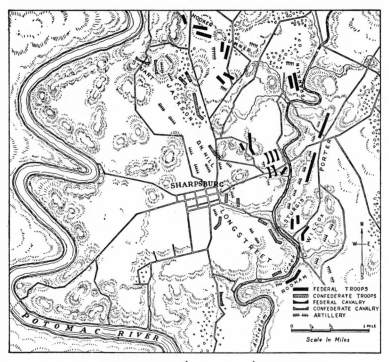

BATTLE OF SHARPSBURG (ANTIETAM), AFTERNOON OF
SEPTEMBER 17, 1862

enough, the ball took off the forelegs of Hill's horse, which
continued, however, to stand until its rider managed to dis-
mount. Longstreet states that this was the second best shot
he ever saw. That he should give the matter consideration
indicates his unexcitable temperament. In fact, he was not
excitable enough. It took a desperate crisis such as Sharpsburg to waken him from his usual apathy and make him for-

[7] *M. to A.*, p. 254.

get himself. For at Sharpsburg Longstreet did well, seconding all of Lee's efforts to hold the line by shifting troops from point to point as needed.

Longstreet was himself exposed, for he never knew the meaning of physical fear. He gives a graphic account of a happening during the fight at the Confederate center:

"We were under the crest of a hill occupying a position that ought to have been held by from four to six brigades. The only troops there were Cooke's regiment of North Carolina infantry, and they were without a cartridge. As I rode along the line with my staff I saw two pieces of the Washington Artillery (Miller's battery), but there were not enough men to man them. The gunners had been either killed or wounded. This was a fearful situation for the Confederate center. I put my staff-officers to the guns while I held their horses. It was easy to see that if the Federals broke through our line there, the Confederate army would be cut in two and probably destroyed. . . . We loaded up our little guns with canister and sent a rattle of hail into the Federals as they came up over the crest of the hill. . . . So warm was the reception we gave them that they dodged back behind the crest of the hill." Then Longstreet had ammunition brought up for the North Carolinians, and the position was safely held.[8]

The third battle of that direful day broke out in the afternoon when McClellan, having failed against Lee's left and center, assailed his right. The Unionists, in massed formation, sought to force a passage of the Antietam Bridge, held by a single brigade under Robert Toombs of Georgia. The stand made here was one of the most heroic of the day, but the Confederate force was too small to face whole divisions, and Burnside finally made his way across the

[8] *B. & L.*, II, 669.

bridge that still bears his name. The day was now wearing away, but the fighting that had begun at dawn was still going on, unabated. A woman of Shepherdstown has left a vivid story of that awful seventeenth of September:

"It seems to me now that the roar of that day began with the light, and all through its long and dragging hours its thunder formed a background to our pain and terror. . . . We went about our work with pale faces and trembling hands, yet trying to appear composed for the sake of our patients, who were much excited. We could hear the incessant explosions of artillery, the shrieking whistles of the shells, and the sharper, deadlier, more thrilling roll of musketry; while every now and then the echo of some charging cheer would come, borne by the wind, and as the human voice pierced that demoniacal clangor we would catch our breath and listen, and try not to sob, and turn back to the forlorn hospitals, to the suffering at our feet and before our eyes, while imagination fainted at thought of those other scenes hidden from us beyond the Potomac." [9]

At length in the late afternoon it seemed that the wavering and yielding but clinging Confederate line was at last broken. After Burnside had cleared the way, whole divisions of Unionists hurried across the bridge and assailed Longstreet, who had few men left because he had sent so many to the relief of D. H. Hill. At that moment, with thousands of Union troops on the west side of Antietam Creek, Lee was face to face with defeat and ruin. But he bore the crisis with the calm fortitude that was always his.

Just then, when the Confederate leaders felt all hope slipping from them, a body of troops was observed approaching from the right rear. For a moment it was feared that

[9] Mary Bedinger Mitchell, "A Woman's Recollections of Antietam," *B. & L.*, II, 690-91.

all was over. Anxiously, though quietly enough, Lee asked who the newcomers were. A staff officer leveled his field glasses while the others waited in an agony of suspense. Through the dust and smoke the officer made out crimson and blue flags borne by the newcomers and recognized the colors of the South and of Virginia. A. P. Hill had arrived from Harper's Ferry.

Thus was defeat turned into victory. Hill's men, forming in line of battle, fell on the exhausted Unionists and drove them back to the banks of the creek. And that was the last of it. The sun set on the Confederate army clinging to the position it had occupied in the morning. There are few things in history finer than the stand of the Southerners at Sharpsburg. It ranks with Thermopylae.

All through that terrible day, with the blasting artillery fire, the sweeping volleys of musketry that laid everything low before them, the thousands of dead and wounded strewn over the ground in front of Sharpsburg, Lee and Jackson had never lost the thought of a counter offensive. Not Longstreet. He was a defensive fighter and he had made a good fight, courageous and skillful. But Lee and Jackson wanted something more. They knew that the Union infantry was fought out; it might be possible to take the offensive in turn. That they considered such a thing possible shows their matchless audacity. But when the Union position was examined, it was found that the right rested near the Potomac River. There was no chance for a flank attack.

As darkness fell on the field, Longstreet, satisfied that the fighting was over for the day, rode along his line, giving instructions for the night and the next morning. He was delayed by aiding in the rescue of the wounded, who were to be found in every nook and corner. On riding into the town of Sharpsburg, he saw a house burning and waited until the soldiers put out the fire. Then he went on to headquarters.

The other generals had reported when he arrived. As Longstreet wearily dismounted, Lee came up to him and put affectionate hands on his shoulders.

"Here is my old war horse at last," the chief said.

All the reports told of the terrible casualties of the day, in which about a third of the Confederate infantry had been killed or wounded. All the officers counseled retreat, not even Jackson opposing. But Lee's blood was up and he was prepared for another day of battle. He refused to retreat that night, and thus to make what might be considered an acknowledgment of defeat. He calmly announced his intention of standing his ground.

His course was vindicated. When dawn broke on September 18, there came a sputter of firing among the pickets but nothing more. No line of battle advanced against the Confederate position as on the day before. The day wore away with nothing to mark it except the bickering of skirmishers.

Lee, however, could not attack and he could not remain longer in his exposed position, especially as he knew that reinforcements were coming up for McClellan. That night, under the cover of darkness, the Confederate army crossed the river and was safe on the other side. An attempt at pursuit was harshly punished.

McClellan has been censured for not renewing the battle on September 18, while Lee was still in position at Sharpsburg. He might have done so with a fair prospect of success, for Porter's corps had not been engaged on the seventeenth. But the Union army was so shattered that he feared to risk it, and indeed in no previous engagement of the war was the Army of the Potomac as near disorganization as at

Sharpsburg. It was surely in poor condition for a vigorous offensive against veteran troops on September 18.

Sharpsburg was a tactical victory for the Confederates, who had held their ground against all assaults. But the campaign was a strategical failure after South Mountain; Lee had no chance to redeem it by fighting a battle in so bad a position as that at Sharpsburg. Consequently, he would have done better not to fight there. If he had fallen back into Virginia without a battle, his prestige would have been lowered, but he would have had an army. After Sharpsburg he can be hardly said to have had an army at all, it was reduced to such small proportions. His prestige was greatly lessened by the Maryland campaign. Whatever the reasons may have been, the world could not shut its eyes to the fact that the invasion of Union territory had been a failure.

For Longstreet, Sharpsburg marks a stage in his development. He had shown tactical skill in defense there, but, unfortunately, he was filled with a sense of the futility of the battle, of the mistake made in fighting there. Consequently, his opinion of Lee's generalship, never perhaps very high, was much lowered. He came from then on to occupy the position of a critic, passing judgment caustically enough on the various phases of Lee's movements.

His condemnation of the hard marches in Maryland and the division of the army by the detachment for the siege of Harper's Ferry is excessive, displaying unusual feeling. The Confederate army, he claimed, went into Maryland strong and triumphant and came out broken and disheartened:

"The razing of the walls of Jericho by encircling marches of priests and soldiers, at the signal of long-drawn blasts of sacred horns and shouts of the multitude, was scarcely a greater miracle than the transformation of the conquering army of the South into a horde of disordered fugitives before an army that two weeks earlier was flying to cover under its homeward ramparts.

"Providence helps those who can avail themselves of His tender care, but permits those who will to turn from Him to their own arrogance. That His gracious hand was with the Confederates in their struggles on the Chickahominy, and even through the errors of the Bull Run campaign, cannot be questioned. When, however, in self-confidence, they lost sight of His helping hand, and in contempt of the enemy dispersed the army, they were given up to the reward of vainglory." [10]

This is one of the funniest passages in military literature. Both Jackson and Lee were long dead when it appeared; one would like to know what they would have thought of it. The picture of the bold and arrogant Lee and Jackson forgetting God in their confidence of success and the pious Longstreet drawing a divine rebuke on them from the misfortunes of the campaign is one of those exquisite ludicrosities that sometimes give relief to the horrors of war. From Sharpsburg on, Longstreet's accounts of the war are largely taken up with detailed descriptions of Lee's errors, which, if they were one half as numerous as he represented them to be, would have damned any general.

Why was this man Longstreet all his life long peering for the mistakes of others and blind to those of his own? He would have done well to consider soberly his own contribution to the failure in Maryland, in delaying at Hagerstown and in failing to take measures to hold the gaps in South Mountain, which were more or less under his jurisdiction.

Singular, too, was Longstreet's incapacity to see nobility in others. He was long in the company of such high spirits

[10] *M. to A.*, p. 283.

as Lee and Jackson without finding much to admire in either of them. Lee he charges with arrogance in the Maryland Campaign; Jackson, he declares, was comforted for the failure by the newspaper applause he received as the conqueror of Harper's Ferry. Privileged to be one of a famous trinity, Longstreet considered himself to be the greatest member of it.

CHAPTER X

GREAT MISTAKE OF FREDERICKSBURG

LEE had made mistakes in Maryland, mistakes that cost him the success of the campaign. Although he had captured Harper's Ferry, with thirteen thousand prisoners and though he had inflicted severer losses than he sustained at Sharpsburg, the balance of the campaign was against him. The Confederacy was, in reality, never as near success again as at the beginning of that September, 1862, when Lee's fame had grown to be world-wide and men conjectured nothing to be beyond the scope of his powers. Later in the year he made another mistake, and a greater, though it is counted one of his successes by those who do not reason by consequences. That mistake, however, was really the government's.

It is simply reading the past in the light of finality to say that the Confederates had no chance to win the war because of the heavier battalions and the greater resources of the other side. Wars do not always turn out according to mathematical computations. Genius and the spirit of nations must be taken into consideration as well as material means. The Germans, although greatly inferior to the Allies in resources, came very near to winning the World War. In the same way the weaker Southern Confederacy, if it had been able to take advantage of circumstances, might have encompassed its independence.

Of all the chances of victory offered the South, that in the autumn and winter of 1862 was the best. There was a chance in 1861, after the First Manassas; there was again a chance after the Second Manassas—an opportunity lost as much by the physical breakdown of the Confederate army as by the errors of the campaign. But the chance that came in December, 1862, was the best of all, and perhaps it really was the last.

The conditions that had prevented success earlier in the war, in August, 1861, or perhaps in June-July, 1862, no longer existed by September and October. The Army of Northern Virginia by that time had become inured to war by one of the hardest summer campaigns any army ever underwent. The weaklings and malingerers had been weeded out; discipline was better; organization was vastly improved; and equipment was becoming modern with captures from the enemy. The spirit of the army was high, and the retreat from Maryland—despite Longstreet's calamity howling—had not materially lowered it. The rank and file had confidence in the leaders, and the leaders were in harmony. Longstreet had not yet fully developed his perverse opinionativeness, which was to become harmful to the cause.

With the Army of the Potomac, on the other hand, everything was wrong. The Confederate administration reposed confidence in Lee; the Union authorities disliked and distrusted McClellan. The latter's political moderation displeased a government now depending on fanaticism for its driving force. Beginning the war for the salvation of the Union, it had come to conducting a liberty crusade. Sharpsburg was followed by the Emancipation Proclamation, which marked Lincoln's surrender to Greeley and the abolitionists. McClellan, a man of the world and not in the least a fanatic, did not fit in with the new scheme. He was a Democrat and cared not a rap about slavery, one way or another. The consequence was that the Washington government decided, before any competent successor appeared, to get rid of him. And just that gave the Confederates their great opportunity. Lincoln was doing the most dangerous of all things, deciding military issues on political grounds.

McClellan was not given his walking papers at once. The Army of Northern Virginia had retired to Martinsburg and thence to Winchester, in which vicinity it remained until late in October. Early in the month Stuart rode around the Union army, which was then near Harper's Ferry. The impunity with which the daring cavalryman thus encircled McClellan for the second time cheered Southern hearts, drooping since Sharpsburg, and angered the North. It may have had something to do with hastening Lincoln's determination to replace McClellan with another commander.

In the autumn of 1862, the Confederate armies were reorganized, greatly to their benefit. The clumsy way of having several major generals serving under an officer of the same rank was discarded for the corps system. Longstreet, Jackson, Polk, Holmes, Hardee, E. Kirby Smith, and Pemberton were advanced to the grade of lieutenant general, the rank of corps commander. The Army of Northern Virginia was divided into two corps, the First under Longstreet, and the Second under Jackson. Increased efficiency was the result of this rearrangement.

On October 26, 1862, McClellan crossed the Potomac River east of the Blue Ridge, with the evident intention of conducting an aggressive campaign; his self-confidence had been greatly raised by Sharpsburg, or Antietam, claimed in the North as a victory. To meet the threat Lee directed Jackson to remain in the Shenandoah Valley and guard the passes of the Blue Ridge, while Longstreet moved on the east side of the mountains. One of the latter's divisions passed through Ashby's Gap to Upperville, moving on thence to Culpeper. Hood at Manassas Gap fought an action with Union cavalry. McLaws, crossing at Chester Gap, also ran into hostile cavalry and had a lively brush. Gradually Longstreet's corps became concentrated in the neighborhood of Culpeper, while the Union army was at Warrenton. It was now a question as to what McClellan would do. Would he cross the mountains after Jackson or move due south after Longstreet? The question was not to be answered, for on November 5 the Washington authorities delivered the long-impending blow. McClellan was relieved and was succeeded by Ambrose E. Burnside, who took command on November 9.

The Confederates were elated by the news, for they counted the dismissal of McClellan as their best victory. But even Lee, with his astute judgment of character, did not fully appreciate the meaning of the change. The Army of the Potomac had been under a commander who was cautious but who had, also, the merits of caution; he was not to be lured into battle at a disadvantage and destroyed. He was now succeeded by the most incompetent man in the high command of the Union army, a man who did not believe in himself and who was regarded as inefficient by his associates. Lincoln made a bad blunder, and it was the part of the Confederates to make it a fatal blunder. Thus Fortune dealt the South a hand of aces and waited to see if the South could play the hand.

At the time of the change the Confederate leaders expected the Union army to move toward Culpeper and were making examinations preparatory to the junction of the two corps behind the Robertson River.[1] But Burnside considered the move risky and determined on another course of action. No doubt, too, he wished to put off contact with the Confed-

[1] *M. to A.*, p. 292.

erate army until he could get accustomed to the saddle. He was well aware of the dissatisfaction in his army over McClellan's removal. Many of the division generals were McClellan's friends and looked on his dismissal, so soon after the great services he had rendered the Union, as little short of a crime. Thus while all was confidence and harmony on the Confederate side, the Army of the Potomac was rent by a dangerous feud. McClellan's friends gave grudging support to McClellan's supplanter.

To Lee the supreme opportunity had come in this mistake of the opposition, and he began to perceive it. His army, now rested and recruited, numbered seventy-eight thousand men, actually the largest force he ever commanded, and it was a veteran and well-organized array. It was at last capable not only of winning a victory but of annihilating an enemy. Everything depended on the way in which it would be handled in the next few weeks.

There were, however, drawbacks. The first was Lee's imperfect knowledge of Burnside, for he did not fully understand his opponent's incompetence and the dissatisfaction prevailing in the opposing army. The main disadvantage, however, lay in President Davis's interference in Lee's plans, for the President had not yet learned to let Lee form his plans without advice.

On November 19, Lee wrote to Jackson: "As to the place where it may be necessary or best to fight, I cannot now state, as this must be determined by circumstances which may arise. I do not now anticipate making a determined stand north of the North Anna. Longstreet's corps is moving to Fredericksburg, opposite to which place Sumner's corps has arrived." [2]

Between the Rappahannock and the James, the North

[2] *O. R.*, ser. I, vol. XXI, p. 1021.

Anna River is the best defensive position, and Lee had, as he said, half way decided to fight there. Most unfortunately, he changed his mind and determined to hold the line of the Rappahannock. Doubtless he was influenced in this by Jefferson Davis's reluctance to having his army give ground before the foe. Davis was a mediocre strategist, and the idea of retreating in order to fight at a greater advantage was beyond him.

From the moment of Burnside's accession to command, Lee expected him to move to Fredericksburg, but it was some time before Burnside showed his hand sufficiently for Lee to prepare to checkmate him. Sumner's advance to the Rappahannock opposite Fredericksburg fully disclosed the Union plans, and Longstreet moved from Culpeper to the town on the river. Jackson did not like the idea of fighting at Fredericksburg. He said the Confederates would win a victory there but would not be able, from the nature of the ground, to follow it up; Jackson wanted something better than a repulse and he was right. Longstreet seems to have favored Fredericksburg, which appealed to his defensive tastes.

On November 18, Longstreet marched with McLaws's division for Fredericksburg, while Ransom's moved toward the North Anna. Thus, even as late as this, Lee was hesitating between the two lines; but when his cavalry, on reconnaissance, reported the whole Union army as moving on Fredericksburg, he himself went to that place.

Longstreet reached Fredericksburg on November 19, and fixed his headquarters on the heights back of the town. On November 21, Sumner, in command of the Union force across the river from Fredericksburg, called on the town authorities to surrender on pain of bombardment, complaining that the place was being used for making supplies for the Confederate army and transporting them. The troubled burgomaster appealed to Longstreet, who suggested that a reply be sent to Sumner promising that the town facilities would not be used for the purposes complained of but that the Confederates would not permit a Union occupation. Sumner thereupon agreed not to open the bombardment at the time designated but made no further promises. Longstreet then advised the inhabitants to leave.

Lee would have preferred for Burnside to follow McClellan's plan of intervening between Jackson in the Shenandoah Valley and Longstreet at Culpeper, in which case he would have sought to envelop the Union host between the two concentrating wings. But eastern Virginia looked easier to Burnside and, besides, offered certain definite advantages. If he crossed the Rappahannock below Fredericksburg, say at Port Royal, he would have an excellent water base of operations for an advance against Richmond. It was unfortunate for the Confederates that he was not able to realize this idea, for if he had advanced southward on the side east of Fredericksburg he would have been drawn away from the Rappahannock and might have become involved in a country where his powerful artillery would have availed him little.

At this time it was by no means certain that a battle would be fought at Fredericksburg. Burnside preferred to cross the river lower down and Lee had no particular relish for fighting there. And he left Jackson out to the west as long as possible, hoping to be able to use him offensively. Only after long study and with reluctance did Lee decide on keeping to the mere defensive along the Rappahannock. For a man as audacious as himself it was a move lacking in spirit.

Jackson came down from the west in the last days of November and was assigned to the right of the Confederate line. He did not like to fight at Fredericksburg and said so, but Lee had decided to hold the line of the Rappahannock against Burnside. That he let his own judgment be overruled by Davis seems certain, for Fredericksburg is not a Lee-like battle at all; it smacks all the way through of Jefferson Davis, whose ideas of war were as strongly defensive as Longstreet's. To wait for attack, to run no risks, that was the defensive ideal.

The hills north of the Rappahannock, dominating the river plain, gave an ideal position for the superior Union artillery and made counterattack almost impossible. Here a Bunker Hill might be won, but the South needed a Cannae, not a Bunker Hill. Southern resources were showing the strain of the war; especially, man power was failing and war demands man power. Never again was Lee to have an army so large and an opportunity so potential.

In the first days of December, the army spread out along the river south and east of Fredericksburg. Longstreet was immediately behind the town, prepared to resist any attempt of the enemy there. Jackson, on the right, was stretched for miles along the river, as far down, in fact, as Port Royal, twenty-five miles below Fredericksburg. It was his task to see that the foe did not slip across the river at some point to the east and move around Fredericksburg instead of upon it.

Jackson performed his work only too well. The Unionists, trying out various points, could find no inviting crossing below Fredericksburg. The banks of the river were precipitous in places and in other places the river broadened out into an estuary difficult to cross by pontons. At length Burnside came to the decision of forcing a crossing immediately at Fredericksburg.

Fredericksburg is one of the picturesque fields of the Civil War. It was even more picturesque than usual in that winter season, for the Union commanders on the high hills north of the river could look for miles across the river plain and see the ascending smoke of the Confederate camp-fires. In the midst of the plain the river wound in folds, and on the south bank the steeples and roofs of the little town arose. Here was an absence of the heavy woods that obscured so many battlefields of the war.

The odds were on the side of the Confederates. An army of 78,000 men, holding a strong position, was about to be attacked by 110,000 men who had to cross a river and advance over an open plain. The Confederates were almost certain to win, unless something went awry, and the Union division commanders seem to have had little hope of success. But what sort of victory would the South win? The Union army, repulsed, would retreat across the river, where its artillery would give it protection against any enterprise of the Confederates. Would the latter be the better off for such a battle? Would it materially alter the situation in their favor?

It was Burnside's hope to be able to get across the river and take the hills on the Confederate right before Lee read his design and concentrated there. But, on attempting to throw pontons across the river in front of the town, the Unionists were so harassed by Confederate sharpshooters that they could make no progress. Whereupon the Union artillery opened fire on the town, on December 11, destroying many buildings and sufficiently advertising the commander's intention. Jackson was brought up from the east, taking position on Longstreet's right. Lee's line ran about five miles, from a point a mile west of Fredericksburg to Hamilton's Crossing on the Richmond railroad, four miles southeast. Of this Longstreet held about three miles, and Jackson the other two.

It was not until the afternoon of December 12 that the Union pontons were laid and a sufficient force conveyed to the south side of the stream to drive away the annoying snipers, who here showed how major operations can be delayed by skirmishers. The town, now deserted by most of the inhabitants, was plundered by the soldiers, who occupied the houses because of the bitter cold of the winter season.

At two points the Unionists clustered thickly: at Fredericksburg itself and at Hamilton's Crossing, four miles southeast. Burnside hoped to carry the hills at Hamilton's Crossing, not knowing that they were now held by Jackson's men. And as a matter of fact the extreme right of the Confederate position was occupied only in the early morning of December 13, when A. P. Hill and Early came up from the east. This was the only assailable part of a line which, for strength, left nothing to be desired. When Joseph E. Johnston, then gone West, heard of the battle of Fredericksburg he wailed, "Nobody will ever attack me in such a position!"

Longstreet was with Lee near the center of the line, about a mile south of the town. There, on an eminence since known as Lee's Hill, the two commanders saw unfolded beneath them a vast panorama as the morning mist lifted. North of the river were the Union batteries, lining the ridges for miles, from which came puffs of smoke at brief intervals. In the town itself moving bodies of bluecoats showed the Unionists clustering for attack while the frosty air brought to the listeners the blaring music of many bands. Off to the east and not far from the river, dense masses of troops stood in column with a hundred flags giving a vivid touch of color to the scene. The road to the east running parallel with the river showed the noses of many field pieces, brought across to support the infantry advance.

The mist had now entirely lifted, the sting gone out of

the sharp air. Snow covered much of the ground, affording a marvelous background to the splendid spectacle. Forty thousand men were massed for the charge on Jackson on the

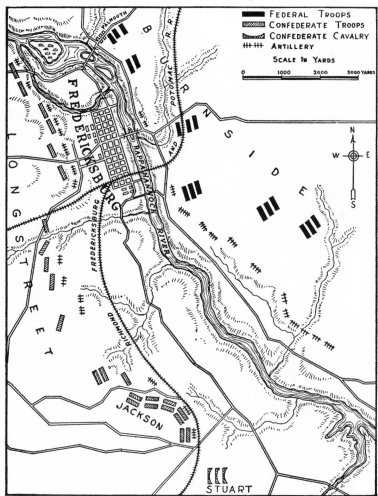

BATTLE OF FREDERICKSBURG, DECEMBER 13, 1862

Confederate right; the great host stood in serried ranks with flags waving and bands playing. Lee, admiring, said to Longstreet, "It is well that war is so terrible, or we should grow too fond of it." The sentiment of a man essentially a soldier, and yet a soldier softened and perhaps a little embarrassed by Christian sentiments.

In spite of the magnificence of the spectacle, the battle was hardly thrilling. Burnside's subordinates had little heart for the adventure when they looked on the frowning heights they were expected to take; the army itself had small confidence in its new commander. Perhaps the Army of the Potomac was never in lower spirits than at the battle of Fredericksburg, December 13, 1862.

The attack on Jackson was the only serious feature of the engagement, and that was not serious long. The Unionists, emerging from behind the high road running southeast from Fredericksburg, which they had made into a kind of field fortification with artillery, moved across the open space toward the ridge held by Jackson's troops. Harassed by a few guns of Stuart's horse artillery, they reached the railroad embankment at Hamilton's Crossing and rushed upward toward the hill crest. At one marshy point, which the Confederates had left unprotected, they broke through and, for a moment, imperiled Jackson's position. But Jackson, immediately calling up reserves, drove them back. Fired on by artillery and infantry along the line of the crest, which blazed like a volcano, the Unionists halted and then reeled back into the plain. The Confederates, pressing forward in pursuit, came under the fire of the fieldpieces along the road and were decimated. The battle on the Confederate right ended in the complete repulse of the Union attack and the repulse of the unorganized Confederate pursuit.

The great force on the Union left had no more stomach for what was seen to be a hopeless venture. The earth was strewn with blue uniforms. The time had come for the attack on the Confederates behind the town, an attack that had not the least chance of success. Reluctantly, the Union troops in the town left the shelter of the houses to advance against the hill known as Marye's Heights. Moving forward at the officers' command, they emerged from the houses and from a railway cut that gave a little protection and came out into the open fields. What was in front of them was Marye's Heights, at the base of which ran a stone wall. When the Unionists approached, the batteries on the hill opened on them. Closing their ranks they went forward and, as they did so, the stone wall blazed and rang from end to end as the Confederate infantry behind it opened fire.

Hopeless as was their task, they stuck to it doggedly, cursing their general and yet not accepting the fact of defeat. In particular, the pluck of Meagher's Irish Brigade was long remembered and was attributed by the townspeople to the men's being dosed with whiskey and gunpowder, as if the Irish ever needed such stimulants to valor.

Merciless was the fire of the Confederates, who discharged their muskets at the foe much as hunters shoot at game; hopeless was the task set the gallant Union army. French's division led the assault at Marye's Heights, followed by Hancock, who was followed later by Hooker commanding the Center Grand Division, composed of Stoneman's and Butterfield's corps. Hooker was in command and he soon saw the impossibility of the task. Nevertheless, by Burnside's orders the attacks were kept up until near the end of the short winter day. By that time the commands were all mixed up, and, while some of the troops lay on the ground helpless, other regiments moved over them to the front. Finally, the attempt was abandoned and the disorganized army fell back into the town, where all was confusion, misery, and recrimination. Never in all its honorable career was the Army of the Potomac so near demoralization as on that terrible night.

The views of the Southern leaders differed as darkness fell on the woeful scene. Lee thought that the attack would be renewed in the morning, and this was Burnside's intention, expressed in an order captured by Confederate pickets. Lee read the Union leader aright but could not know that Burnside's lieutenants, almost at the point of mutiny, would combine against him and overawe him. Longstreet seems to have been satisfied, for Fredericksburg, with its heavy cost to the Unionists and its much smaller loss for the Confederates, was his ideal battle.

It was not Jackson's. The sun had hardly set on the field before he went to Lee with proposals for a night attack. He urged that his men be stripped to the waist, to distinguish them in the darkness, and be launched in a bayonet attack on the confused masses in the town. It was a risk, of course, but what is war but the running of risks? It offered hopes of large captures of men and material. Lee demurred. He was sure that Burnside would try again. Then Jackson, in his eagerness to take advantage of the opportunity, seems to have made other suggestions. According to local tradition, he wished to blow up the dam in the river above the town and thus sweep away Burnside's pontons. Again Lee objected. At length Jackson desisted, unable to get his way.

The next day, December 14, the lines remained quiet when the winter morning broke. The day wore on and nothing happened but the firing of pickets. The sun set, and Burnside had not attacked again. That night, by all the rules, the Confederates should have tried something, some kind of a counterattack.

Another night passed and another Confederate opportunity. Then came December 15. That night was stormy, and the howling wind stifled merely human sounds. Under cover of the storm and darkness, while the Confederate pickets crouched at their posts, half frozen, the Union host recrossed the river on its pontons. The next morning, when the Confederate skirmishers cautiously crept forward, they found no responding enemy. Entering the town, they came on nothing but dead men and the thrown-away relics of a defeated army.

The Union army had escaped. The Confederates would have no such opportunity again. The South rang with Lee's praises over the new victory, but Lee himself was dissatisfied and depressed. The futility of his success was evident to him almost as soon as it was won. The Union army could not drive him from his position, but he could not drive the Union army from its. Thirteen thousand men had fallen on the Union side against five thousand on the Southern. That was the only gain. All that the Confederates had really accomplished was the ruin of their best friend, Burnside. He would never lead an army to battle again. Politics or no politics, he was not competent to command, as the authorities in Washington now knew. They would not remove him summarily, but they would get rid of him before it was time for another advance. For, in spite of Fredericksburg, the Unionists were thinking of advance, not retreat. All that the December battle accomplished was to postpone the advance from the winter season to the spring.

CHAPTER XI

INDEPENDENT COMMAND: SUFFOLK

THE month of December, 1862, marked the high tide of Confederate strength. In Virginia Lee mustered a fine army of seventy-eight thousand men and won the too easy victory of Fredericksburg, marked by no fruits of importance. In Tennessee, at the same time, Bragg had a chance to dispose of the opposing army under Rosecrans. On the last day of the year he almost won a great battle at Stone's River but did not quite win it, with the result that he lost it and fell back before his opponent in the opening days of 1863.

From that time the fate of the Confederacy was declining in spite of the dazzling victory of Chancellorsville, which was, like Fredericksburg, without important gains to the victors, and was made terrible by the death of the irreplaceable Jackson. The Confederate course was downward henceforth, partly because the Richmond government after this time directed the strategy to a considerable extent. Up to the battle of Fredericksburg, Lee largely dominated the strategy in the East, that is, from March, 1862, to November, 1862. After that time the arm-chair strategists in Richmond began to work, and the first result of their endeavors was the inconclusive victory of Fredericksburg. Politics played its part in the inconsequentialities that followed the bold movements of 1862, politics reinforced by Longstreet's insatiable ambition. For about this time he had the vision of a realized ambition.

Longstreet had done well at Fredericksburg, where he

had actually handled his part of the Confederate line better than Jackson had his. Jackson's loss had been considerable; Longstreet's had been negligible. His growing opinion of his own powers was accentuated by his lessening opinion of Lee, who, by the Maryland Campaign, had forfeited his admiration, if he had ever really admired Lee, which is doubtful. When a man speaks of the "errors" of such a military masterpiece as the Second Manassas, as Longstreet does, it is evident that he is lacking in appreciation of the generalship that directed it.

Longstreet had become weary of serving under Lee and desirous of demonstrating his own strategic powers, which, it is needless to say, he rated highly. He fancied himself in the rôle of commander and was elated when fate finally threw in his way the opportunity of independent command.

In December, 1862, the Confederate government was being worried by North Carolina. The long coast line of that state, exposed to sea raids, had always been a weakness, which was being accentuated as the war went on. The raids, or rather the fear of raids, were bringing protests from the North Carolina authorities, who demanded the keeping of a large force in the state for protection.

In this coastal region lie Norfolk, Portsmouth, and Suffolk in Virginia, and Elizabeth City, Washington, and Edenton in North Carolina. It had been occupied in part by Union troops since early in 1862, while the Confederates held the area just to the west, extending from Petersburg, Virginia, to Goldsboro, North Carolina. The naval power of the Unionists made it possible for them to dominate the tidal rivers and estuaries, but for some time they had made no forward movement into the region picketed by the Confederates.

In this bitterly cold winter of 1862-63, the Army of

Northern Virginia and the Army of the Potomac watched each other across the Rappahannock River at Fredericksburg. Burnside was not satisfied with the one battle he had directed and was eager to redeem himself; late in January, 1863, he made another attempt to cross the river, this time above Fredericksburg. But incessant rain brought the "Mud March" to naught, and, finding that he had lost the confidence of his government, he resigned. He was, however, man and patriot enough to agree to remain as the head of the Ninth Corps, a decision that relieved the government, which dared not throw him into the discard as it had done the New York Democrat, McClellan.

It was not deemed wise to have Burnside in the same army with Joseph Hooker, who superseded him in command and who had been his persistent critic. Consequently, the Ninth Corps was withdrawn from the Army of the Potomac and sent to Hampton (Fort Monroe). As soon as the Confederate authorities learned of this move, they began to fear for the Virginia-North Carolina coast. Lee, to quiet apprehensions, detached Pickett's division of Longstreet's corps and sent it toward Richmond, where it would be able to move easily to reinforce a threatened district. That was at the middle of February, 1863.

A few days after Pickett's departure, Hood followed him. Then since two of Longstreet's three divisions had left for other pastures, Longstreet and his staff were sent after them. This was a disastrous move, perhaps the most unfortunate move Lee made in the war, but he could hardly help himself, with North Carolina apprehensive and the Richmond authorities twittering. Longstreet was granted his long-desired opportunity.

The resignation of Gustavus W. Smith brought this about. Smith had been one of the failures of the war. Given high command at the beginning, he had shown his incapacity for responsibility at Seven Pines, where he had suffered nervous prostration. After his recovery Smith was detached from the main army, which had no place for him, and sent to take command of the Department of Southern Virginia and North Carolina. Always apprehensive, he made the Richmond government and Lee miserable by incessant demands for troops to guard against raids in North Carolina. On November 28, 1862, Lee, then facing the certainty of a battle, answered one of these calls for reinforcements as follows:

"While it is necessary to make every preparation against the operations of the enemy south of James River, we cannot hope to meet him at every point with anything like equal force. I think with you that efforts will be made to get possession of Wilmington, and perhaps other points of the railroad south of James River. I think, though, at present these demonstrations are intended as feints; but should they find us weak at any point, they will be converted into a real attack. I wish it were possible to reënforce you from this army; but if it is weakened by detaching men to the several points named by you, I see nothing left for it but to fall back before the enemy. We must risk some points in order to have a sufficient force concentrated, with the hope of dealing a successful blow when opportunity favors." [1]

Unable to get the troops he wanted, a concession that would have reduced Lee to impotence, and believing himself discriminated against by the government, the disappointed half-day commander of the Army of Northern Virginia shook the dust of Virginia from his feet. Going to Georgia, he took the command of Governor Joe Brown's state army, which included thousands of men who had no

[1] *O. R.*, ser. I, vol. XXI, p. 1038.

stomach for fighting. As their leader, Smith accomplished nothing of a military character but, at least, had the satisfaction of suffering practically no casualties. His wrathful departure left the Department of Southern Virginia and North Carolina without a commander.

Lee had been so harassed by the greatly exaggerated reports of the number and activity of the Unionists on the James River that he actually contemplated the withdrawal of his army to the vicinity of Richmond, where he could face both ways, against the Army of the Potomac coming from the north, and against the imaginary army described as being about to move up the James River and attack the capital from that side. These inaccurate reports of incompetent observers on the lower James, emphasized by the disgruntled Smith, were destined to lead to the unfortunate Suffolk campaign and the consequent fatal weakening of Lee's army at the moment of crisis. If the Unionists had had any idea of the disintegrating effect of their presence on the lower James, they would have made a strong demonstration on the river, for if they had done so, they would have brought about the abandonment of the line of the Rappahannock by the Confederates. They would have accomplished more by excursions and alarums than by fighting.

Davis, harassed by the necessity of keeping the people of all sections quiet, was to play the game, so characteristic of a politician, of scattering troops to defend all points, leaving no sufficient force at any one place to win a decisive victory. This strategical system was, to some extent, the cause of the downfall of the Confederacy. If Davis could have closed his ears to the chorus of squawks from every direction and concentrated enough men to give Lee a large army, he might have won the war. And it was worth trying, for, as things turned out, he lost the war.

The Richmond authorities were in hysterics over fleets and armies moving up the James. The North Carolina government was having fits over the threats of Unionists to penetrate the deep estuaries that reach far into that lovely state. On January 12, 1863, Governor Zebulon B. Vance urged President Davis to send Lee to North Carolina to survey the situation. Davis forwarded the message to Lee without other comment than, "Your presence there would be important; indeed, seems necessary." But poor Lee could not oppose the main enemy and at the same time look out for raids at distant points. He judged, rightly enough, that his presence was needed with his army. A week later Burnside made his abortive effort to cross the Rappahannock, thus proving Lee's wisdom.

Longstreet was glad enough to try another field, especially as he thought nothing of importance would take place on the Rappahannock before spring. Writing to Jackson, on January 18, 1863, he expressed that opinion, adding, "Our line is stronger now than it was when he advanced before." Just about this time the first withdrawals were made for the purpose of protecting the James River and North Carolina. It was the beginning of the breaking up of Lee's fine army.

The main trouble with the South was that it could not maintain any strategic system for any length of time. Lee's and Jackson's ideas of strategy were offensive. Lee knew that it is necessary to take great risks to gain great ends. If his ideas had prevailed, the South might have won the war. But Lee's own ideas were often in direct opposition to those of Jefferson Davis, who was essentially defensive. Davis did not believe in taking risks and, therefore, could not win great victories. Yet if the defensive system had been followed consistently, it might have succeeded by wearing out the North; but as offensive and defensive strategy were mixed, the chance of victory was obscured.

In passing judgment on the administration of Jefferson Davis, allowance must be made for the opposition he met at the hands of politicians. While Lincoln received hearty support from most of the war governors of the Northern states, Davis found in his war governors one of the obstacles to success. This was particularly the case of Governor Joseph Brown, of Georgia, and in no much smaller degree of Zebulon B. Vance of North Carolina and other governors.

It is easy enough to blame these executives, but they, like Davis, were the victims of states' rights. While the Confederacy was in the first flush, national feeling obscured states' rights; but as the war lengthened and grew burdensome, the states remembered their sovereignty. When the Union armies penetrated to the interior or Union fleets menaced the coast, there came demands for troops from every section that would have taken five times the man power of the Confederacy to fill. Vance, for instance, saw nothing beyond the horizon of his own state; the general situation did not interest him. His requisitions would have left Lee with a corporal's guard if Davis had listened to them, and Davis was damned if he did not listen.

Thus harassed on every side, Davis himself found the situation to be one compelling the sending of troops to the defense of Wilmington, Charleston, Savannah, and other points. And a problem not much less embarrassing was the matter of supplies. Virginia was pretty well exhausted by 1863, and the logical place to secure food for Lee's army was North Carolina. Unfortunately, by that time the inhabitants of the Old North State were not eager to exchange articles of value for Confederate currency, which, considering the dubious prospects of that currency, was but natural.

Yet the authorities in Richmond had an idea that food supplies were to be obtained in the section of North Carolina
along the Chowan River and in the eastern counties of Virginia in Union occupation. As a matter of fact, little was left
anywhere in Virginia and no great deal in North Carolina,
when, on February 10, 1863, Secretary of War Seddon wrote
Vance that Lee's army might, in its extremity, become de-
pendent on the latter state for food.

Davis and Seddon, filled with the vain hope of securing
food supplies from the area controlled or threatened by the
Unionists, were beginning to disperse Lee's army by drawing
on it for detachments. Wilmington was represented to Lee
as being in dire danger of attack, which was not the case at
all. But some excuse was needed to get troops from Lee, and
the threat of attacks on Wilmington, chief port of the Confederacy, was always effective. As one reads the dispatches,
he is struck by the sagacity and honesty of Lee and by the
folly and something like disingenuousness of the men with
whom he dealt. Struggling against the drains made on him,
feeling that they were not wise, he was nevertheless betrayed
by his loyalty and soldierly habit of obedience into compli-
ances with the demands of politicians and bureaucrats, plus
his ambitious lieutenant, which reduced his army to a point
where he was obliged to take desperate risks. It is a curious
case.

Lee, on February 4, writes Seddon who is fishing for
troops, "I am trying to be prepared for any movement that
may be made by General Hooker, but if the pressure on
Wilmington is the more urgent it should be reënforced."
Seddon had asked Lee's views about sending troops to North
Carolina but had not recommended it. In the middle of
February, Lee sent two of his best divisions (Hood and
Pickett) to the southward, a move that greatly reduced his

army and placed him in a dangerous position if they should be long absent.

It would have been better if he had done what he often thought of doing, but rejected—fallen back to the North Anna River. In that case he would have given up some territory of little value and his railroad communications with the West would have been menaced; but he would have been near enough to Richmond to relieve the fears of the authorities, who always visioned armies of Unionists coming suddenly up the James River, and near enough to North Carolina to have resisted the demands of that state for depleting his army. But Davis would have opposed abandoning the Rappahannock, just as he had done in November before; he would keep a few troops there, a few troops everywhere, enough at no point for decisive victory.

Another great scare agitated the authorities in February. Burnside, on being relieved of the command of his army, had retained the Ninth Corps. He was sent away from what was now Hooker's army, and his first station was near Fort Monroe. On February 17, Seddon wrote Lee that twenty thousand men had landed at Newport News and that it was believed Hooker was about to abandon the line of the Rappahannock. Lee himself thought for a moment that this might be true. Helpless in the hands of the enemy in Richmond, Lee on February 18 directed Longstreet to go south to join his two divisions, sent ahead and now destined for service in North Carolina if needed. Longstreet was glad enough to get away from Lee and reluctant to return. His reluctance was destined to cost the Confederacy dear.

On February 22, Longstreet was in Richmond, conferring with the authorities and hearing of the vast numbers of Unionists at the mouth of the James River. A few days later he wrote Lee that scouts reported forty or fifty thousand

Union troops at Newport News (Hampton). On February 26, he assumed command of the department from which Smith had resigned. It is significant that in taking the reins he speaks of the "Department of Virginia and North Carolina." The word "Southern" is left out. This omission was prophetic of his ambition to become the main Confederate leader in the East. Lee he fancied in a subordinate capacity, for which he considered Lee fitted. On March 1, Longstreet wrote Lee that he had a sufficient force for the purpose of securing supplies in North Carolina, the original reason for detaching troops.

It was early in March that Davis and Seddon cooked up a plan destined to have the most disastrous consequences. Seddon asked Longstreet to make a reconnaissance toward Suffolk with a view to attacking it. The town was held by Dix with a considerable Union force and was a thorn in the Confederate flesh, but it was so surrounded by deep water that its retention by the Confederates, if captured, was impossible. Seddon was not thinking of retaining it; he was dreaming of drawing supplies from a region the Unionists had occupied for months, a futile scheme.

About the same time Lee became a little skeptical of the reports of enormous Union forces at Hampton, Virginia, and in North Carolina, with which he had been stuffed. As the March days passed, Longstreet still cogitated over the move to Suffolk proposed by Seddon; he thought it would be a good play provided he was given cavalry and war vessels.

Finally Longstreet, rather suddenly, resolved to push his line eastward to the Blackwater River, which is not far from Suffolk. Seddon at once approved the plan, in which he saw carried out his idea of a campaign against Suffolk. (Or was it Davis's idea? It sounds like one of Davis's fatuous strategic ideas, this futile supply-hunting campaign against a point of no consequence in itself.)

On March 16, Lee tells Longstreet he thinks the enemy will try to cross the Rappahannock in his front and asks the latter to be ready to join him when needed. Longstreet answers, "I will be ready to join you with Hood's division at any moment unless there is a fine opportunity to strike a decided blow here, in which case I think I had better act promptly and trust to your being able to hold the force in your front in check until I can join you." In other words, Longstreet did not wish to go back to Lee; he much preferred his present position of departmental commander, and it would appear that he seized on the movement against Suffolk, about which he never showed much enthusiasm, as an excuse to keep from joining Lee's army with his divisions. He was now actually proposing for Lee to fight the great Army of the Potomac, more than a hundred thousand strong, with his depleted force, while expeditions were to be attempted against the enemy in North Carolina. "All things considered," he wrote, "I now think that our better plan would have been to fight the enemy on the Rappahannock with the force that you have there, *or slightly diminished even* [italics ours], and to leave the force that was here to drive the enemy in North Carolina and draw out the supplies there. I cannot divest myself of the opinion that an obstinate resistance on the Rappahannock will hold that line, and the force that I had here would then do to drive the enemy out of North Carolina, where it seems we must get our supplies. . . . If it is necessary to give ground anywhere it seems to me that it would have been better to retire your force across the Anna." [2] The last suggestion was not inapt. Lee would have done better on the North Anna with his

[2] *O. R.,* ser. I, vol. XVIII, p. 924.

army in hand than on the Rappahannock with a depleted host.

On March 19, Longstreet answers Lee's query about supplies, for very few provisions were being collected in North Carolina in spite of the imposing force kept there. Again Longstreet suggests that Lee should fall back to the Anna rivers. He says he thinks he can obtain supplies, provided he can have the use of all his force, but if his divisions rejoin Lee he can do nothing. The enemy had forty thousand men, he the same number. In reality, he had perhaps fifty thousand troops at that moment, almost the same number with which Lee was opposing the vastly larger Army of the Potomac. Indeed, Longstreet may have had even more than fifty thousand under his command.

Longstreet was not only resolved to keep his two divisions away from Lee; he was actually angling to get his third division, leaving Lee only one corps, Jackson's, with which to confront Hooker. On March 21 he wrote Lee, "I believe that an advantageous battle could be made at Suffolk in the next fifteen days, but at least one division in addition to what we have would be necessary." Suffolk was the excuse for drawing still further on Lee; Longstreet, as we have seen, never was vitally interested in Suffolk or thought particularly well of the expedition against it. But if Lee could be soothed by the idea of something being done at Suffolk, he might send Longstreet the third division. That would have left Lee forty-odd thousand men with which to oppose Hooker's great army and would have given Longstreet sixty thousand men with which to repel a raid or two somewhere in North Carolina and pick up a little corn and bacon. In other words, the wily Longstreet was fully engaged in the process of reducing Lee to the second place in the Confederate service while he, Longstreet, occupied the first, with an army larger than Lee's.

On the same day (March 21), Lee protested to Longstreet that he could not understand why the latter should need Pickett and Hood in North Carolina, "as from the information I received the enemy between the Roanoke and Tar is feeble." Yet Longstreet was left free to act if he could do anything. Lee was beginning to believe that he might have to fall back southward toward Longstreet.

Longstreet now became committed to the enterprise against Suffolk to facilitate the gathering of supplies. On March 27, Lee agreed with him that Suffolk might be taken by a sudden attack but was far from satisfied that the move would be worth while. Longstreet himself had little stomach for attacking Suffolk and wrote Lee, on March 30, "There are no particular advantages in giving battle at Suffolk."

Now comes perhaps the worst feature of the whole business. One reason that Longstreet had advanced for the drains on Lee was the threat of Burnside's presence at Newport News. In the beginning of April, Lee writes that Burnside is reported to have gone to Kentucky. A little later this news becomes certainty; Burnside, with the whole Ninth Corps, has gone West. It is Lee who informs Longstreet of this, not Longstreet who tells Lee, although Longstreet should have known something of troop movements on the James unless his scouts were totally worthless.

On April 3, Longstreet informs Lee that he has been to the Blackwater River to make arrangements to cross for a move against Suffolk. He has the audacity to ask for more men, alleging that Lee could hold the line of the Rappahannock with one corps. He could not see why Lee should think of falling back to the North Anna, even if his army is depleted by further drafts. Longstreet is now full of the prospect of operating independently of Lee and becoming an army commander.

He was dreaming of something bigger than a paltry excursion against the Union post of Suffolk. He was thinking of the move to reinforce Bragg in Tennessee that was carried out in the autumn of 1863. To his restless ambition that seemed a better chance than to fight with Lee, where he was not only eclipsed by the commander himself but by Jackson as well. In other words, in the Army of Northern Virginia Longstreet was third, while elsewhere he might be first. Significant of this is an endorsement Jefferson Davis wrote on a dispatch sent by Lee to Cooper in which Lee announced that Burnside had gone West and added that he had made inquiries of Longstreet. Davis wrote, "Why inquire of Longstreet? This may be an error in dispatch, or it may be a suggestion of that which is to my mind indicated—the movement of Longstreet to reënforce Bragg." That was on March 28.

Davis was now pecking away at Lee's army, trying to get troops to send definitely away. On April 6, Seddon asked Lee for Pickett to reinforce Bragg. Since Union troops had gone West, they must be met there by withdrawals from Virginia. That was Davis's idea of strategy. Lee demurred, naturally enough. He, most honest man, while he did not fathom Longstreet's scheme of drawing sufficient troops from him to give the latter command of the largest army, was yet ill at ease, feeling that something was out of gear, believing that Longstreet and Seddon were allowing themselves to be frightened by bugaboos. Lee himself was holding up the Confederate cause on his broad shoulders while his subordinates and the authorities were not supporting him. Cooper chimed in a few days later, asking for troops to send West. Lee's answer is a revelation. How can he send troops away, he inquires, when Hooker has seventy thousand effectives and he, Lee, only thirty-eight thousand? At this moment, mid-April, Longstreet must have had forty thousand effectives under his command. It is easy to see how Lee is being silently eclipsed, relegated to inferiority by intrigue— intrigue for which he never had any talent himself, being the most straightforward of men. Poor Lee, harassed by Longstreet for more men to use against Suffolk and by the authorities for troops to send to Bragg! If Lee had not become impatient, he would have been left with only a handful at Fredericksburg, confronting an army of a hundred thousand.

Longstreet now begins his move toward Suffolk. To deceive the enemy, the report is given out (which he wishes were the truth) that he has gone West to join Bragg. No such luck for him; he has no other opening as an independent commander than this small affair at Suffolk. It will at least serve to keep him in command of an army, his objective.

Longstreet approached Suffolk and began a mild investment of it, throwing up earthworks across the principal roads. Nothing whatever was to be gained by the movement. The town was of no importance to the Confederates and could not be held, if taken, because of its position near the great estuary of the James filled with Union gunboats. Few supplies were to be found in the vicinity, which had been combed by the Union garrison long before. The Unionists themselves were amazed at the Confederate strategy. Keyes wrote to Halleck, "I can see nothing in that quarter [Suffolk-Goldsboro area] to tempt the enemy to weaken his attack on Hooker." The real reason for Longstreet's move is that it gave him an excuse for not rejoining Lee. He hoped to be sent West if he did not go back to the Army of Northern

Virginia. This is proved by his repeated suggestions to the authorities to reinforce Bragg in Tennessee.

On April 11, the Confederates, having crossed the Blackwater, approached Suffolk and felt out its defenses. The Union garrison was not large but it was on the alert, and Longstreet could find no opening anywhere for an attack that promised good results. He then invested the place, which leads to the belief that he hoped to be away from Lee for some time, as an investment of a fortified position is not an affair of a day or two. On April 14, the Confederate guns opened fire on Union gunboats in Nansemond River with some success, but a few days later a Confederate battery on the water front was cleverly surprised with loss. The net result of the operations was entirely negative. The Suffolk campaign is another name for futility.

Meanwhile April was nearing the end, and Hooker was making preparations, no longer to be hidden, to cross the Rappahannock. Lee, realizing what was about to happen, began to appeal to Longstreet to return, but the latter always had some good excuse for not doing so. At last Davis, perhaps at Lee's solicitation, took a hand, as the Confederate government suddenly became aware of the threatening situation on the Rappahannock, where Lee was vastly outnumbered. On April 29, Lee telegraphed to Richmond that Hooker was crossing the Rappanhannock and asked for all available forces. The next day Cooper ordered Longstreet to rejoin Lee. Longstreet took his time to move. His excuse was that he could not leave his wagon trains, which were scattered. In view of Lee's repeated warnings the excuse is not valid; Longstreet did not move because he did not wish to move. He had no desire to rejoin Lee. He did not move until it became evident that a great battle was being fought without him and that the government itself was growing restive over his conduct. Moving deliberately, he reached Lee several days after the battle of Chancellorsville had been fought.

In his extremity Lee had fully exerted his genius and his audacity and had won the greatest victory in American history in the dense woods of Chancellorsville, May 1-5, 1863, but at the price of Jackson's life. That was the penalty exacted by having to fight Hooker with an army less than half the size of the Army of the Potomac. His insufficient forces had permitted Hooker to escape across the Rappanhannock just as Burnside had escaped some months before. The Union campaign had been wrecked, but the Confederates had lost heavily, and Jackson, the incomparable Jackson, was dead.

How needless it all was! The critics have condemned the Confederate authorities for not shifting troops East or West as the need was, using the interior lines of communication. But it would have been far easier to concentrate the troops in Virginia and North Carolina. If Lee had fallen back to the North Anna it would have been possible to bring together a hundred thousand men there with which to confront Hooker. Lee and Jackson, with a hundred thousand men, might well have accomplished the overthrow of the Union host. A rudimentary conception of strategy would have enabled the Confederate authorities to win such a victory as would conceivably have brought about the success of their cause. But these mighty possibilities were thrown away for the purpose of maintaining troops in North Carolina to repel raids and to aid Longstreet in his ambition to become an independent commander, while at the same time the line of the Rappahannock was held. Richmond headquarters strategy—and Longstreet—had brought this about.

CHAPTER XII

LONGSTREET SEEKS TO IMPOSE HIS WILL ON LEE

WHEN Longstreet rejoined the army at Fredericksburg, Lee informed the government that he would need his lieutenant with him thereafter. The government acquiesced. Longstreet had done nothing of value as the commander of a department, and his services were considered of more moment as attached to Lee's army. Indeed, he would have been an efficient and useful corps commander if his vanity had not always pictured him to himself as the presiding genius of the Confederacy and Lee as secondary.

D. H. Hill was made commander of the Department of Southern Virginia and North Carolina, in which difficult position he did little better than Longstreet had done. In fact he was not adequate to the administrative labors of such a post, being essentially a fighter, one of the best, but nothing else.

Longstreet was chagrined that Lee had won a great battle without his assistance; considering himself a vital part of the army, he found that the army had done so well without him that his absence was not felt except that he might have made the victory decisive instead of indecisive. Longstreet took pleasure in pointing out in his book, written many years later, that the Confederate losses were very heavy. This was inevitable, inasmuch as Lee was forced to take the offensive against Hooker's fortified position. If Longstreet's divisions had been there, the Confederate tactics would have been different.

Longstreet seldom has praise for Lee, and Chancellorsville is no exception. In order to find material for criticizing one of the most remarkable feats in military history, Longstreet borders on the nonsensical. He condemns Lee for not following his superior advice, as follows:

"It is only apropos to this writing to consider the plan of battle as projected some four months previous—i. e., to stand behind our intrenched lines and await the return of my troops from Suffolk.

"Under that plan General Lee would have had time to strengthen and improve his trenches, while Hooker was intrenching at Chancellorsville. He could have held his army solid behind his lines, where his men would have done more work on the unfinished lines in a day than in months of idle camp life." [1]

Truly the desire to criticize and find fault leads us into absurdities. One reading this extract might imagine that Longstreet was ignorant of the rudiments of strategy, but it is only Longstreet indulging in his usual diversion of passing judgment on Lee. How could Lee have remained in his trenches at Fredericksburg with Hooker south of the Rappahannock at Chancellorsville, on his flank and in a position to break his communications? Indeed, the moment the Union army crossed the river Fredericksburg became untenable, as Lee and Jackson perfectly understood. They had fought the battle in the only possible way short of falling back to the North Anna and giving up a strip of territory. But the battle had not been fought according to Longstreet's ideas, and consequently it was all wrong and was to be classed as a failure.

The death of the lamented Jackson left Lee with the terrible task of finding his successor. No one in the army ap-

[1] *M. to A.*, p. 329.

proached the great Stonewall in reputation or ability. Finally Lee decided to divide his army into three corps instead of two, feeling that no officer he had was competent to handle so large a force as the original corps.

Because of the rather slender success of the two corps commanders now selected, Lee has been criticized for his choice. Foremost among the critics, as one might expect, is Longstreet, always eager to point out Lee's incompetence. He also illustrates the petty jealousy of Virginia that animated many Lower Southerners. One might imagine, from their attitude toward the Old Dominion, that it had led the way in secession and hoped to profit by it instead of making inconceivable sacrifices in order to stand by the Lower South.

Longstreet remained in command of the First Corps, now somewhat reduced. Richard S. Ewell became the head of the Second Corps, and A. P. Hill of the Third. Both Ewell and Hill were distinguished officers, but they had not stood out above other soldiers in the army. Ewell was handicapped by a wooden leg, the result of a wound received at the Second Manassas. He was supposed to have been close to Jackson and was undoubtedly selected partly for that reason. He was not a good choice. An adequate division commander, he never measured up to the height required of the head of a corps. Hill had been associated with most of the campaigns and battles of the army from the beginning of the war. He was also a good division leader but lacked the capacity for higher command.

Later critics have thought that Lee would have done well to place Stuart in Jackson's place; and it might have been a better choice than Ewell or Hill, for Stuart had handled Jackson's troops with skill after the great commander was laid low on May 2; but his name seems not to have been considered. Besides, Lee no doubt felt that Stuart was essential to the cavalry. As a matter of fact, he would probably have made a better corps commander than a cavalry chief, since he would have had only to carry out Lee's instructions, while as a cavalryman he initiated movements, some of which resulted unfortunately.

Longstreet advances the charge that Lee chose Ewell and Hill because they were Virginians. He makes the statement in his book that the appointment of Ewell and Hill was resented by other officers because these men were Virginians. Ewell (but not A. P. Hill) was a senior major general and, by the rules of seniority, entitled to promotion. Besides them "was a North Carolinian, General D. H. Hill, and next a Georgian, General Lafayette McLaws, against whom was the objection that they were not Virginians." [2]

Habits of criticism lead one insensibly into glaring inconsistencies. Longstreet, habitual critic of everyone but himself, did not realize this, but the fact becomes apparent that he was unfair in his judgment and wholly inconsistent, when we understand that D. H. Hill had just been assigned to the North Carolina district, with its troublesome governor, and was hardly available as a corps commander in Lee's army. Besides, D. H. Hill himself went beyond Longstreet in his criticism of others, being unrestrained by any considerations from condemning his superiors; and, lastly, he was not in good health. As for McLaws, Longstreet found him so unsatisfactory as a division commander that he put him under arrest and preferred charges against him. Yet he thought that McLaws was suited as a corps commander! Longstreet admits that McLaws was not in good health at the time.

The crisis of the war had now arrived. It was evident that Davis's idea of the strategic defensive was not working well. Chancellorsville had been a fruitless victory. On the Mis-

[2] *M. to A.*, p. 332; *B. & L.*, III, 245.

sissippi, Vicksburg was besieged by Grant and in danger of capture. In Tennessee, Bragg and Rosecrans neutralized each other. At Jackson, Mississippi, Johnston was assembling a small army. West of the Mississippi were considerable bodies of Confederate troops, but that was another department.

The Confederates had to decide on what course they would follow, especially since the victory of Chancellorsville had given them the chance to take the initiative. To stand still was to lose, but it was by no means easy to say what was the best offensive action to take. Critics since the war, notably General A. P. Alexander, Confederate artillerist, have pointed out that the Confederates might have used their interior lines of communications and shifted troops from East to West and *vice versa* as the need arose; in that way inferior forces might have become superior at the point of contact. The suggestion is so obvious that many students censure the Confederate authorities for not adopting it at an early period of the war, and particularly in the summer of 1863.

Longstreet had early been of this opinion, chiefly because he wished to get to fields where he would not be towered over by the taller forms of Lee and Jackson; he had hoped, when he left Lee in February, 1863, that he was going West to join Bragg and, possibly, to supersede him. And in his writings he dwells on the great advantages to be obtained by sending a part of Lee's army West.

There were two serious objections, however, to the weakening of Lee's army in the summer of 1863 to reinforce Bragg. One was the bad state of the railways, which made the transportation of a large body of men and their baggage a matter of difficulty; it took an interminable time to shift

Longstreet and a part of his corps to Tennessee in September, 1863.

What was still more serious was that there was no general available competent to give any assurance of victory whatever. Bragg was already considered a failure by nearly everybody but President Davis and General Johnston. To weaken Lee in order to give Bragg troops to use in an attack on Rosecrans would have been suicidal. To give troops to Johnston at Jackson, Mississippi, would not have helped materially unless a whole corps were sent, since Johnston would never have attacked Grant unless relatively as strong.

Lastly there was Longstreet, of course. But Longstreet had shown no signs of ability in his conduct of the Department of Southern Virginia and North Carolina and had made a futile campaign against Suffolk at a moment when he was direly needed elsewhere. What reason was there, then, to take him at his own valuation as the most useful officer in the South and put him in command?

There was one alternative, and that was that Lee should go West. Davis had thought of this and had asked Lee to go. Lee had declined. He was fighting for Virginia, preeminently, and he did not wish to command in fields where everything was strange to him. Besides, he was far from well, for he had suffered from pleurisy in the winter and was troubled now by infected tonsils. Moreover, if he went West, he who upheld the Southern cause by his ability, what would happen to Virginia and the capital of the nation? Lee considered the whole matter thoughtfully and put the gist of it to Davis: it was a question of losing either Mississippi or Virginia.

Lee planned an invasion of Pennsylvania. Or, rather, he decided to make the invasion that Jackson had already planned and for which the latter had had a most extensive map prepared, for Jackson was, in a certain sense, a more scientific soldier than Lee. Lee hoped to accomplish much, but alas! he did not have Jackson any longer to sketch the strategy of the invasion, and that Lee relied on Jackson for strategic advice is certain.

Lee hoped to accomplish three things: to gain food for his almost starving army and relieve Virginia for a season of the military locusts devouring it; to draw Grant from Vicksburg by a threat against Harrisburg and Philadelphia; to win a victory on Northern soil that would lead to foreign recognition of the Southern nation and perhaps cause the North to abandon the contest.

Under the circumstances, this was the best course. The capture of Vicksburg was the greatest feat of the war, but it would not have had its overwhelming effect if countered by a Confederate victory in Pennsylvania and the occupation of Harrisburg. What broke the strength of the South was the coincidence of great defeats in the East and the West at the same moment.

Seddon at first preferred to send troops West but he deferred to Lee, as did Davis. At a cabinet meeting held on May 26, 1863, the government took the fateful step of deciding on the invasion of Pennsylvania. Once the step was taken, preparations were in order.

Longstreet tells us that he, reluctantly, consented to the invasion of Pennsylvania instead of the relief of the West. In his several accounts of the event he speaks in the tone of an army commander. He "consented" to the move but he bound Lee, according to his story, by a promise to make the campaign offensive but the battle defensive. Here, as always, Longstreet's natural penchant for the strict defensive asserted itself.

He was right in preferring the advantages of the tactical

defensive on the enemy's soil, but it is one of the unsolved mysteries of his generalship how he proposed to bring about this desired consummation. His solution of the difficulty at Gettysburg was hardly practicable under the circumstances; the one solution that was promising he never even suspected.

He was right, however, in seeking to temper Lee's natural taste for the offensive, "headlong combativeness," as he calls it. The man power of the Confederacy was rapidly waning and it was necessary to conserve Lee's army to the point of extreme caution before accepting battle. Yet the Confederates were in no position for extensive maneuvering. Lee's hope was to relieve hard-pressed Vicksburg, and to do that swift action was necessary. This was the weak point in the campaign—that Lee might be forced to accept battle on disadvantageous terms because of the time element. Longstreet gave no consideration to this. He seems to have thought that Lee could penetrate the enemy's country and give battle wherever and whenever it suited him. This fixed preconception was one of the factors that wrecked the campaign and lost the battle.

The month of June saw Lee pull skillfully out of his earthworks about Fredericksburg and head northward. Hooker, feeling that something was in the wind but not knowing its nature, launched his cavalry on the Confederates at Brandy Station near Culpeper by way of reconnaissance. One of the great cavalry actions of the war followed, June 9, 1863. Stuart was hard pressed; indeed, the honors of the day were perhaps really with the Unionists. They also learned what they sought to know, that large bodies of Confederate infantry were in the vicinity of Culpeper. Hooker realized that Lee was going toward the Potomac.

Early of Ewell's corps led the way, Hill followed, safe behind the wall of the beautiful Blue Ridge, which here runs north and south. The campaign was beginning propitiously, but already there were deficiencies and miscarriages that Lee could not guard against.

In the first place, Davis did not much like the offensive campaign; he had consented to it reluctantly because Lee after Chancellorsville was so powerful that his plans could not be denied. But Lee was not given the force needed to insure victory; a hundred thousand men might have been concentrated in this great effort to win the war instead of the seventy thousand he actually had. True to form, Davis was mixing the cautious defensive with the bold offensive; failure was the probable outcome.

Lee had asked for something in order to confuse Union strategy and keep Hooker south of the Potomac while he requisitioned north of it. He had requested the forming of a skeleton army at Culpeper under Beauregard; that officer's reputation, together with a small body of troops, would give weight to the report that a second Confederate army was prepared to intervene between Hooker and Washington if Hooker went in pursuit of Lee. Lee had cautiously opened this plan, but the Confederate authorities never gave it serious consideration. A dispatch from Davis to Lee, announcing that nothing could be done, was captured and taken to Meade, who was relieved of any fears for his rear. Davis, in bed with one of his terrible attacks of neuralgia, was too exhausted to do justice to Lee's strategy.

The Confederates moved up the Shenandoah Valley. Ewell, rather skillfully, ejected the Union commander, Milroy, from Winchester, taking a number of prisoners. Once more the people of that oppressed district thrilled at the sight of Confederate soldiers and the red Confederate flags.

And now there occurred an untoward event that had a

sinister bearing on the campaign. Mosby, the bold guerrilla, went to his superior, Stuart, with a suggestion that the latter might get in the rear of Hooker's army, now heading north, and accomplish something. It was just such an enterprise as suited the youthful Stuart, who naturally preferred dashing rides to the dull routine of outpost duty.

Longstreet had remained east of the Blue Ridge while Hill crossed the mountains behind him and moved on to Winchester. Then Longstreet himself crossed by the northern gaps of the Blue Ridge and joined Hill, about June 20. Throughout this movement Stuart screened the infantry with his cavalry, fighting many severe actions and demonstrating the importance of cavalry in any large army movement. But, fired by Mosby's proposal, the young cavalryman was dreaming of a great raid that would crown him with glory.

Stuart proposed to Lee to leave a brigade or so of cavalry with the army and, with the rest of his force, to cross the mountains and ford the Potomac in Hooker's rear, passing around the Union army. That would mean separation from his own army in the critical hour when it was moving into the enemy's territory, and why Lee entertained such a plan, so dangerous to his strategy, it is impossible to say. He seems to have had such confidence in Stuart's judgment and ability that he did not give the proposal the serious consideration it deserved. He agreed, provided that Longstreet could spare the cavalry, which was screening his front at that moment.

Longstreet himself agreed for the curious reason that "the passage of the Potomac by our rear would, in a measure, disclose our plans." It seems to have been his idea that Stuart, by moving eastward at the very time that the army was about to cross the Potomac, would confuse Hooker as to Lee's aims, a very far-fetched conclusion and a decision most disastrous to the Confederate cause. However, Longstreet stipulated that Hampton was to be left with the cavalry accompanying the army, but Stuart did not comply with this. He left W. R. Jones and Robertson but did not give them orders to report to headquarters. In other words, the cavalry with the army was practically left without instructions while Stuart started off on his ride around the Union army. Longstreet comments thus: "So our plans, adopted after deep study, were suddenly given over to gratify the youthful cavalryman's wish for a nomadic ride." But Longstreet himself was to blame in the matter, for his explanation, over-elaborate and difficult to understand, leaves one with the impression that his own conscience was not clear.

Beyond doubt Longstreet expected Stuart to keep close to him. "My orders to him were that he should ride on the right of my column as originally designed, to the Shepherdstown crossing," says Longstreet. Stuart had not expected to have to pass around the whole Union army, but Hooker was farther north than the former thought him to be; Stuart had to move farther east than he had proposed and had to put himself in such a position that the enemy was between him and Lee. That made necessary a long detour, and Stuart, bringing captured wagons, did not rejoin Lee until the second day at Gettysburg. Lee, thinking that Stuart had given instructions to the cavalry left with the army, sent no orders; and Stuart, thinking that Lee would give orders, gave no definite orders. The result was that Robertson remained guarding the passes of the Blue Ridge long after the army had crossed the Potomac, when the possession of the passes was of no moment whatever. Only a small force of cavalry accompanied Ewell, the advance

guard of the invasion. The Southern army had divested itself of its cavalry screen at the very moment when that
screen had become of paramount importance in preventing the enemy from learning its movements.

Ewell had crossed the Potomac first. He was followed
by Hill, and Hill by Longstreet. The two latter corps met
at Hagerstown and continued on to Chambersburg, Pennsylvania, where they remained from June 27 to June 29.
Ewell now moved over the mountains past Gettysburg, halting at Carlisle on June 29. Gordon, of Ewell's corps, went
as far as Wrightsville on the Susquehanna, which he would
have crossed but for the burning of the bridge by Unionists.
Ewell was gathering provisions and cattle in leisurely fashion, and the invasion of Pennsylvania was beginning to wear
the aspect of a raid rather than that of an important strategic move. But Lee's strategy was always hampered by
commissariat considerations, and those considerations led him
to take risks. It was a grave risk to send Ewell so far east as
Carlisle while the position of the Union army was entirely
unknown.

Lee had no information whatever of Hooker's movements; he was working in the dark. He might have known,
though he evidently did not, that the presence of an invading army in Pennsylvania would galvanize the Unionists
into quick, almost frantic, action. There was no chance that
he would be permitted to garnish his larder without resistance in the fields of Pennsylvania, and he should have
realized it. But Hooker had been paralyzed for some time,
and, thinking that Hooker was still in command, Lee
counted on his remaining inactive for a while to come.

Then suddenly there came the return to reality. In the
night of June 28, Harrison, Longstreet's favorite spy—
scout, he calls the man—appeared at the latter's headquar-

ters at Chambersburg. He brought important news. Hooker had been superseded in command of the Army of the Potomac by George Gordon Meade, and the army was already north of the Potomac River following fast on the Confederates. Lee, aroused from slumber to hear the news, did not immediately credit it. He seems to have been incredulous of the passage of the river by the Unionists; but the report was perfectly true and, after some reflection, it was accepted.

It was now necessary to concentrate without delay, as a collision might occur at any moment. Lee in his report expressly states that he did not wish to fight an offensive battle; so far Longstreet had influenced him. He feared, however, that Meade would cross South Mountain and intervene between him and Virginia. To prevent this and, at the same time, to remain in a situation to fight a defensive battle he took the proper course, but not with sufficient definiteness. He began to move on Cashtown, immediately east of South Mountain. There he would be in a position to turn either east or west as circumstances demanded, while he would fight with advantage if attacked. Matters seemed to be shaping toward the defensive tactics that Longstreet sought to combine with offensive strategy. One circumstance, however, defeated it: Lee did not determine to cling to South Mountain, his refuge, but was considering concentration at Gettysburg, to the east, which he did not suppose was in Union hands. But it was already in Union hands, and this mistaken supposition was destined to wreck the whole campaign. If Lee had known at this time of the presence of Union troops at Gettysburg he would have kept his army in hand at Cashtown.

CHAPTER XIII

GRAND TRAGEDY OF GETTYSBURG

IT WAS on June 29 that the Confederates learned that Union troops occupied Gettysburg. On that day Heth, sent toward the town on the quest for provisions and shoes, of which the Southerners stood in dire need, found the town occupied by the enemy. Whereupon he fell back without a fight on his corps at Cashtown. From this circumstance arose the legend that the battle was brought on by troops hunting shoes. Hill now made the blunder that ruined everything; he told Heth to return the next day to Gettysburg. Hill's orders from Lee had authorized him to move eastward, orders that Lee should never have given in ignorance of what might be at Gettysburg.[1] The commander had done a dangerous thing: he had permitted his most impulsive corps commander to go forward, though expressly cautioning him not to bring on a battle.

Hill, without conferring with Lee though aware that Unionists were at Gettysburg, left Cashtown in the morning of July 1 and moved eastward toward the former town. Probably he merely intended to explore, hoping to find only a small cavalry force at Gettysburg. If that were the case he would brush the enemy aside and occupy the town. He knew its importance as the junction of many roads, especially of roads to Washington and Baltimore, and desired

[1] Hill had been ordered to move on Harrisburg, but the order was suspended. He may have interpreted his second order as a renewal of the first. It seems to have been ambiguous.

to seize it. He acted on his own initiative instead of going
to Chambersburg and consulting Lee.

Coming within two miles of Gettysburg, Hill found a
large Union infantry force in position waiting to dispute the

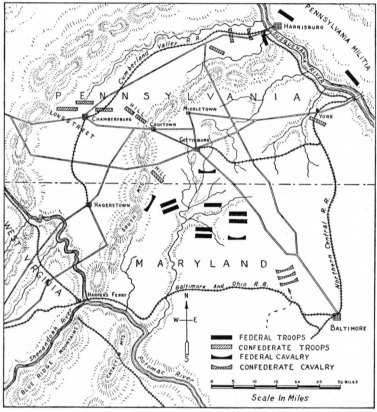

GETTYSBURG CAMPAIGN, TROOP POSITIONS, JUNE 29, 1863

way. This should certainly have induced him to haul off
until Lee came up. But it is difficult to make a reconnaissance
of infantry without being drawn into action, and now Hill,
probably without intending it, became involved. This was
the price the Confederates paid for the absence of cavalry.

In the early afternoon of a hot July day the opposing

blue and gray lines came into contact, and a bitter struggle followed. The Unionists, posted on the ridges west of Gettysburg, resisted with the utmost gallantry the advance of the Confederates, who were thrown back with heavy loss. It appeared that Hill, after becoming involved in the action he had been expressly warned to avoid, was about to be defeated.

Help was at hand, however. Ewell, obeying his orders to return from Carlisle to Cashtown or Gettysburg, had marched to the sound of the guns and was coming on the field. The brave Unionists were about to be caught between the fires of two converging forces. And right here is one of the problems of Gettysburg. It has been generally supposed that Lee took no part in the events of the first day's fight until the late afternoon, but Harry Heth states that at this phase of the battle Lee was near enough to the field to direct movements. Heth's account has been followed by Freeman in his admirable description of the battle. If it is true, Lee's responsibility for the outcome of the engagement is greatly augmented since it was in his power to break off the action if he had so desired. Up to that moment it had been nothing but a reconnaissance in force; from that time it became a battle. Probably Heth was mistaken.

At all events, whether Lee directed movements or not, Heth went forward instead of backward, while Ewell formed line of battle at right angles with the other Confederate corps. The Unionists were enclosed between the two Confederate lines and enfiladed. The right end of the Union line, caught as in a vise, was shattered. Before long the Unionists gave way and came streaming through the streets of Gettysburg with the Southerners in hot pursuit. The chase was so keen that five thousand Union soldiers were caught and sent to the rear; two corps were badly broken. Thus the accidental junction of two Confederate corps on the field of battle had resulted in the defeat of two Union corps with unusually heavy loss. Yet the Unionists were defeated, not routed, and with fine pluck they went no farther than they were driven, rallying on Cemetery Ridge just south of the town.

This was Ewell's opportunity to win fame. It was his part to go ahead, since his own corps had not suffered heavily while Hill's was partly disorganized by its fierce combat. A vigorous attack on the gallant but shaky troops holding the ridge would probably have resulted in their dislodgment and the securing of the position by the Confederates. Lee would have won the battle of Gettysburg. What that would have meant is difficult to say. A part, but only a part, of the Union army would have been defeated. Meade would have taken position on Pipe Creek, his original intention, and Lee would have had to attack him there if a complete victory was to be won. Would he have won or would he have lost? Nobody knows. The point is that the moment Lee left the shelter of South Mountain and moved east he was almost certainly committed to battle on the offensive, just the thing that both he and Longstreet desired to avoid.

Lee now made the cardinal error of his career: he gave Ewell orders to attack Cemetery Ridge or not according to his judgment. Lee should never have acted in this indecisive manner after being committed to battle. Since he was committed, he should have pushed the opportunity to the limit. Yes, it is easy to say so. But only two of his corps were up and one of them was in no condition to press the action. His best corps, Longstreet's, was behind. There was no telling how large a Union force was at hand. If Ewell went forward he might find the whole Union army. Lack of information of the enemy's movements, lack of knowledge of the terrain handicapped both Lee and Ewell. Everything was a leap in the dark.

Perhaps a little after four o'clock Lee came on the field. Several hours before, following on Hill's track from Cashtown, the commander had heard the roar of artillery, succeeded a little later by the ominous rattle of musketry. He had been greatly disturbed, because he expressly wished to avoid battle before he gained information of the enemy's position. But his own breadth of orders was responsible, for he should have kept his army close in hand at Cashtown until he had learned how the land lay. Instead of doing this, he had permitted Hill to move east and away from the mountain. And from this sad mistake everything else followed. Now he found himself engaged in a great battle on a field of which he knew virtually nothing. It was a terrible situation.

Longstreet was with Lee, though his corps was some distance in the rear. Up to this moment the former seems to have been in complacent mood, imagining that everything was going well, even in the absence of Stuart and information. But from this time his mood suddenly and radically changed.

From the summit of Seminary Ridge the two commanders anxiously raked with their field glasses the opposing Cemetery Ridge, on which the distant bluecoats preparing for attack appeared like bustling ants. Presently Longstreet, lowering his glasses, turned to Lee.

"If we could have chosen a point to meet our plans of operations," he said, "I do not think we could have found a better one than that upon which they are now concentrating. All we have to do is to throw our army around by their left, and we shall interpose between the Federal army and Washington. We can get a strong position and wait, and if they fail to attack us we shall have everything in condition to move back to-morrow night in the direction of Washington, selecting beforehand a good position into which we can place our troops to receive battle next day. Finding our object is Washington or that army, the Federals will be sure to attack us. When they attack, we shall beat them, as we proposed before we left Fredericksburg, and the probabilities are that the fruits of our success will be great." [2]

But here Lee broke away from the tutelage Longstreet fancied he had established.

"No," said Lee, positively. "If the enemy is there, we must attack him." [3]

Nonplussed by this sudden revolt, Longstreet argued his view, declaring that a move around Meade's left would give the Confederates the control of the roads to Washington and Baltimore and force Meade to attack them in their own chosen position.

"No," Lee returned, unshaken in his resolution. "They are there in position, and I am going to whip them or they are going to whip me."

The continuance of the battle of Gettysburg was then and there decided on.

Here is raised, of course, the question of the wisdom of Lee's decision and the practicability of Longstreet's alternative. Nothing is more fascinating than speculation in the field of might-have-beens, though few things are more profitless. Since Lee lost the battle and, with it, the war, one might argue that he should have taken some other course, no matter what, that something else could not have been more fatal than what was. And it may be fair to say that Lee should

---

[2] *B. & L.*, III, 339.

[3] Longstreet's statement of Lee's language varied in his later accounts. This is his first.

have done one of two things, neither of which he did: he should either have pressed the attack in the evening of the first day or he should not have attacked again. The odds were so great against Southern success after that first fateful evening that continuing the battle entailed too grave risks.

This does not mean, of course, that Longstreet's suggestion to pass around Meade's left wing and intervene between him and Washington was the solution of the difficulty. It possibly would have turned out worse than the course Lee took. Everything would have depended, in a sense, on the psychological factor. If Lee had essayed this course and succeeded in moving eastward of Meade, what would have followed?

Lee would have been in a most perilous position, north of an unfordable river with his communications completely cut. His food must have been obtained by foraging, a difficult operation in the presence of the enemy. All that Meade would have needed to do to ensure the destruction of the Southern host would have been to hold off from attacking it.

But could he have refrained from attack? Would the Union government and public opinion have permitted the Union commander to remain quiescent with the enemy in striking distance of Washington and lying across the railway arteries? That is a question no one can answer. For that reason no one can say that Longstreet was right; all that one can say is that Lee was wrong. That is the conclusion toward which the facts drive the impartial student despite the emphatic denials of Lee's admirers, who hold others and not himself responsible for the loss of Gettysburg.

Longstreet states that his fateful conversation with Lee on Seminary Ridge took place about 5:00 P. M. of July 1. It was before this that Lee had sent word to Ewell that he might or might not attack as he saw fit. Probably Lee hoped Ewell would consider the assault practicable and order it, but this unfortunate message (which was not a command, in a crisis that demanded definite orders) left Ewell bewildered and helpless. Instinctively he felt that the commander-in-chief should not place on his shoulders the burden of deciding whether or not the battle should continue, and he was right. Lee acted unwisely.

While the Confederates halted in the flush of success and their ardor cooled as they watched the preparations being made for their reception, the Unionists recovered from their defeat and began to arrange their position on the ridge they had decided to hold. Lee, not satisfied with the option he had given Ewell and anxious to learn something of the enemy's position for himself, sent his staff officer, Long, to examine Cemetery Ridge and report on the chances of taking it. Long, after such a study as he could make in the hurry and confusion of the moment, returned to Lee with the discouraging news that the Union position was strong and defended by a stone wall. In fact, the stone wall seems to have affected Long's imagination unduly. Under the circumstances, with Ewell showing reluctance to advance and with a staff officer reporting adversely on its practicability, Lee decided to hold off until next morning. It was one of the most fatal decisions he ever made, if not the most fatal. An hour or more of daylight remained, followed by a moonlit night, and the Confederates were still inspired by victory, the Unionists still somewhat depressed by defeat.

The fact is seldom noted by historians that the decision not to continue the battle in the late afternoon of July 1 was made by Lee on Long's report and not by Ewell. Nevertheless, Ewell has borne the blame for not making a decision that was properly the commander's; a subordinate should not be tasked with the responsibility of deciding for or against action in the chief's immediate presence. At all events, Lee resolved to do nothing more that day, although he felt irrevocably committed to battle.

In the early evening Lee, seeking to learn something of the ground and preparing plans for the next day, held a conference with Hill, Ewell, and Early, from which Longstreet was absent. All three subordinates showed extreme reluctance to attack, a fact that might have warned Lee but did not. They reported the Union position in their immediate front as being most formidable but declared that it was weaker toward the right, where Longstreet was. They simply shifted the responsibility to the absent Longstreet, who could not speak for himself. Lee, listening to them and finding them so half-hearted, decided to let Longstreet make the assault; doubtless, he had more confidence in the latter than in the two new corps commanders. Still he grumblingly commented on Longstreet's slowness. Longstreet seems to have been depressed. At supper that night he spoke of the enemy's position as being "very formidable."

Now comes the most controverted point on Gettysburg. Longstreet's critics maintain that Lee gave him definite orders in the night of July 1 to attack early in the morning of July 2 and that he deliberately disobeyed these orders, failing to move until the afternoon. Therefore Longstreet is blamed for the adverse outcome of the battle. This is the almost universal Southern belief.

The facts are otherwise. Longstreet was able to show, in 1875, by letters received from Lee's staff officers, that no such orders were ever issued to him; there can be no question that he was technically right. It appears, however, that Lee, following his rather unfortunate method with subordinates—which had resulted badly that very day in Ewell's case—*suggested* to Longstreet that he attack as early as possible the following morning. Lee had more than Southern politeness and disliked to give the brusque orders soldiers usually receive and almost always prefer. So he indicated to Longstreet what he wanted done and let it go at that.

Longstreet, receiving no positive orders and hoping to avoid the battle he so greatly dreaded, made no dispositions in the night of July 1; he was still counting on persuading Lee to abandon the offensive. He says that the stars were still shining when, on the morning of July 2, he sought Lee at his headquarters and opened the debate again. Again he urged the movement toward Meade's left but he found Lee impatient and disinclined to listen, for the commander had decided to fight and wanted no more councils of war. Lee, indeed, seems to have been somewhat disconcerted at Longstreet's reluctance. He rode off to the left to consult Ewell about the possibility of the latter's attacking Meade's right. Ewell and Early were thoroughly unsatisfactory; they did not want to attack and yet they held out hopes of doing something. By this time Lee had learned that his line was too greatly extended and wished Ewell to move toward the right, but for some reason, the latter did not wish to draw in. So the line remained too long, one of the causes of defeat. Lee then, perhaps about 11:00 A. M., returned to Longstreet and, without further ado, directed him to make the attack.

Longstreet thus found himself committed to the offensive action he so intensely disliked, and under the most unfavorable circumstances. A soldier whose main idea was never to fight except at advantage, he was now called on to assault a position than which none could be stronger. Dismayed, resentful that his supposed influence with Lee did not exist, he procrastinated, he killed time, he did nothing for a while. His lack of confidence in Lee, abated while he supposed Lee was being led by him, returned in full force.

As for Lee, he had temporarily lost his splendid poise. All his strategic gifts had been wasted by the untoward progress of the campaign. Hoping to accomplish much by maneuver, he had run into the enemy in the blindest fashion and was now committed to battle under such circumstances as reduced the chances in his favor to less than the chances for the Union. In all his accounts Longstreet speaks of Lee's excitement, and his story is confirmed by Scheibert, a Prussian officer with the Confederate army. The latter says that Lee's obvious nervousness communicated itself to the other officers and affected them unfavorably. Thus the men around Lee, who had to conduct the battle, were anxious and lacking in confidence.

Lee was exasperated by the absence of his cavalry and his consequent ignorance of the enemy's position and numbers. Appreciating much more fully than the others the gravity of the crisis and the need of immediate action, he found his subordinates diffident, unready, reluctant to act. Yet it should be remembered that the Confederates had not been exactly surprised by the Union force at Gettysburg. Hill had known the day before that bluecoats were there and, in that knowledge, had deliberately advanced and let himself be drawn into battle. In so doing he had played into Meade's hands. It was unbelievable luck for the new Union commander that instead of having to seek Lee in a formidable position, he was being sought by Lee in about as good a defensive position as any commander could desire. For Meade had advanced to the vicinity of Gettysburg in the belief (and hope) that Lee would strike at Washington. Lee, compelled by circumstances, had done just what Meade desired. The former was no longer, as in the past, forcing the Union strategy; he was now being forced.

Lee seems to have felt that he had no choice but to fight. He and his staff were in serious error in one respect, and that error has come down in history. They thought that Meade was surprised and only partially concentrated when, as a matter of fact, his army was more completely in hand than Lee's. Consequently, the current Southern impression that if Longstreet had advanced early in the day he would have found a much smaller force to oppose him than later is only partly true. The Union army was in position before all of the Southern troops were up.

Lee was mistaken in another particular. In his report he says that he was constrained to fight because he found himself in the immediate presence of the enemy, from which he could not withdraw his wagon trains across the mountain without difficulty. As a matter of fact, most of his wagons were west of the mountain and he would have experienced little trouble in retiring if he had so chosen.

The trouble was that withdrawal after the action of July 1 would have been taken as an admission of defeat and would have relieved the North of its panic. Lee felt that victory was indispensable, with Vicksburg at the last gasp and to be rescued only by a great success in Pennsylvania. It is true that Vicksburg could not have been saved by anything that might happen in Pennsylvania but Lee did not know that. He had to take into consideration the situation in Mississippi as well as in the East.

Longstreet, most reluctant to fight and greatly apprehensive of the result, did not have definite plans to offer in substitute. His suggestion of a move around Meade was vague; sometimes he speaks of passing around the Union left, then again around the right. It seems evident, how-

ever, that he really meant to move eastward around the
Union left and in the general direction of Washington. Lee
resolutely rejected the idea; in fact, he never seriously considered it.

The Union position, as the Confederate officers viewed it
at midday of July 2, was very strong, so strong indeed that
one feels a certain sympathy with Longstreet's reluctance.
Certainly something was amiss with the generalship that
had brought the army all the way from Virginia only to
dash it against steep heights held by thousands of infantry
and rows upon rows of frowning guns. That something was
the compliance with which both Lee and Longstreet had
allowed the cavalry to slip away from them on the very eve
of a most perilous enterprise.

As a matter of fact at midday of July 2 it may have been
Lee's best course to fall back to Cashtown and let Meade
follow him, for Meade would have had to follow. But Lee,
in his unusual state of excitement, appears to have felt that
there was no other possible course but battle; he had high
hopes of success based on the result of the first day's encounter. His strategical mistake had been made in leaving
South Mountain; he did not think of returning to its shelter
and playing the game of hide-and-seek he knew so well how
to play. So he decided on a frontal assault on the Union
position and sought to make the arrangements despite the
pessimism of all three of his corps commanders.

The Union position at Gettysburg may be likened to a
fishhook enclosed within a semi-circle by the Confederate
position. The Northerners held a continuous ridge marked by
two protuberances on the left, Little Round Top and Round
Top. It was short and compact, and it afforded every facility
for moving troops from one point to another. The Southern
position, on the other hand, stretched out for miles over

rough and broken ground. To shift troops from flank to flank would take hours; coöperation among the three corps was difficult. That was one reason the Confederates failed; their line was too greatly extended.

The setting was picturesque that hot July day of 1863, the crisis of the war. Gettysburg, a sleepy little market town with a divinity school perched on Seminary Ridge, stands in a lovely limestone country of fertile farms tilled by industrious husbandmen of German ancestry. It is a land of bumper crops and of inspiring piedmont scenery. Few American battlefields are more interesting. The extreme right of the Union position, the point of the fishhook, was the rough eminence known as Culp's Hill. Thence the high ground runs westward to Cemetery Hill (the bend of the hook), the town's burying ground, which at one angle was even then not far from the town itself. The ridge continues, growing steeper toward the left end of the Union position, which was marked by the height of Little Round Top, precipitous and covered with granite boulders, and beyond by Round Top, a small mountain. A strong position, probably most vulnerable at Cemetery Hill, directly in front of the town.

Lee had decided to attack the Union left, probably because Longstreet was there and his corps was fresh for the fray, having been in the rear the previous day. Possibly he resented Hill's precipitance, which had committed him to battle under unfavorable circumstances. At all events the burden of the attack was put on the unwilling, almost rebellious Longstreet. Yet as early as 7:00 A. M. Longstreet was directing McLaws, a point not generally known.

Soon after midday of July 2, under a burning sun unmitigated by clouds, Longstreet's troops moved toward the Union left, the point of attack. It is significant that they were guided to position by officers of Lee's staff, not Long-

street's. Lee was, in fact, taking the movement to a certain
extent under his own supervision, though only partially.
Longstreet was in immediate command.

The most authoritative account of the movement to the
Union left wing is that of Major General Lafayette Mc-

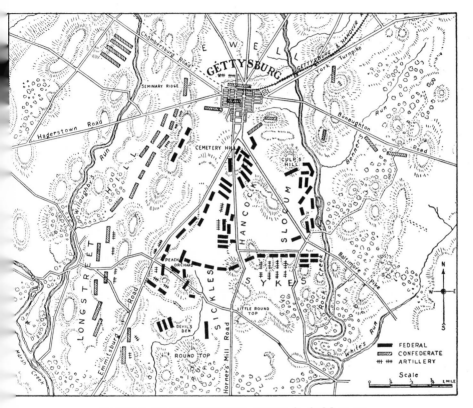

BATTLE OF GETTYSBURG, JULY 2, 3:00 P. M.

Laws, who wrote in 1879 when the events were still fairly
fresh in his memory. Soon after his arrival at Gettysburg
on the morning of July 2, Lee sent for him and showed him
on the map the position for his command in the impending
battle. Lee made a mark on the map perpendicular to the
Emmitsburg road, asking McLaws if he could reach the

point. The latter requested permission to reconnoiter. Lee answered that a staff officer, Johnston, was about to make the reconnaissance, on which McLaws declared that he would go with him.

At this moment Longstreet, who was pacing up and down near by, intervened. "No, sir, I do not wish you to leave your division," he said to McLaws. "I wish your division placed so," indicating a line on the map perpendicular to that made by Lee.

"No, General, I wish it just the opposite," Lee objected.

McLaws repeated his request to go with the reconnoitering party, but Longstreet again forbade it and Lee said nothing. "Longstreet," adds McLaws, "appeared as if he was irritated and annoyed, but the cause I did not ask."

McLaws then returned to his command and waited for several hours, watching the Unionists come into position on the opposite heights. About one o'clock his division was put in motion, with the staff officer, Johnston, guiding it. The leaders wished to conceal the movement from Union eyes, but as the signal station on Round Top commanded the whole country around this was difficult to do. Much time was lost in attempting it, until Longstreet finally abandoned the futile effort and doubled the marching columns in order to make haste.

The reconnaissance had been so hastily and imperfectly made that both Lee and Longstreet were ignorant of the real conditions. As the column neared its destination, Longstreet asked McLaws, "How are you going in?" to which the latter replied that that depended on what he found in front. "There is nothing in your front," Longstreet returned. "You will be entirely on the flank of the enemy."

But when McLaws came to the position he was to take he found himself in the immediate presence of the enemy instead of on the flank. Here seems to be Lee's mistake, that he expected Longstreet to reach a point where he would be beyond the Union left wing and then to move along the Emmitsburg road to attack it. However, the Union line extended all the way to Round Top, where it rested on the slope.[4]

E. M. Law, commanding one of the brigades of Hood's division, which was on McLaws's right, then made the discovery that Round Top was only partly occupied by the enemy and that immediately in its rear were the medical and ordnance trains of the Union army.[5] Here was offered a chance to slip around the Union flank and get in the rear. Law told Hood and Hood sent a message to Longstreet requesting permission to make the movement. Longstreet refused, declaring that Lee had ordered an attack to be made along the Emmitsburg road and that orders must be obeyed. Hood repeated his request, which was again denied. The point is that the attack could not be made as Lee had directed because the conditions were not what he supposed them to be. The attack by the Emmitsburg road, instead of being the flank operation he expected it to be, could be nothing but a frontal assault on an enormously strong position held by a far larger number of the foe. It would seem that Longstreet here lost an opportunity to do somewhat the same thing he desired to do, to move around the Union left, though in his plan he did not contemplate any attack but only a wide turning operation. General Alexander, the artillerist, thinks that Hood's proposed movement would not have succeeded, since the Confederate line was already much too extended, but it could not have been worse than a frontal attack on such a height as Little Round Top. It seems

[4] *Southern Historical Society Papers*, VII, 68-90.
[5] *B. & L.*, III, 318-30.

certain that Lee would never have made the attack if he had been on the spot, but he was not there and his orders were carried out while he remained in ignorance of the circumstances. At Gettysburg he was never at the right place.

The Confederates moved into the low ground immediately in front of Little Round Top, known as the Wheat Field and the Peach Orchard. Even this terrain was broken by rock formations such as the Devil's Den. Sickles, in command of the forces on the extreme Union left, thrust forward his men to meet the Confederate advance, occupying the Wheat Field. Hood and McLaws, deploying in line of battle, ran into the waiting line of bluecoats, greatly superior to the Confederates in number.

The action that followed was one of the severest fights that ever took place on the American continent, if it was not the severest. Seasoned troops animated by the highest feelings of duty and patriotism faced each other. Firing and loading and firing and loading with such rapidity that the muskets grew almost too hot to hold, the two swaying lines, drawn close together, poured a terrible fire into each other's faces. The carnage was awful. The Confederates included Hood's famous Texas brigade and other commands only just less noted, experts with weapons and as tough and hardy as men can be. At length their individual superiority began to tell, though the Unionists fought with magnificent valor. The Southerners were not to be denied. The bluecoats began to go back, slowly at first and then more rapidly. The victorious Confederates drew near the steep height of Little Round Top. They had suffered fearfully in that awful infantry duel; the ground was strewn with their dead and wounded. But two corps of the Union army had been fought out and success would have crowned the blood-red flags of the Southerners if it had not been for the vast strength of the Union position and the promptness with which the Union leaders hurried troops from the center and right to the gravely threatened left.

That was the moment that should have been looked for; then it was that Ewell and Hill should have advanced resistlessly against the Union center and right and, perhaps, won the battle. But at that moment nothing was going on except on the Union left.

The Confederates continued to advance. Despite the terrible fire of the infantry holding Little Round Top and the enfilading Union guns, which were volcanoes belching shell at the Confederates, the dauntless men from the Lower South began to climb the steep sides of Little Round Top, dislodging squads of Union infantry from the cover of the boulders as they did so. Hood's incomparable Texans reached the crest of the height, but their ranks were thin now and the men were worn out by heat and exertion. On the summit of Little Round Top they found dense lines of Union infantry awaiting them. They were unable to do more, heroes though they were. The Confederates came to a stop under the ridge as the thickening darkness of the summer night told them that the battle was over for the day. Longstreet had been at the front all the time, even leading a charge on a battery.

It is possible that the day was saved for the Union by Longstreet's delay in moving and by the alertness of Warren in occupying Round Top when its importance was at last realized. If the Confederates had taken it, as Hood suggested, they might have won the battle by enfilading the Union line from its lofty height. Its occupancy by the Confederates, however, would, as has been pointed out, have extended their already long and thin line.

It was Lee's plan for the whole army to participate in the

battle. In conformity with it, Ewell on the left advanced troops against Culp's Hill, though not until very late in the afternoon. This force carried the Union trenches at the foot of the hill but did not storm the hill itself. If the movement had been made when Longstreet was launching his attack it might have served to confuse the Union defense. Indeed, Lee's best chance to win the battle seems to have been to take Culp's Hill or Cemetery Hill while Longstreet was making his powerful assault on the Union left.

Lee, however, could not be everywhere, and he appears not to have exerted much influence on the operations of the day. At the very close of the battle, Early, of Ewell's corps, made an attempt on Cemetery Hill and almost took it, but he was not supported by Rodes, who was to have joined in the attack, and was driven back. The situation as night fell on the butchery of a day in which twenty thousand men had fallen was that the Confederates had struck a mighty blow at the Union left and a slight blow at the Union right but had failed at any point to dislodge the Unionists. The Union line was shaken but not broken.

It must have been early in the night of July 2 that the full horror of the situation burst on Lee. In the two days' fighting he had lost fourteen thousand of his sixty thousand infantry and his army was consequently much weakened. The Union army had lost even more heavily, but its eighteen thousand casualties and prisoners were deducted from ninety thousand infantry. The odds were now terribly against the South.

Beyond doubt it was a night of agony for Lee, who had the vision to understand, as the other officers did not, the full significance of his failure. Everything had been risked on the invasion of Pennsylvania, which was a gamble made to relieve Vicksburg and win the war by a single stroke. Instead of a victory that would endanger Washington and that might bring the North to terms, all had gone wrong and defeat stared him in the face. Lee had had failures before, as at Malvern Hill in 1862, but he had never definitely lost a battle. And now he was about to lose the greatest battle of all.

It is no wonder that he was no longer able calmly to estimate the chances of failure and success, that he refused to concede defeat. He would not acknowledge that he was beaten; he determined to try one more cast of the dice. Perhaps they would decide in his favor after all. He had failed at the Union left and right, at Little Round Top and Culp's Hill. It remained to try the center, which was the best point of attack if properly approached through the town itself. But so ill-informed were the Confederate officers that they prepared to assault Cemetery Ridge, just beyond Cemetery Hill, across fields enfiladed by whole batteries of artillery. Under the conditions, it was in the nature of a forlorn hope. It was ominous that the Confederates could not even hold the works at the foot of Culp's Hill but were driven out in the early morning of July 3. With all of his lieutenants more hesitant and uncertain than ever, Lee's chances of success were slim indeed.

The point selected for launching the assault of July 3 was across nearly a mile of open fields interspersed by stone fences. It seems hardly possible that the attack could have succeeded even if conducted by a larger force than that employed, but Lee was justified by the desperate nature of the case in making one last bid for victory.

The attack centered about the single remaining fresh unit of the army, Pickett's division of Longstreet's corps, just up. Probably because this command belonged to Longstreet, the attack was entrusted to him. Indeed, it is likely that Lee still felt greater confidence in Longstreet than in Ewell and Hill, who had done so little the day before.

Longstreet, however, on the morning of July 3 was even more unconvinced than he had been on July 2. On meeting Lee, he began all over again his plea for the movement around Meade's left, though such an operation was now absurd in view of the losses the army had sustained and the small amount of ammunition left. Again Lee paid no attention to the suggestions of his disgruntled lieutenant.

"No, I am going to take them where they are, on Cemetery Hill," Lee said. "I want you to take Pickett's division and make the attack. I will reënforce you by two divisions of the Third Corps [Hill's]."

"That will give me fifteen thousand men," Longstreet replied. "I have been a soldier, I may say, from the ranks up to the position I now hold. I have been in pretty much all kinds of skirmishes from those of two or three soldiers to those of an army corps, and I think I can safely say there never was a body of fifteen thousand men who could make that attack successfully."

Longstreet was right. The force given him was not sufficient to storm a hill held by forty thousand Union troops and protected by innumerable guns so set as to enfilade the approach from every angle. The fact is recognized, but Longstreet has been blamed for not using Hood's and McLaws's divisions as well. His answer was that he could not withdraw them from the portion of the line they held without opening the army to a counterattack and, besides, that they had suffered so severely the day before that their efficiency was impaired. As both divisions had been terribly cut up on July 2, the plea seems sound. Under the circumstances success was not possible, and for that reason Pickett's charge was a tragic blunder, famous as it is as the most heroic episode in American military annals. Yet if the charge had been made at dawn and through the town, it might possibly have succeeded. Meade's army was shattered by desperate fighting, and a resolute assault carrying some element of surprise might have gained the position.

Longstreet's reluctance, so pronounced the day before, had now reached the point almost of paralysis. It was planned that the attack should be preceded by a cannonade, which the Confederate leaders hoped (though for what reason is not apparent) would silence the hostile artillery on the opposing heights and enable Pickett to cross the intervening space without being torn to pieces by canister and shell. As the Union artillery was better posted, better handled, and better supplied with ammunition, this hope was surely futile. Indeed the Confederates, possibly from lack of information, had not placed their batteries to the best advantage, neglecting opportunities to gain an enfilading fire on the Union line. Among the failures of Gettysburg was Pendleton, Lee's artillery chief, who began the accusation of Longstreet's losing the battle. He was practically superseded on the battlefield, for Longstreet entrusted the placing of the guns for the grand bombardment to young Alexander, an officer in whom he had much confidence. This incident may have had something to do with Pendleton's dislike for Longstreet.

Longstreet did not believe it possible for the assault to succeed; he had little faith in the chance of suppressing the superior Union artillery. In fact, he was so reluctant to sacrifice his men in what he felt was the most desperate of chances that he actually sought to pass on to a subordinate the responsibility. Alexander was told to give Pickett the signal to advance when the fire of the Union artillery should have so lessened that the column could move forward.

Alexander, alarmed, answered that it was for Longstreet to decide whether or not there was any alternative to attack, but that he would send word when the Union fire slackened.

The cannonade was the most spectacular artillery combat that ever took place in America. For an hour the rival batteries on the opposing heights spouted flame at each other while the ground trembled under the concussion. At length the Union fire lessened. The guns were not silenced but the leaders decided to save their ammunition for the infantry assault they knew was about to come. When the cannonade dribbled off to occasional shots, Alexander sent word to Pickett to advance if he intended to do so, since the ammunition was running so low that he could not much longer support an attack. Pickett, imperturbable, turned to Longstreet, who was so overcome by emotion that he could not speak. He merely nodded. At the signal the waiting Confederate line advanced from its cover and entered on its hopeless endeavor.

Pickett's division, the spearhead of the assault, was composed of Virginia troops, tried veterans of many fields. They were supported by North Carolina troops (Trimble's division) who have not generally received the credit due them for their equal gallantry. Perhaps seven thousand men in all made the full charge; some thousands more, intended to accompany them, drifted off in the confusion of the scene. There was no hope that this small force could dislodge the far larger body of seasoned Union veterans on the hill, but the Southerners advanced with calm mien and admirable discipline to their doom, one of the finest sacrifices to duty and patriotism in all history.

They had nearly a mile to go and there was not the least cover. Before they had advanced far the Union guns opened on them from every side. Closing the gaps in their line like the true men they were, they moved stolidly on until they neared the stone wall at the foot of Cemetery Ridge, which blazed from end to end as the Union infantry opened fire. Still the Southerners pressed on.

" 'Give them the cold steel, boys!' cried Armistead, one of the brigadiers, putting his hat on his sword as a guide. The thin gray line swept over the wall and seemed, for the moment, to have carried the position."

Longstreet, however, sitting on a fence intently viewing the scene, declared that the charge was a failure. It so fell out under the eyes of the onlookers. Two of Pickett's brigadiers were killed; the third was terribly wounded. When the Confederates gained the wall, a mass of Union infantry poured down the hillside and engulfed them precisely as a wave devours a sand hill. Pickett's division disappeared as a body. Groups of survivors might be seen hurrying back across the fields under the fire that swept down from the heights in terrific volume. The assault had failed; the battle was lost; the South was ruined.

Fremantle, an English officer with the Confederate army, has given us a stirring account of the scene. He reached Longstreet's side just as Pickett's charge failed. "I wouldn't have missed this for anything," he said, thinking that the Confederates had gained a success. Longstreet, atop of the fence appearing perfectly unperturbed, laughed and said, "The devil you wouldn't! I would like to have missed it very much. We've attacked and been repulsed. Look there!"

Fremantle, looking, saw that the plain was covered with small parties of retreating Southerners returning under a heavy artillery fire. Longstreet told him that Pickett had carried the enemy's position and had remained there for twenty minutes but had been forced to retire when Heth and Pettigrew on his left fell back. "No person," he says, "could have been more calm or self-possessed than General Longstreet under these trying circumstances, aggravated as they now were by the movements of the enemy, who began to show a strong disposition to advance. I could now thoroughly appreciate the term bulldog, which I had heard applied to him by the soldiers. Difficulties seem to make no other impression upon him than to make him a little more savage."

Longstreet, fully aroused by the magnitude of the disaster, made vigorous efforts to meet the counterattack that was to be expected. To Pettigrew, who declared he was unable to bring his men up again, Longstreet said sarcastically, "Very well. Never mind, then, General. Just let them remain where they are. The enemy's going to advance, and it will spare you the trouble."

Longstreet asked for a drink, which he doubtless needed. Fremantle gave him rum out of a silver flask, which he desired Longstreet to accept as a remembrance. The general smiled and received the flask. Presently he went off. Lee meanwhile had come up and was making telling appeals to the soldiers to stand firm for the anticipated attack.

The Unionists did not take advantage of the Confederate discomfiture to make a charge in turn. Meade has been censured for not pushing his success, but all accounts attest the rapidity with which the Confederates recovered from their repulse. The Union army was itself almost fought out. If it had advanced across the open plain, under the fire of the Confederate batteries, victory might have been followed by a severe repulse. Probably Meade was wise in not attempting to do anything more than hold his own.

All day of July 4, the two armies faced each other without fighting. In the morning Fremantle met Longstreet, who seemed to be in good spirits in spite of the reverse the army had suffered. A flag of truce had just come over from the enemy with the message that "General Longstreet was wounded and a prisoner, but would be taken care of." Longstreet, much amused, sent back an appropriate answer. Fremantle here comments, "The iron endurance of General Longstreet is most extraordinary. He seems to require neither food nor sleep." [6]

In the afternoon Fremantle visited Longstreet in his camp, which had been moved back some distance. The latter gave the Englishman his views of the battle, saying that the attack of the day before should have been made with thirty thousand men instead of fifteen thousand. That night the inevitable retreat began. Though much harassed by Union cavalry and threatened by infantry attacks, Lee succeeded in falling back into Virginia without further material losses.

Since Gettysburg has been generally considered the most decisive battle of the war, a vast literature has grown up about it, particularly on the Southern side. A reason for this is that it stands as the challenge to Lee's claim to be considered one of the world's great commanders. Southerners, venerating the memory of the grandest Southerner, have explained Lee's failure by the failure of his subordinates. His plans were sound, they say, but were neutralized by poor execution. Somebody blundered, thereby bringing Lee's finewrought schemes to naught.

The scapegoat, by general consent, is James Longstreet, to whose hands was committed the battle of July 2 and July 3. His slowness, his reluctance to carry out his orders, are blamed for the defeat that cost the South its chance of winning the war.

It is interesting to note that contemporary accounts do not

[6] Arthur James Lyon Fremantle, *Three Months in the Southern States, April-June, 1863* (Mobile, Goetzel, 1864), pp. 257-70.

put any particular blame on Longstreet; the general opinion of the Confederate army was that it had been called on to carry a position that was too strong for it. And it is possible that Longstreet would not have acquired his position of pre-eminent demerit but for his career as a Radical Republican in the period following the war; that supplied a powerful motive for the condemnation of him as the blunderer who lost the great battle.

The controversy began about 1873 and enlisted Pendleton, the artillery commander; Early, a division commander at Gettysburg; John B. Gordon, a brigadier there; A. L. Long of Lee's staff; Colonel William Allan, and many others. They accused Longstreet of disobeying his orders of July 1 to advance in the early morning of July 2, to which disobedience they attribute the defeat.

Longstreet answered his critics effectively by showing that he received no orders in the night of July 1. Moreover, he demonstrated that the idea entertained by the Confederate staff that the Union army was not concentrated in the morning of July 2 was largely erroneous. The whole Union army was on the battlefield or near it.

It is on the premise that Longstreet must have succeeded if he had advanced at an early hour of July 2 that Lee's supporters base the argument of his responsibility for the loss of the battle. Probably the chance of success would have been greater if the movement had been made at an earlier time. Yet there can be no certainty that the Confederates would have carried a strong position held by a strong infantry force and a powerful artillery at any hour. They might have carried the position, say in the forenoon, but then again they might not have done so. Nobody knows. It was a great risk to attack such a position held by such a force as the Army of the Potomac, and the real question as to the blame for the defeat at Gettysburg must rest on the necessity or non-necessity of making that attack. And that is a difficult point to decide.

The evidence is very conflicting, but much may be said for the view that the Confederates lost little by making the assault in the late afternoon instead of at an earlier hour. McLaws, who went through it all, declared that it would have been better if the Confederates had waited until more troops came up. According to him, the chief trouble was that the Confederates made practically no reconnaissance of the left side of the Union position. It was intended that Longstreet should turn the left flank, attacking it along the line of the Emmitsburg road. But, according to McLaws, the staff officers guiding the Confederates led them out into the fields in front of Little Round Top and directly facing masses of Union infantry drawn up in line. He declares that the only possible chance of success lay in moving around Round Top, as Hood suggested, and thinks that the attack would never have been made if Lee had realized the situation. It is evident that Lee, after giving Longstreet his orders, exerted no influence on events and, indeed, seems not to have been aware of what was going on. He certainly was not himself at Gettysburg.

The battle witnessed a conflict of wills between Lee and Longstreet from the evening of July 1 to the late afternoon of July 3. For some time Longstreet's overmastering force of character had deeply impressed itself on Lee. Longstreet's resistance to Lee's wishes had caused the Second Manassas to tremble in the balance. His willfulness had partly wrecked the Maryland campaign and brought Lee to battle in the dangerous position at Antietam Creek. His refusal to consider Lee's urgings had forced Lee and Jackson to fight against terrible odds at Chancellorsville. Yet these eccentricities of conduct had not lost Lee's confidence; on the contrary, Lee had actually let him dictate the methods by which the Pennsylvania campaign was to be conducted.

Then, suddenly, in the evening of July 1, Lee had revolted against his behind-the-throneship. Lee's will had asserted itself and he rejected Longstreet's counsel to maneuver, deciding on instant battle. According to Longstreet, his combativeness ran away with him, he was overwhelmed with the blood lust. That this is untrue every circumstance of Lee's character attests. But we can well believe that Lee, thrust unawares into a most perilous position, lost his calmness of mind and failed to exercise those eminent qualities of generalship he customarily exhibited. Determined to fight, he did not know where to make his attack and then made it without due examination of the ground and so in ignorance of the circumstances. No doubt his confusion of mind was increased by Longstreet's opposition and subsequent reluctance, but it would seem that the latter's cantankerousness was actually less harmful than on other occasions. One is impelled to believe that Lee would probably have failed to carry the left of the Union position at Gettysburg, no matter at what time the attack had been made or by whom. Those who argue otherwise forget that the Army of the Potomac was a very valiant body of men occupying a very strong position.

In certain ways the most interesting question raised about Longstreet in connection with Gettysburg concerns Pickett's charge on the last day. There are indications that Lee in after years was inclined to blame Longstreet for permitting the charge, which means, if true, that Longstreet was granted a certain discretion in the matter. Were his orders so binding that he was forced to make the charge after discovering that the Confederate artillery could not silence the

Union guns? Or was he so incensed by Lee's rejection of his advice that he went ahead with the charge, although he had an option to call it off if apparently hopeless?

Nobody knows. The probability is that Lee left Longstreet no discretion, and yet there is something in the latter's accounts of the battle to lead one to suspect that his conscience was not altogether clear as to Pickett's charge, though clear enough about the fighting on July 2. But his story of what happened, growing as it did into an elaborate *apologia* under the savage attacks of his enemies, leaves one in the dark as to what he really thought.

Curiously enough, Hill and Ewell have not been blamed greatly for their delinquencies at Gettysburg, though there has been some censure of the latter for his failure to push his success on July 1. Of all the three corps commanders Hill was probably the most blameworthy. It was his precipitancy and incaution that committed the Confederates to battle under such disadvantageous circumstances. He should have held off from advancing on Gettysburg until Lee came up. After bringing on the battle he did almost nothing to win it on the two subsequent days, though it is only fair to say that his inaction on July 3 was fortunate inasmuch as it prevented the casualties from being larger than they were and insured one comparatively fresh corps at a moment of great crisis. If both Longstreet and Hill had been wrecked, Lee's position on July 3 would have been desperate indeed.

Lastly comes the question of Lee's blame, the blame he so magnanimously accepted—Longstreet says he took the blame because he deserved it. This is a harsh, ungenerous way of putting what is partly true. Lee expected too much from reluctant subordinates and he made battle on the most sketchy and inaccurate information. He expected three rather mediocre corps commanders to show the energy and genius of the lost and lamented Jackson. Never afterward did he call on corps generals for movements demanding marked initiative. After Gettysburg, Lee was both strategist and tactician.

It was in the field of strategy that he failed in Pennsylvania after opening moves of genius. Permitting Stuart to ride off from the army on one of his gorgeous raids around the Unionists was worse than an indiscretion; it was a blunder. Lee, of course, did not expect Stuart to lose himself but he should not have taken chances in such a desperate adventure as the invasion of the North. From this grave error the great misfortune followed.

In sending Ewell on to Carlisle and Harrisburg, east of South Mountain, Lee took a terrible chance, for there was a grave risk that the Unionists might intervene between the wings of his army. No general should have his troops wandering about the country when ignorant of the enemy's position. Utterly in the dark as he was as to the movements of the Army of the Potomac, Lee should have had his army close in hand and on the *western* side of South Mountain. Longstreet was quite right in insisting on a defensive battle. If Lee had held the passes of South Mountain and levied supplies to the west of it, Meade might have been forced to attack him, and then Lee would have enjoyed the advantage that was his opponent's at Gettysburg.

It was an error for Lee to consider concentrating at Gettysburg at all; he should have clung to Cashtown, his proper strategic position. By allowing his generals the option of moving to Gettysburg, Lee gave Hill the opportunity of bringing on the battle prematurely and making it offensive instead of defensive. All the advantages of Lee's superior generalship were cast away when the Confederates were called on to assault a formidable position held by a larger force. Strategic victory lay with Meade the moment that the Confederates became involved at Gettysburg; it was not difficult to add tactical victory as well. After all, the failure of the Pennsylvania campaign was the failure of the Confederate high command. Lee blundered into battle at Gettysburg and then showed no genius in the manner in which he conducted it, making no feints and relying on frontal attacks on a formidable position. All commanders, even Napoleon, have fallen into mediocrity at times; it was Lee's ill fate to do so at the very moment of crisis, the crucial struggle. He was great before Gettysburg and greater afterward; at Gettysburg he was not the captain he showed himself on other fields.

All the Confederate leaders, with the staff, failed in the Pennsylvania campaign: Lee, Stuart, Longstreet, Ewell, Hill. The one who did not fail was the Confederate soldier. Rarely in the history of the world have men fought with greater bravery and devotion than was shown by the Southerners at Gettysburg, which, in consequence, is an even greater monument to them than to the conquerors. After all, the chief glory of Gettysburg is Pickett's.

CHAPTER XIV

WESTWARD HO! TO CHICKAMAUGA

WHEN the Confederate leaders took stock of the situation in August, 1863, its full gravity burst on them. The failure of the Gettysburg campaign, for which great exertions had been made, was a paralyzing blow, even though the newspapers concealed with words the magnitude of the defeat. Moreover, in the West, the Confederacy had suffered a catastrophe no less cataclysmic than Gettysburg in the fall of Vicksburg, with nearly thirty thousand men, and the severance of the Southern republic by the Mississippi River, now in the control of the Union for its whole length.

Lee, feeling keenly his frustration, offered his resignation, which was declined by Davis in a letter of noble confidence. But sympathetic words could not conceal the fact of his failure and the unwillingness of the authorities for him to try his fortune in another invasion of the North. Indeed, another Pennsylvania offensive movement was out of the question with the whole of Tennessee slipping from the grasp of the South. Something had to be done there, and that soon, to change the fortunes of war, now so decisively setting against the South.

The war had stood still in Middle Tennessee for some months, while the eastern and western parts of the state had fallen into complete Union control. After the terrible battle of Stone's River, fought at the very threshold of the new year, Bragg, the Confederate commander, had dropped back to Tullahoma, where he faced the Union army under Rosecrans at Knoxville. In June the stalemate was ended by the advance of Rosecrans against Bragg. The latter, a little inferior in numbers to the Union army, retreated. As we shall see later, he even abandoned the important city of Chattanooga, a strategic center, without making a stand. This convinced Rosecrans that all the fight was out of the Confederates and that he could maneuver without regard to them. Never was a commander more mistaken.

President Davis had been troubled about the West for a long time. He had never been absolutely convinced of the wisdom of the Pennsylvania invasion and he was now satisfied that something must be done to better matters before Tennessee was entirely lost to the South. As resources were limited, the only possible addition of moment to Bragg would be a subtraction from Lee. Longstreet had urged a reinforcement for the West from the East early in the year, before Chancellorsville, but his advice had been disregarded, largely because Lee did not relish being weakened for a move of dubious utility. Nor did he like being weakened now, but his prestige was lowered and he saw that something must be done somewhere to help the failing cause. Lee went to Richmond to confer with the authorities and came back prepared to ship a part of his army to Tennessee. Longstreet, whose fame had not been much dimmed by Gettysburg, which had not then been refought by the veterans a thousand times, was assigned the duty of leading the detached force, partly because he was the best known of Lee's subordinates and partly because he had always advocated such a move. It gave him a chance to get away from Lee.

Longstreet was the second reinforcement sent West. As early as July 13, 1863, with the Gettysburg campaign just closed, President Davis visited Major General D. H. Hill in Richmond and commissioned him to go to Tennessee. At that moment Hill was doing nothing, he tells us, but reflecting on Lee's folly in invading the North, for he was always a caustic critic of Lee. For some months Hill had been in command of the Department of Southern Virginia and North Carolina, in which he had been called on to do nothing more important than repel raids. His reputation was rapidly declining as a result, but the President knew that Hill was one of the most resolute fighters in the service and resolute fighters were needed in Tennessee.

"Rosecrans is about to advance upon Bragg," Davis said to Hill. "I have found it necessary to detail Hardee to defend Mississippi and Alabama. His corps is without a commander. I wish you to command it."

Hill accepted the commission when he was given the temporary grade of lieutenant general, which qualified him for the command of a corps. Going westward, he reported for duty to Bragg on July 19. The condition of the railroads connecting Virginia and Tennessee was so bad that he and his staff left their horses behind.

Hill found everything dismal at headquarters. Bragg could not conceal his gloom and nervousness, which in turn affected his subordinates. A commander must show, above all things, a bold and confident front. Bragg, eaten by his fears, was out of place at the head of an army facing a stronger adversary; every factor of the situation suggested the wisdom of his replacement. But Bragg, supported both by President Davis and Joseph E. Johnston, departmental commander, continued in the place he did not entirely fill, though he was a man of some ability.

Bragg was irritable and querulous. He had declined to such a point in the army's esteem that he could not get his orders promptly obeyed, though this was partly because he seldom saw that they were carried out. His intelligence system was poor, since he had no scouts and since the cavalry screen in front of the Union army prevented his obtaining much information.

Hill was not the man to bring the commander confidence, for Hill himself declares that he had given up hope after Gettysburg; he was simply fighting now to do his duty, a different thing from fighting for victory. He was assigned Hardee's corps, consisting of Cleburne's and Stewart's divisions, veteran and steady commands. In Cleburne he had under him one of the best officers in the service. Bragg was a little east of Chattanooga when Rosecrans appeared before that place. Although the town was fortified, Bragg dejectedly abandoned it on September 8, retreating without a fight. No wonder Rosecrans thought that all the spirit had gone out of the Confederate commander! Without concentrating in the captured city, the Union general sent out his forces in scattered detachments in search of the retreating Confederates.

It was on August 15 that Longstreet had called Seddon's attention to the dangers confronting the country. On August 23 Lee went to Richmond at Davis's request and remained there for two weeks. It was at this time that it was decided to send Longstreet to Tennessee to reinforce Bragg.

On September 2, Longstreet wrote to Lee as follows:

". . . I do not know that we can reasonably hope to accomplish much here by offensive operations, unless you are strong enough to cross the Potomac. If we advance to meet the enemy on this side, he will, in all probability, go into one of his many fortified positions; these we cannot afford to attack.

"I know but little of the condition of our affairs in the west, but am inclined to the opinion that our best opportunity for great results is in Tennessee. If we could hold the defensive here with two corps, and send the other to operate in Tennessee with that army, I think that we could accomplish more than by an advance from here . . . and concentrate with one corps of this army, and such as may be drawn from others, in Tennessee, and destroy Rosecrans' army. I feel assured that this is practicable, and that greater advantage will be gained than by any operations from here." [1]

About this time the government decided to send Longstreet West. Lee concurred, probably rather reluctantly.

On September 12, Longstreet wrote Lee from Richmond suggesting the possibility of having to give up Richmond, temporarily at least, but insisting on holding the fortifications at Drewry's Bluff and Chaffin's Bluff even if the city should be lost, a most impracticable proposition. He concluded:

"I hope to start west on Monday morning. If I can do anything there, it shall be done promptly. If I cannot, I shall advise you to recall me. If I did not think our move a necessary one, my regrets at leaving you would be distressing to me, as it seems to be with the officers and men of my command. Believing it to be necessary, I hope to accept it and my other personal inconveniences cheerfully and hopefully. All that we have to be proud of has been accomplished under your eye and under your orders. Our affections for you are stronger, if it is possible for them to be stronger, than our admiration for you."

Longstreet was actuated in this matter by his genuine belief that more could be accomplished in Tennessee than in Virginia and by his longing for an independent command.

[1] *O. R.*, ser. I, vol. XXIX, pt. II, pp. 693-64.

His non-success in the Suffolk campaign had not lessened his belief in his capacity to command an army or quenched his thirst for glory. He desired to get away from Lee, as he had done for a year. He saw now a chance to leave the Army of Virginia and at the same time secure the command of an army for himself. His letter to Lee of September 5, 1863, proves this, though he says nothing of it in his book.

"I do not know enough of our facilities for transporting troops, etc., west, to say what time would be consumed in moving my corps to Tennessee and back.

"Your information will enable you to determine this much better than I. I believe, though, that the enemy intends to confine his great operations to the west, and that it is time that we were shaping our movements to meet him.

"If this army is ready to assume offensive operations, I think that it would be better for us to remain on the defensive here, and to reënforce the west, and take the offensive there. We can hold here with a smaller force than we would require for offensive operations; and if it should become necessary to retire as far as Richmond temporarily, I think that we could better afford to do so than we can to give up more of our western country. I will say more; I think that it is time that we had begun to do something in the west, and I fear if it is put off any longer we shall be too late.

"If my corps cannot go west, I think that we might accomplish something by giving me Jenkins', Wise's and Cooke's brigades, and putting me in General Bragg's place, and giving him my corps. . . . We would surely make no great risk in such a change and we might gain a great deal.

"I feel that I am influenced by no personal motive in this suggestion, and will most cheerfully give up, when we have a fair prospect of holding our western country.

"I doubt if General Bragg has confidence in his troops or himself either. He is not likely to do a great deal for us."[2]

Longstreet was partly successful in his plans. The government decided to make its main effort in Tennessee and Lee was relegated to the defensive for some time to come. That was as Longstreet desired. But what he most ardently wished he did not attain. Bragg was not relieved of his command and brought East to serve under Lee, and Longstreet was not assigned to command the Army of Tennessee in his place. It followed that he went West dissatisfied and in a condition of mind to pick flaws in Bragg and his army. The critic who was always finding fault with such masters as Lee and Jackson would certainly have occasion for extensive condemnation of the Army of Tennessee and its unfortunate commander, who had no idea what he had to encounter in Longstreet, the man that desired his place.

Longstreet had gained such an ascendancy over Lee that the latter seems to have acceded to his ambition to become commander in the West. But President Davis was by no means satisfied that Longstreet had the qualifications for command and wished to test him. It was thus with the double purpose of relieving Tennessee and of giving Longstreet a better opportunity of demonstrating his quality as a general that he was sent West. But to Longstreet, who thought that he had long since won his spurs, the situation was unsatisfactory. And unwittingly, the government had assured Bragg's ruin by sending him the two chief malcontents and critics from the East, Hill and Longstreet. Both of these men, who considered Lee a second-rate commander, were sure to fall upon the mediocre but well-meaning Bragg like wolves upon a deer. It should not have been; Longstreet

[2] *O. R.*, ser. I, vol. XXIX, pt. II, p. 699.

should have been given the command, the chance to prove himself.

The vicinity of Chattanooga is one of the most beautiful regions, scenically, in the United States. Lookout Mountain towering just over the clear and winding Tennessee River makes a vista of almost incomparable loveliness. Less cultivated then than now and more generally wooded, the scenery has lost somewhat in the interval since 1863.

The Union corps commanders, satisfied that they had nothing to fear from Southern aggression, pushed into the mountain region south of Chattanooga with a recklessness that invited disaster and would have entailed it but for the psychological condition of the Southern corps and division generals. They had become semi-mutinous without intending it. That is, they were so dissatisfied with Bragg as a commander and so distrustful of his judgment that they exercised reservation in obeying orders, and the wretched commanding general had no means of enforcing obedience. With none of his subordinates does he seem to have been on friendly terms.

The dispersal of the Union army gave Bragg the most unusual opportunities to cut off detachments, and he sought, writhing in his torment, to grasp one of these chances. But he could not; something always went awry. On September 10 there was to have been a mountain battle, an overpowering of a Union division, but the affair did not come off. Bragg attributed the failure to the disobedience of Hindman, who had it in charge. On September 12, Polk was to attack Crittenden's Union corps at Lee and Gordon's Mills on Chickamauga Creek, but, instead of attacking, Polk contented himself with taking up a defensive attitude and informing Bragg of it. Bragg, stupefied that his orders were not obeyed, went to the front to find that the enemy had recrossed the Chickamauga, removing the opportunity. Polk's defense was that Bragg's orders were premised on conditions that did not exist and so could not be fulfilled. This is probably true, for Bragg seldom knew what the enemy was doing, but Polk could have made his orders fit the situation if he had desired to do so.

The main trouble was that Bragg's devolution as a commander had proceeded to the point where he could get little done himself although he could prevent others from doing anything. If his generals had dared to do so, they would have deposed him and conducted the campaign according to their own ideas. This would have been rank mutiny, but it might have been better than the existing condition of affairs. That an army utterly without confidence in its commander or liking for him should have won the most dramatic and bitterly-fought battle in American history is a mystery. By all the canons of military art, by all the rules of human affairs, Bragg should have been defeated by the larger and far better equipped army that opposed him. But there was a quantity x in the problem, and that quantity was the valor and steadiness of the individual Confederate soldier, almost enough in itself to turn the tide of conflict and reverse the dictates of fate.

One of the Union detachments, under McCook, had wandered far south of the Confederate position and was in imminent danger. McCook was taken aback by learning that Bragg had halted his retreat; when he received an order to rejoin Thomas, who was in a mountain valley known as McLemore's Cove, he began a hurried return. With great difficulty he passed over Lookout Mountain and made his junction with Thomas on September 17. The Confederates here lost a marvelous opportunity to destroy one of the units of Rosecrans's army and thus reduce it to numerical inferiority.

On the morning of September 14, Bragg gave to his four corps commanders, Polk, Buckner, Walker, and Hill, his idea of the positions of the enemy's forces. Being entirely wrong as to McCook's whereabouts, the commander seems to have been in fear of a rear attack from him and thus failed to take advantage of the opportunity to assail Crittenden and Thomas before they were reinforced. The poor man was in a frenzy of uncertainty—uncertainty as to the enemy's position, uncertainty as to what to do, uncertainty as to the staunchness of his army, for Bragg had little more confidence in his army than his army had in him. The unresponsiveness was mutual.

Bragg had his army in hand but hesitated to attack, hesitating away the golden hours and yet determined to fight when he could bring himself and the army to it. Meanwhile Rosecrans had learned his error, discovered that Bragg, instead of retreating, was advancing and offering battle. He at once issued orders for a concentration and, by September 16, his army was in position from Lee and Gordon's Mills on Chickamauga Creek to Stevens's Gap, stretched out for about eleven miles and facing west. Bragg was on the west side of Chickamauga Creek facing the Union line and overlapping its left wing, just as the Union troops at Lee and Gordon's Mills overlapped the Confederate left. As Hill points out, on September 17, either commander could have flanked the other by moving around the left wing.

Finding Bragg on the aggressive, Rosecrans determined to fight on the defensive, confident of his ability to repulse the Confederate attack. Although the two armies were near Lookout Mountain, with its wide vistas, they confronted each other along Chickamauga Creek in woods of such thickness that the generals saw but a small segment of their lines. The Unionists took advantage of the trees to make defenses of logs, which played a considerable part in the battle. But for them the rout of the Union army would probably have been complete. The result was that Bragg finally, with about forty thousand infantry, assailed a fortified position held by perhaps forty-five thousand infantry; he had not only numbers but fortifications against him. This was due to his inability to impose his will on his subordinates and make them carry out orders not well digested and perhaps almost impossible of execution under the circumstances. Bragg's lack of accurate information seems to have filled his lieutenants with distrust of him—that and his habit of finding a scapegoat for every failure.

After waiting a long time Bragg was now in a hurry to attack, when nothing was to be gained by hurry. The Union army was well concentrated, while Bragg was looking hourly for Longstreet and his brigades from the Virginia army. Nevertheless, the Confederate commander began the battle without them.

On the night of September 18, Bragg's troops were disposed as follows from left to right: Hill, Polk, Buckner, Hood. The Union army lay along the Chattanooga-Lafayette road from Lee and Gordon's Mills on Chickamauga Creek for several miles. Crittenden's corps was on the right, Thomas's in the center, and two divisions of McCook's corps on the left. Missionary Ridge was directly behind. In the morning of September 19, Thomas, at the Union center, advanced toward Reed's Bridge on Chickamauga Creek. Brannan's and Baird's divisions drove back a small Confederate force but were attacked by Liddell's division with such fury that they were thrown back in confusion. Union reinforcements, however, came up at this moment and enabled the

Union commander to repulse Liddell in turn. Then Cheatham's division was sent forward by Bragg and swept everything before it until it was, in turn, driven back by Thomas, who had called up reinforcements. The engagement continued all the afternoon, with varying fortunes but inclining toward the South. The Unionists found to their surprise that the Southerners were fighting with a concentrated fury they had never shown before and tended to give back before it. Indeed, if the Confederates had been handled with skill in a concerted assault instead of being sent forward in detachments, Bragg might have won a decisive victory on the first day of the battle. Hood, with his division and Bushrod Johnson's, crushed a part of the Union center, gained the Chattanooga road, and captured some artillery. But three Confederate divisions could not defeat six Union divisions.

At 3:00 P. M., Hill received an order from Bragg to send Cleburne's division to assault the extreme left of the Union line. Crossing the creek and marching six miles, Cleburne's men in the twilight struck the Union left, driving everything before them and capturing prisoners and guns. But log breastworks barred their way, and when these breastworks were finally captured night had come on. So the first day ended with considerable Confederate success and with the Union leaders, who had suffered from over-confidence, now gravely anticipating the outcome of the morrow.

It was in the night of September 19-20, 1863, that Longstreet finally reached the scene of action. He had left Lee at Gordonsville after a final conference in which the feelings of both men were touched. At his departure Lee followed him to say a last farewell. He seems to have been more than usually moved as he stood beside Longstreet while the latter mounted his horse.

"General, you must beat those people," Lee said.

"General," Longstreet answered, rather ungraciously, "if you will give your orders that the enemy, when beaten, shall be destroyed, I promise to give you victory if I live. But I would not give the life of a single soldier of mine for a barren victory."

What Longstreet meant is not entirely clear, but it would seem to be something of a criticism of the small fruits garnered by Lee from his victories. Lee was too magnanimous to care for, or perhaps even to see, the implied censure.

"The order has been given," he said, "and will be repeated."[3]

It was not until September 9 that the first troop train came to Orange, where the army was. A disaster at this moment brought delay. Buckner, the Confederate commander in East Tennessee, moved south to join Bragg, leaving only a small force at the important Cumberland Gap, where Virginia touches Kentucky. The troops at Cumberland Gap surrendered to Burnside, thus closing the short railway line from Virginia to Tennessee. This made necessary the transporting of Longstreet's command through the Carolinas to Augusta, Georgia, and thence by way of Atlanta to Ringgold, near which Bragg's army lay. The result was that the artillery did not arrive until September 25, after the battle of Chickamauga. But Hood's division, sent ahead, reached Bragg on September 18 and 19 and thus was able to take part in the great battle.

Longstreet and staff reached Catoosa early in the afternoon of September 19. Their horses arrived two hours later. These were saddled, and Longstreet, accompanied by two members of his staff, Sorrel and Manning, set out to find Bragg's headquarters in a country utterly unfamiliar to them. The battle of September 19, the first day at Chicka-

[3] *B. & L.,* III, 652.

mauga, was still going on, and the sound of the guns came plainly to the anxious officers seeking the commanding general.

Night came, with a bright moon, while the party continued to ride along the woodland roads. Suddenly they stumbled upon men and were challenged, "Who comes there?" "Friends," was the answer. Noncommittal, Longstreet strove to see whether he had encountered a Confederate or Union picket. One of the officers asked the outpost to what command the men belonged. The answer gave a numbered brigade and division. That told the watchful officers that the picket was Union, as Confederate commands were known by the names of commanding officers and not by numbers.

Longstreet's party was in a quandary. The moonlight was so bright that if they turned and attempted to ride back they would make perfect targets. Longstreet solved the problem with ready wit, for he was never better than when peril forced him to think quickly.

"Let us ride down a little way to find a better crossing," he said aloud.

The outpost let the officers move off without disturbance, and presently Longstreet and his companions were under cover and safe. But it had been a narrow escape. A little more alertness on the part of the outpost and the commander of the First Corps would have been killed or captured.

Longstreet finally reached Bragg's headquarters at 11:00 P. M. Reporting to the chief, he received orders for an attack early in the morning. Bragg, at midnight before a dawn attack, was making arrangements for the next day. The arrangements for September 20 were entirely different from those of the preceding day. It was a very late date for a reorganization of forces. Dividing his army into two wings, Bragg gave the right to Polk, who had under him Hill's and Walker's corps and Cheatham's division, and the left to Longstreet, consisting of Buckner's (in part) and Hood's and Hindman's divisions. Bragg's plan was cumbrous and not particularly good: a series of attacks from right to left. It was to be initiated by a single command and every other command was to join in, successively, until the whole army was engaged. Late at night the plans had not been completed, and Hill spent much time looking for Bragg to get instructions. He states that it was not until 2:00 A. M. of September 20 that he learned he had been put in Polk's wing for the battle. Hill further maintains that he was told nothing of the assault to be made at dawn, that Bragg's order for the attack never reached him. At 7:25 A. M., Hill was shown an order intended for Polk instructing the latter to order his major generals to begin the attack. Hill informed Polk that he was adjusting his line and his men were getting their rations. Polk, coming up, assented to the delay, for which Polk and, particularly, Hill were censured. Indeed, the failure to attain greater results was laid to Hill's not moving in the early morning. If Hill's account is true the blame was not his; the fault lay with circumstances. Bragg had made his plans late in the night, amidst the confusion following a hard-fought battle, and it was too much to expect that the orders would be carried out as issued. Indeed, poor Bragg never succeeded in getting his orders accurately obeyed.

At eight o'clock Bragg rode up and angrily demanded of Hill why the attack had not been made at daylight. Hill answered that this was the first he had heard of a dawn attack. Bragg, angry and worried by this initial failure of his plans, declared that he had found Polk reading a newspaper two miles from the line of battle. Later on, he said that one of his officers told him Polk was reading the paper.

As a matter of fact, everything was haphazard on the

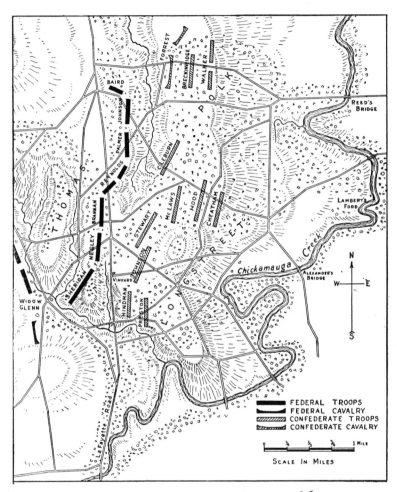

BATTLE OF CHICKAMAUGA, SEPTEMBER 20, 1863, AT NOON

Confederate side and defeat was all that could be expected, for Rosecrans, standing on the defensive, had no such elaborate arrangements to make; all he had to do was to hold his line. All night long the waiting Confederates heard the

ringing of axes on trees as the Unionists worked like mad
to strengthen their fortifications against the morrow's fray.
The Confederates, aligned in the woods without proper
staff supervision, were in much confusion. Hill was standing north and south, parallel with the Union position, while
Cheatham's division was at right angles to him. When the
line was adjusted, Cheatham was immediately behind Stewart and had to be taken out and placed in reserve. Kershaw's brigade, of Longstreet, was also out of line and was
put in reserve. Thus in rather disordered fashion, and with
many gaps and displacements, the Confederate army deployed for the coming battle. Everything was wrong with
them but the quality of the men, and that could not have
been better. Manhood was to win the day but was not to
reap the fruits of victory.

The Confederate line ran from north to south: Hill on
the right, then Stewart, then Hood behind in reserve, then
Bushrod Johnson, then Hindman on the extreme left, with
Preston in reserve. Wheeler's cavalry was on the left flank,
Forrest's on the right.

Bragg gave Longstreet a map of the vicinity, which enabled him to understand something of the nature of the
ground. It was not until dawn that he found the left wing.
It was composed of Buckner's corps (Stewart's and Preston's
divisions), Bushrod Johnson's division, Hindman's division,
and three of Hood's brigades. The command stood thus:

Stewart   Johnson   Hindman   Preston
            Hood

Preparing for the battle, Longstreet did not yet know
where the right wing was. Stewart, sent to discover it, moved
half a mile to the right and found himself in advance of the
right wing. This move lengthened Longstreet's array and
enabled him to bring Hood up from the rear and place him

in the line. The troops were now formed in two lines with the exception of Hood, whose five brigades, intended as shock troops, were placed in column.

Scouting the woods, the Confederates found that their right wing overlapped the enemy's fieldworks for some distance and that the road to Chattanooga was free from obstructions. Most of the Union army was in line behind its breastworks and confronting the Confederates, but Gordon Granger, with a considerable force, was behind the left, covering the gap in Missionary Ridge at Rossville. Bragg hoped to cut off the Union army from Chattanooga and sever its line of supply.

The discovery that the road from the Union left to Chattanooga was open and unguarded gave the Confederates a chance to go around the Union left flank and attack in the rear. But Bragg held to his order of battle, that is, successive attacks from the Confederate right to the left.

The Confederates faced a desperate adventure. Slightly inferior in the numbers of their infantry and much inferior in artillery, they were called on to carry a position fortified along most of the way by works of logs and rails, quite formidable in that day. The Union artillery, on the lower slopes of Missionary Ridge, had a far better field of fire than the Confederate guns in the woods. Altogether the conditions and the chances of success were against the Confederates.

About 9:30 A. M., the attack began by the Confederate right under Hill. Two of his divisions, Breckinridge's and Cleburne's, moving around the Union left, attacked the flank, while other troops assailed the breastworks in front, losing a gallant brigadier, Benjamin H. Helm. The first attack failed. An assault was then made by Cleburne on the breastworks, and so energetic and fierce were the advancing

Confederates that George H. Thomas, commanding the Union center and left wing, began to call for reinforcements. In fact, on no other field of the Civil War, by the troops on either side, was such desperate gallantry shown as by the Southerners at Chickamauga.

The successive order of battle of the Confederates called into the assault command after command. The fighting was desperate, the losses terrible; the battle swayed back and forth on the Union left without issue. Breckinridge, Cleburne, and Stewart were all assailing the Union line, which was bending but not breaking. And troops were being rushed from the Union right, still unassailed, to the relief of the hard-pressed left wing.

About noon Longstreet's wing advanced to the attack. By this time the persistent assaults on the Union left and the reliefs sent to that point had resulted in the opening of a gap between the center and the right. Stewart's division penetrated the Union line but was driven back by the fire of the artillery. The Confederates were on the Chattanooga road and the peril of the Union army was imminent.

Into the gap left by the shifting of the Union forces, Longstreet's advancing line stepped. Longstreet had arranged his troops in three lines so as to form a column. It seems that Bushrod Johnson's division was the first to penetrate the gap, and some writers have been inclined to give him the credit for the victory. But it also appears from the evidence that Longstreet was close behind and in control of Johnson's troops.

At eleven o'clock Longstreet sent word to Bragg that his column would probably be able to break the enemy's line if the commander cared to have him go in at once. By that time the successive order of attack from right to left, complicated and difficult, had broken down. If Longstreet continued to wait for it, the other wing might be defeated before he entered the battle. Bragg sent word back to Longstreet to attack, but before the latter could do so Stewart, advancing, came into close contact with the Unionists and pressed them so hard that the gap in the line resulted. Longstreet, moving some time later, found the gap open and availed himself of it.

Immediately in front of Longstreet's moving column were shattered fragments of the Twentieth and Twenty-first corps of the Union army. As the lines of brown-clad men came rushing through the forest and into plain view, the Union infantry and artillery opened on them with deadly effect. The leading brigade was cut to pieces, but the divisions of Johnson and Hindman pushed forward on Hood's left; suddenly the Union line was broken through and the Confederates found themselves among the captured guns of several batteries. Hood himself was so fearfully wounded as to be thought killed, a loss to the army.

It was at this moment that Longstreet showed his great quality, his imperturbability in the midst of ruin and death, for he was never quite himself until his sluggish nature was aroused by scenes of bloodshed and the imminent presence of catastrophe. Benning, a brigadier, coming up to him, declared, "General Hood killed, my horse killed, my brigade torn to pieces, and I haven't a man left." Longstreet, utterly unaffected by hysteria, asked the distracted officer if he did not have at least one man left. Benning was quieted and immediately set to work to collect his scattered command.

In fact, at the moment the prospects were highly favorable to the Confederates. The first line of the Union army had been broken by the charge; a gap was now in the second line, and Bushrod Johnson was in the gap. Stewart and Hindman were advancing.

As the Confederates approached the second Union line, Johnson's men struck it while the Union troops were in the process of changing front. The Unionists were routed; the survivors of the Twentieth and Twenty-first corps fled to the rear over Missionary Ridge, carrying other troops with them. Then there came the necessity of making an instant decision, and Longstreet had the faculty of deciding swiftly and rightly in an emergency. The Confederate right wing was held by the Union left wing, which had been reinforced to such an extent that the gap had opened in the line. As the Confederates could not advance on the right, the continuance of Bragg's successive order of battle from right to left was not possible. Longstreet found that much more could be accomplished by moving toward the right and against the flank of the Union left wing than by attempting to move toward the left and against the Union right wing. Into the gap command after command now pressed, turning toward the right and pouring their fire on the flank of the Union left wing. The fighting went on, fast and furiously, as the Unionists attempted to stay the advance of the Confederates.

The leaders themselves had only vague ideas as to what was going on. "On the most open parts of the Confederate side of the field," Longstreet says, "one's vision could not reach farther than the length of a brigade." As he had many brigades in line, his range of knowledge was very limited, but he was fighting from instinct and from right instinct. When Longstreet forgot strategy and maneuvers and came down to fighting, he was magnificently efficient.

It was now past one o'clock and Longstreet was hungry; he was one of those steely persons whose natural functions are undisturbed by any excitement or contingency. In the midst of the hellish noise and confusion of that awful battle, he ordered his lunch spread out while he rode with Buckner back and forth in the effort to get information.

"I could see but little of the enemy's line," he says, "and only knew of it by the occasional exchange of fire between the lines of skirmishers, until we approached the angle of the lines. I passed the right of our skirmishers and, thinking I had passed the enemy's, rode forward to be accurately assured, when I suddenly found myself under near fire of his sharpshooters concealed behind the trees and under the brush. I saw enough, however, to mark the ground line of his field-works as they were spread along the front of the right wing." Uninjured, Longstreet rode back among the trees to safety. As there was no chief of artillery, he asked Buckner to bring up a twelve-gun battery to enfilade the enemy's line and rode off to lunch. He had bacon and sweet potatoes, the last a luxury unknown to Virginia soldiers. A shell fragment knocked over Manning of the staff, who lay gasping on the ground apparently in the agonies of death. But Longstreet, coolly perceiving that the officer was choked by the potato he was eating, had him relieved, when he was found to be only slightly hurt.

While eating, Longstreet received a request from Bragg to join him. Bragg, some distance in the rear and apparently not fully aware of what was going on, was told of the change Longstreet had made in the order of battle. The latter suggested another alteration in the plan: to leave the right wing where it was, draw off other forces to the left and attempt to occupy the gaps in Missionary Ridge behind the Union left. It was bold counsel, but Longstreet was bold when his blood was up and he forgot his theories and ambitions. Bragg, however, seems to have been disheartened even in this moment of promise.

"There is not a man in the right wing who has any fight in him," Bragg said (according to Longstreet).

If he did say this it illustrates Bragg's pettish humor better than anything else. To attribute lack of fight to men who had stood in line for hours receiving the most terrible punishment is to illustrate Bragg's ignorance of what was going on and his demoralization. Without expressing approval or disapproval of Longstreet's action, he rode off to his headquarters, where he seems to have remained for the rest of the battle. But Longstreet's account of it may not be entirely accurate.

Longstreet had to make the best of the situation. The Confederate right wing was no longer pressing forward. This was unfortunate, as it might have held the Union left in close grips in the critical moment of the battle. Longstreet prepared to push Johnson, Hindman, Hood, and Preston through the gap and decide the issue. Johnson, moving ahead through the murky woods lighted by the flashes of guns and burning trees, drove artillery and infantry before him. At this moment Granger, in reserve at Missionary Ridge, moved toward the swelling noise of battle now fast approaching him, passing near the Confederate right wing. No report was sent Longstreet of the arrival of Union reinforcements. It was growing toward evening and the sun was declining behind the mountains.

By now Granger's reserve had gained the important position known as Snodgrass Hill. The Confederates, advancing through the woods in pursuit of the scattered and fleeing Unionists, suddenly came under the fire of the reserve, which was strongly posted, and in turn were driven back. They rallied and brought up guns. Under the fire of batteries Thomas's position no longer could be held. The Unionists were withdrawn from their fieldworks for retreat.

The direct road to Chattanooga was thought to be closed by the Confederate right wing, which had had ample opportunity to seize it. The Union entrenched line crumbled to pieces quite suddenly. Granger's reserve was now hotly engaged in the effort to hold the gap in Missionary Ridge for withdrawal. It was one of those great moments of opportunity that come to commanders but that must be grasped immediately. If the whole Confederate line had been thrown forward at that instant the greatest victory of the war would, in all probability, have rewarded the valor and endurance of the Southern troops. But two separate battles were fought by the right and left wings and the lack of coöperation prevented complete success.

Longstreet, ordering up his last reserves, attacked Snodgrass Hill, where the Union reserve was holding out heroically. It melted away before the Confederate attack. The left wing of Southerners continued its advance while the right wing gained the Chattanooga road. Some hundreds of prisoners were taken. At length the severed Confederate right and left wings met and made the woods ring with their victorious shouts. The most surprising victory of the war was won.

Thomas, whose stubborn stand had prevented the rout of the Union army, had clung to his position as long as possible. But Longstreet's batteries enfiladed his line, and Thomas at about 5:30 gave orders to his subordinates to prepare for retreat. After sunset Rosecrans himself issued an order for withdrawal. Night was well advanced when the last Union commands left the field. Most of the troops, disorganized and in some cases demoralized, were falling back rapidly to Chattanooga.

The battle was won by the Confederates, but they had failed in one of their main objectives—to cut off Rosecrans from Chattanooga. He still held the town that was the prize of the contention, though he was in dire peril from the army that had stormed his fortifications and beaten his troops in the field. Chickamauga was the hardest-fought, most desperate engagement of the American Civil War. The casualties totaled about thirty-five thousand, slightly more on the side of the Confederates, who were the attackers. The loss in the Confederate infantry was fully 40 per cent of the numbers engaged, a loss unprecedented in American warfare. Longstreet puts down the loss in his own wing at 44 per cent; in some cases regiments on both sides lost 50 per cent. The Tenth Tennessee regiment reached the enormous figure of 68 per cent. Seldom have men shed their blood more freely for their cause than was the case with both sides at Chickamauga. The Confederate infantry demonstrated, if further demonstration were needed, its incomparable dash and vigor in attack. In fact, the battle was won, not by generalship, which certainly in Bragg's case was not high, but by the fighting qualities of the rank and file. Longstreet himself had done well. Just how far he deserves the credit for taking advantage of the gap in the Union line and how far that credit belongs to subordinates cannot be determined, but he was in command and close to the firing line, as was his wont; and the excellent handling of his troops must have been in considerable degree due to his own tactical skill. He at last showed marked ability as an offensive fighter, something he had not done before. Chickamauga was the high-water mark in Longstreet's career. He had nobly redeemed himself for his failure at Gettysburg. The hopes of the South flared up once more as the telegraph wires burned with the news of the great victory before Chattanooga. The sad frustration of those hopes marks the real beginning of the end.

CHAPTER XV

COLLAPSE IN THE WEST

THE generals in front knew that a great victory had been won when, in the early nightfall, the Union fortifications were found to be deserted by all except the dead and wounded, and they desired to take advantage of the opportunity, the first presented in the West, to pursue a beaten and fugitive Union army. Forrest, the cavalryman, alive with somber energy, reported that his cavalry alone could drive the fleeing Unionists into the Tennessee River and urged immediate advance. But it was night in the forest, all of the Confederate commands had sustained terrible losses and were more or less disorganized, and there was reason in not pursuing foes who had given such evidence of their prowess and who would be certain to have strong rearguards at every important point.

The morning of September 21, however, was different. The Confederates were rested and reorganized and the whole army was thrilled with triumph and filled with that feeling of superior courage and efficiency that comes to men who have stormed a strong position and driven the enemy before them. Then was the hour for an immediate advance. Thousands of stragglers might have been picked up, if nothing more could have been done, but more could in all probability have been accomplished. The Union troops were for the moment, but only for the moment, completely non-plussed by the reversal of form in the Southern ranks. Looking on themselves as the hunters seeking the retiring Confederates, they had found themselves to be the hunted, a psychological change that must affect any army for a time. The battle ruined Rosecrans as a commander; it might have ruined his army if the advantage could have been utilized.

At sunrise on the morning of September 21, Bragg came to Longstreet's bivouac.[1] The commanding general asked the subordinate's advice as to the next step to take, speaking of the defensive works at Chattanooga as if in no mood to attack the town. Longstreet made the correct and rather obvious proposal to cross the Tennessee River north of Chattanooga and move against the enemy's communications. If Rosecrans retreated, as would likely happen, the Confederates could either pursue him or move against the Union force near Knoxville under Burnside.

Bragg seems to have been glad to receive suggestions, having no plans of his own, and he accepted Longstreet's offering. The right wing of the Confederate army was ordered to take up the march for the river; the left wing was to follow when the way was clear, utilizing the wait in caring for the dead and wounded.

It was night when the last of the right wing took the road, and Longstreet postponed his march until the morning of September 22. On his arrival at Bragg's headquarters on that day, the commander directed that a division be diverted to follow the enemy toward Chattanooga. When Longstreet asked him if he had abandoned the proposed movement, Bragg said "the people would be greatly gratified to know that his army was marching through the streets of Chattanooga with bands of music and salutations of soldiers." Longstreet replied that it would give the people greater pleasure to know that Rosecrans had been driven from

[1] *M. to A.*, p. 461.

Chattanooga in flight, with the Confederates hammering away at his flanks.

Bragg's change of plans may have been due to the bad feeling that had already arisen between him and Longstreet. The latter was prone to express his opinions bluntly, even to Lee, and his bald manner of speaking grated on the sensitive, unstrung Bragg. On the morning after the battle the two generals had had words. James N. Coggin, a brigadier general, was the witness of the meeting.

"Just at the head of our brigade we noticed a crowd of men collected, some of whom were on horseback. Among them we could plainly distinguish the tall form of John C. Breckinridge and our bull-dog leader, General James Longstreet, Lee's famous war-horse. Tom Wallingford, one of my company, called me, and we walked to where they (Longstreet and Breckinridge) were. I think General Buckner was also there, on horseback. General Bragg was on foot. Longstreet and Bragg were in earnest conversation —the latter calm and quiet, while the former spoke in an excited manner—his voice clear and distinct, yet very angry. We could not hear what Bragg was saying; he spoke slowly, and in low tones. Longstreet said: 'General, this army should have been in motion at *dawn of day*.' General Bragg made some reply, to which Longstreet said: 'Yes, sir; but all *great* captains follow up a victory.' Another remark from Bragg was followed by these words from Longstreet: 'Yes, sir, you *rank* me, but you cannot cashier me.' " [2]

Whether from irritation with Longstreet or prostration after his intense strain, Bragg did not make the move to the Tennessee River, afterward characterizing it as impracticable. All that was done was to follow the enemy toward Chattanooga on September 23. The result was that Rose-

[2] *Southern Historical Society Papers*, XII, 223.

crans did not evacuate Chattanooga, as he would otherwise
have been forced to do, but strengthened his fortifications
and reorganized his shattered army. Bragg did nothing more
than stretch out his army in a semicircle of six miles southeast of Chattanooga, from the base of Lookout Mountain to
the Tennessee River. Longstreet's command (McLaws,
Hood, and Walker) held the left of the line of investment.

Bragg shelled the town from his batteries on Lookout
Mountain but without effect. Finding the Unionists growing stronger in the invested city, he sent Wheeler off on a
cavalry raid against their communications. The cavalry made
a number of captures but failed to break the Union communications. Another effort of Bragg's, to prevent the bringing of provisions into the town by the fire of sharpshooters,
also failed. No fruits whatever had been gained from the
greatest victory of the war, and the position of the Confederates, though victors, was becoming increasingly hazardous.
The Union army, while on short rations because of Bragg's
investment, was not starved and had only to wait for reinforcements to take the offensive again. The Confederate
army had no reinforcements to expect.

By this time Bragg's subordinates were on the verge of
mutiny. The commanding general was simply in the way.
He had contributed little to the winning of the victory and
he had prevented the victory from being utilized. Unpopular with his officers before because of his petulant disposition and his tendency to place the blame for every
miscarriage on somebody else's shoulders, he was now hardly
on speaking terms with his lieutenants.

To this tense situation Longstreet contributed his full
share. Accustomed to speaking his mind without reserve, to
criticizing Lee in severe terms, he found the conditions in
the Army of Tennessee intolerable. To Longstreet, Lee

seemed rather incompetent; how did he find the dyspeptic, irritable Bragg who never knew his own mind and was constantly sending orders to his subordinates that he never took the trouble to see fulfilled? To the intensely critical Longstreet who always knew his own mind, even when he was wrong, Bragg was simply impossible as the head of an army. He did not hesitate to say so to the officers around him.

Thus encouraged, some of the generals came to Longstreet and asked him to intervene with President Davis in regard to Bragg, who they all thought should be removed from command. Longstreet answered that he was not in Davis's confidence but agreed to present the case to Secretary of War Seddon and to Lee. At the same time a round robin was drawn up by the rebellious officers, written by D. H. Hill, and sent to President Davis. Hill, accustomed to the comparative efficiency of the Army of Northern Virginia and the able methods of Lee, was, like Longstreet, scandalized by the uncertainty of Bragg's ways and the inferior organization and equipment of the Army of Tennessee. On October 4, Longstreet sent a note to Hill: "Colonel Chesnut, the President's aide-de-camp, has just passed my headquarters on his way to the mountains. In a ten minutes' conversation I told him of our distressed condition, and urged him to go on to Richmond with all speed and to urge upon the President relief for us."

Bragg retaliated by striking at his critics. Polk was put under arrest for failing to begin the battle at dawn of September 20, to which failure Bragg attributed the escape of the Union army from destruction. Hindman, who had fought with great valor and efficiency, was relieved of command on charges of misconduct in the effort to crush a part of Rosecrans's army in the operations before Chickamauga. And others were mentioned for rebuke or court-martial.

The situation was so acute that Davis felt it incumbent on him to visit the camp and diagnose the trouble. On October 9, the Southern President reached headquarters and called for a conference of the generals. In the presence of Bragg, Davis asked the officers, one after another, for their opinion of the commanding general. Longstreet attempted to evade the question but, when Davis insisted, answered briefly that he thought Bragg would be of greater service elsewhere, explaining that the fruits of victory had not been gathered. Buckner gave somewhat the same answer, as did Cheatham. D. H. Hill was emphatic in his agreement.

The next day, October 10, Davis had a private conference with Longstreet that lasted for most of the day. Longstreet says the President expressed the thought of assigning him the command of the army and that he answered that the day had passed for it, that he should have been given the command as soon as sent West, in time to learn something of the army and to gain the confidence of the officers and men before fighting. As it was, the battle had been fought, the army was engaged in a sort of siege, and was now discouraged and disaffected. Grant was moving to reinforce Rosecrans, and the situation was serious. Longstreet did not think it would be just to himself to call him to the command under the existing circumstances. The army was in Joseph E. Johnston's department, and should be used in combination with his forces in Alabama and Mississippi. Under him Longstreet would serve in any capacity. The mention of Johnston's name, according to Longstreet, aroused Davis's ire and brought forth a severe rebuke.

Possibly Longstreet was mistaken in his recollection that the command of the army had been offered him. It was well known that the authorities in Richmond had long considered the possibility of giving him the command of the main Western army and, in reality, sent him to Tennessee to put him on probation. But Davis never seems to have been satisfied of Longstreet's capacity for command of an army; and, if so, his doubt was justified by the facts. Longstreet had it in him to be a magnificent corps general, but he lacked the breadth of knowledge necessary to a successful army commander. He did not realize it himself but he was essentially a subordinate, a lieutenant. Always dissatisfied, always longing for an independent command, always feeling himself discriminated against, he proved a complete failure when given a chance to show what he could do. Yet it is fair to say that he did not have a very good opportunity.

Probably Davis was influenced against Longstreet, as he was against Hill, by learning that these two fully concurred in the dissatisfaction of the officers of the Army of Tennessee with Bragg. The President may not have been so blindly devoted to Bragg as is supposed but may have thought him under the circumstances the best choice where any selection involved difficulties.

In that interview with Longstreet, Davis referred to his troubles with politicians and noncombatants, their ceaseless criticisms. Longstreet answered that if Davis gave the country success the webs of the politicians would break. Then he says he offered his resignation. Davis objected to the effect of the resignation on Longstreet's troops, to which the latter answered that he would go for the winter to Texas and send in his resignation from there. Davis did not agree. Longstreet asked him to assign a commander in place of Hood, terribly wounded, suggesting either Micah Jenkins or Law, but the President made no choice.

As the sun was setting Longstreet left the President.

Davis "walked as far as the gate, gave his hand in his usual warm grasp, and dismissed me with his gracious smile; but a bitter look lurking about its margin, and the ground-swell, admonished me that clouds were gathering about head-quarters of the First Corps even faster than those that told the doom of the Southern cause."[3]

A day or two later Davis called another conference at Bragg's headquarters, expressing a desire to take the army out of the lines of Chattanooga and put it into active field service once more. Longstreet repeated his suggestion of a move against Rosecrans's communications. That would force the Union army, he maintained, to fight or retreat. Bragg proposed a somewhat similar plan but apparently rather vaguely. Davis ordered the scheme offered by Longstreet to be put into effect. A day or two later he left.

He had brought Pemberton with him, intending to put the latter in command of a corps but found the sentiment of the army bitter against the surrenderer of Vicksburg. Hill was relieved of duty and Buckner was given a leave of absence. Hardee took command of Polk's corps in place of Cheatham. As these officers, Hill, Polk, Buckner, and Cheatham, were the chief opponents and critics of Bragg, their removal meant the endorsement of the latter by the government.

Experience was teaching Longstreet many things he had not known. Detached from Lee, attached to an army far inferior to Lee's in command and equipment, he was beginning to realize that Lee was not the incompetent general he had before sometimes felt him to be. Now Longstreet wanted Lee to come West and wrestle with problems that he realized were too hard for him to solve. He wanted Lee

[3] *M. to A.,* p. 468.

to grapple with the task and risk his reputation. As for himself, Longstreet desired to go back East and command Lee's army while the chief was straightening matters in Tennessee. In fact, Longstreet already wished himself back in Virginia. He wrote all this to Lee, who answered from his camp on the Rappahannock on October 26:

". . . As regards your proposition as to myself, I wish that I could feel that it was prompted by other reasons than kind feelings to myself. I think that you could do better than I could. It was with that view I urged your going. The President, being on the ground, I hope will do all that can be done. He has to take a broad view of the whole ground, and must order as he deems best. I will cheerfully do anything in my power.

"In addition to other infirmities, I have been suffering so much from rheumatism in my back that I could scarcely get about. The first two days of our march I had to be hauled in a wagon, and subsequently every motion of my horse, and indeed of my body, gave much pain. I am rather better now, though I still suffer." [4]

Lee closed with an account of his Bristoe campaign and a wish for Longstreet's return.

Meanwhile Longstreet was having a wretched time with Bragg, whom he now thoroughly disliked and despised. That makeshift general could never satisfy the hypercritical Longstreet. The latter had concurred reluctantly in Bragg's quaint idea of preventing supplies from reaching Chattanooga by the fire of sharpshooters and had sent a brigade to support the sharpshooters. Longstreet complained of the negligence of the cavalry, which Bragg defended. Then Longstreet did something that should have been done before: he established a signal station to communicate with

[4] *M. to A.,* p. 469 n.

his headquarters. That irritated Bragg, who declined to credit the messages so received.

Rosecrans, ruined by his defeat, which could not be concealed from the keen eyes in Washington, was superseded by his notable subordinate, Thomas. Under him W. F. Smith moved to break up the investing line of sharpshooters. On October 27, he landed troops at Brown's Ferry some miles down the river. Taking possession of the other side of the river bank, Smith entrenched himself there, and the siege of the sharpshooters came to an end.

Bragg desired to recover the river bank and directed Longstreet to confer with him on plans. The latter met the commander on the point of Lookout Rock in the morning of October 28. While they were talking, a messenger came for Longstreet to report that the enemy were moving along the base of the mountain. Bragg angrily denied the report, but the messenger asked him to ride to the west side of the mountain and see for himself. Riding there, Bragg and Longstreet saw Hooker's Twelfth Corps marching along toward Brown's Ferry.

Longstreet estimated the hostile force at five thousand men and the rearguard at fifteen hundred. It bivouacked immediately under the mountain whereon the Confederate commanders stood. Bragg began to make plans for capturing this rearguard by a night attack. Longstreet was to do it with McLaws's and Jenkins's divisions. Details were left to him.

But the plan went awry. McLaws never received the order to move. After waiting for him for some time, Jenkins determined to act alone. But in the darkness everything was wrong. The Confederates attacked and a fierce engagement followed with nearly a thousand casualties on both sides, almost equally distributed. The attack was a failure and led to bitter recriminations among some of the Confederate officers. Longstreet thought that Law was mainly to blame, though it appears that he himself was careless and handled matters poorly.

The truth is that Longstreet had lost all hope of accomplishing anything under Bragg and longed to get away—anywhere, if only away. He states that it was about November 1 when it began to be rumored in the camps that he was to be sent to East Tennessee against Burnside's force. Longstreet hardly credited the report, as it seemed madness for Bragg to weaken his army at the very moment that Sherman was hurrying from Memphis to join the Union army shut up in Chattanooga. All the same, the report pleased him, and he says, "So I set to work to try to help his plans in case the report proved true."

That Longstreet should seek to forward plans which he himself regarded as unfortunate and fraught with peril to the army does not reflect credit on him, but the relations between himself and the commanding general had become so strained that effective coöperation was impossible. Longstreet indeed was wild to get away, trying to find some excuse for leaving an army surely doomed under such a commander.

It took no great prescience to see that the army was doomed. Davis, accepting Bragg's assurances at face value, had sent away Bragg's chief antagonists, in the fatuous belief that that would heal the discontent in the army. But the disaffection had spread beyond the generals and was now widespread in the rank and file. The whole army, officers and privates alike, was sick of Bragg, bitterly critical of the President for visiting the camp and not recognizing the necessity of change. Indeed the army was so discontented that its fighting power, wonderful at Chickamauga, was rapidly declining. All that was needed to complete the demoralization was to detach Longstreet, thus leaving the wretched remnant of the army with the conviction that it was to be sacrificed to official incapacity. One quality American soldiers have nearly always lacked, and that is the capacity for fighting successfully under unpopular and untrusted generals; the American soldier demands competence in his commanders. And now the Army of Tennessee, whether justly or unjustly, had lost confidence in Bragg and respect for him. It was perhaps the most deplorable mistake ever made by Davis, a man with a magnificent ability for making mistakes, that he did not recognize the handwriting on the wall and put somebody else—anybody else—in Bragg's place. But he had weakly yielded to Bragg's argument that if the head malcontents were removed all would be well with the army.

Bragg called Longstreet into conference with Hardee and Breckinridge and announced his intention to send the first named against the enemy at Knoxville, pausing to await comment. Longstreet, always ready with suggestions, declared that the move was feasible but that it would be risky to detach a strong force from the army while it lay in a semicircle of six miles around Chattanooga. He urged a concentration of the main army behind Chickamauga Creek while he himself should make a hasty campaign against Burnside and return before Sherman reached Chattanooga. Longstreet evidently was moved by a desire to leave Bragg, for more fatuous reasoning never was. How could he, with the poorest transportation facilities, expect to move into East Tennessee and fight a battle and return, all while Sherman, hastening from Memphis, was still on the way? It seems inconceivable that experienced officers could ever have seriously expected such an outcome, that they did not see and recognize the fact that the army was about to be sacrificed to its internal dissensions, to Longstreet's desire to be gone and to Bragg's determination to have him gone—him the disturber, the free critic, the contemner of his chief. And indeed in one sense Bragg was right; if he was to continue to command the Army of Tennessee it was necessary to get rid of Longstreet, for perhaps nothing had so affected the mass of soldiers as the openly expressed contempt of the noted corps general from the Army of Virginia for the commander of the Army of Tennessee.

The decision was made, the madness was completed. Longstreet was assigned his two divisions, batteries and Wheeler's cavalry. It was expected that a force from Southwest Virginia would join Longstreet, but this hope was as chimerical as the campaign. What anybody expected to result from it is difficult to see. If Burnside should be forced from Knoxville, little or nothing of importance would be accomplished. The Union army at Chattanooga had several possible supply lines and that with East Tennessee meant little. That Longstreet should have consented to such a movement would set a seal on him as an incompetent strategist if we did not understand his peculiarities and recognize the fact that nothing was permitted to stand in the way of them. He was unhappy and apprehensive with Bragg and determined to leave. The Knoxville campaign gave him the desired chance to get away, and the probable fate of the disjointed, half-mutinous army in his absence did not disturb him. Moreover, he was going to have another chance at independent command. He had done nothing at Suffolk, but he did not think that anything could be accomplished there. It was going to be different now. He would defeat Burnside, drive him from Knoxville, perhaps capture his command. Nothing was possible with Bragg but defeat. Victory beckoned Longstreet from the mountains of East Tennessee.

To do Longstreet justice he seems to have warned Bragg that, unless the move against Burnside were made speedily, Grant's army would arrive before he could return. But Bragg only smiled sardonically.[5]

As a matter of fact, Grant was already on the ground when Bragg made his suicidal move. He had arrived in Chattanooga on October 22, and Sherman was close behind. But Bragg seems to have been animated by the single consideration of getting rid of the offensive Longstreet, who had antagonized him constantly from that very first interview in the night of September 19.

Longstreet's detachment, which was destined to ruin Bragg and shatter almost the last hope of the Confederacy, was a forlorn hope indeed. He had in all something more than fifteen thousand men with whom to attack and defeat the twenty-five thousand veteran troops commanded by Burnside in a strongly fortified position.

Longstreet's force was to travel part of the way on railroads; by November 4 his men were ready. The trains did not come until the next day. The troops arrived at the terminal, Sweetwater, on November 6, 7, and 8. The last battery of artillery did not reach the station until November 10. Part of the troops. for whom trains did not come, moved by the roads.

Bragg now began to complain of the delay in Longstreet's movements; the latter's comments show how bitter the feeling was between the two men: "He knew that trains and conductors were under his exclusive control, but *he wanted papers that would throw the responsibility of delay upon*

[5] *M. to A.*, p. 481.

other shoulders." [6] On November 8 and 9 the marching infantry reached Cleveland, where the trains were to meet them; it was not until November 12 that the last of the commands were at Sweetwater. By that time the move against Knoxville was hopeless if it had not been hopeless from the first. After the farrago of generalship resulting from Bragg's broken-down condition and the dissensions that had ruined the army, catastrophe was about to descend in person. And Longstreet was deftly out of the way of discredit. This was his weakest act, this agreement in a madness of the commanding general, this disinclination to remain and share the fate of the Army of Tennessee. The diversion of forces from Lee's army to Tennessee had been Longstreet's work. Prompted partly by military considerations and partly by ambition, he had urged, and successfully urged, his transferal to the West. Now that things were going badly and his trained observation led him to understand the doom that was about to descend on the blind Bragg and the unfortunate army, he was thinking only of getting away.

Bragg seems to have been moved by no other consideration than his desire to get rid of the critical Longstreet. When the latter's troops reached Sweetwater (the railway terminus) on the way to Knoxville, they expected to find rations there. Supplies were there, but, according to Longstreet, Carter L. Stevenson in command refused to give his troops any of them, averring that he was under orders to ship all stores to Bragg. The lack of coöperation between the Confederates in the West, their endless feuds and quarrels, had reached the point of suicide. Longstreet comments:

"Thus we found ourselves in a strange country, not as much as a day's rations on hand, with hardly enough land

[6] *M. to A.*, p. 483.

transportation for ordinary camp equipage, the enemy in front to be captured, and our friends in rear putting in their paper bullets."

Longstreet had expected to cross the Little Tennessee above its junction with the great river and take position on the east bank over against Knoxville, which would have brought the town under the fire of the Confederate batteries. But when the pontons arrived they came without a wagon train for hauling them, and so were useless. Longstreet had to cross the river elsewhere and after some delay.

Bragg, though he had ordered the detachment of Longstreet to East Tennessee, was anything but easy in mind, knowing that the Union army in Chattanooga was growing stronger. He urged Longstreet to keep in telegraphic communication with him and repair the railroad, as it might be necessary to recall him at any moment. Longstreet commented on these instructions rather petulantly, on November 5:

"In reviewing your instructions of yesterday it appears that you intend that in driving the enemy out of East Tennessee I must surely keep railroad communication with your forces at Chattanooga. . . . My understanding of the move was that I should gain possession of East Tennessee, and, if possible, the army there, as the primary condition, and in doing this as far as practicable keep the communication with Chattanooga open, but to get East Tennessee and to get rid of the enemy's forces there. . . .

"I think that you greatly overestimate the enemy's force at and around Chattanooga. I have seen the force every day for the time it has been here and cannot think it exceeds your force without Stevenson's division, and the greater part of it has been badly beaten in battle not long since." [7]

[7] O. R., ser. I, vol. XXXI, pt. III, p. 636.

Thus he sought to lull Bragg's fears while he went off on his own campaign, an independent commander at last.

On November 9, the anxious Bragg sent a dispatch to Longstreet to hurry his movement. At the moment Longstreet was at Sweetwater endeavoring to draw more troops to himself. He answered tartly:

"The troops are not here yet, the supply train is not here, nor have my troops any meat rations."

Longstreet states in his book that Bragg was attempting, by his repeated injunctions to hurry, to build up a "paper" case against him. There is no reason to believe this is true. What happened was that Bragg realized, almost as soon as Longstreet was detached, that he had made a false move and that he was in a position of great peril. He wished Longstreet to hasten to do what he could do and return. But he had made an irreparable blunder in ever sanctioning so harebrained a movement and he had to pay the penalty. Longstreet's deliberation, and he did everything with the utmost deliberation, did not make the unhappy commander of the Army of Tennessee feel any better. He tore his hair as he watched the growing Union strength in Chattanooga and realized that Longstreet could not be driven, that that mulelike personage would do only what he pleased to do and as it pleased him. On November 11, the unfortunate Bragg wired Richmond that Sherman, with twenty thousand men, was approaching and that Longstreet should be over the Tennessee. "But I hear nothing from him," he added.

Bragg was astonished when Longstreet's dispatches of that day reached him. He answered on November 12:

"All your infantry left on Sunday last, the most of your artillery on Monday night, and the last gun yesterday morning. Transportation in abundance was on the road and subject to your orders. I regret it has not been energetically used. The means being furnished, you were expected to handle your own troops, and I cannot understand your constant applications for me to furnish them." [8]

On November 13, Longstreet replied that Bragg's dispatch was the first notice he had that he had authority over transportation. Beyond doubt everything was distracted, at sixes and sevens, but there seems no reason to believe that Bragg did not wish Longstreet's success. He was not deceived as to his own situation and he ardently desired Longstreet's return to the weakened and disaffected army. Longstreet, no doubt, had reason to complain of imperfect arrangements, and arrangements could not have been anything but imperfect under the circumstances; but a part of his delay was due to his desire to draw extra troops to himself. Finally, when his men were all up, he moved forward.

On November 13, Wheeler was sent to surprise Maryville near Knoxville and capture the Union cavalry force there and then push on to Knoxville and attempt to secure a commanding position. Wheeler, moving to Maryville, surprised and scattered the detachment there but failed to gain any of the heights around Knoxville. Longstreet himself crossed the Tennessee River at Huff's Ferry on November 13-14. On the afternoon of November 14, Union troops, advancing from Knoxville, skirmished with the Confederates. The next day the enemy retired.

Longstreet now made a flank movement, hoping to surprise a part of the Union force, but failed. The Unionists fell back on their chain of forts around Knoxville, leaving heavy skirmish lines out in front. With these skirmishers McLaws's troops fought a brisk action, driving them back on the defenses. Wheeler, crossing the Holston River, joined Longstreet on November 20. As the Confederates had

[8] *O. R.*, ser. I, vol. XXXI, pt. III, p. 686.

brought no tools with them and were faced by the necessity of fortifying lines in front of the Union forts, they found captured picks and shovels of great value. However, the fact that he intrenched showed that Longstreet was repeating the tactics of Suffolk. He could not assume the offensive de-

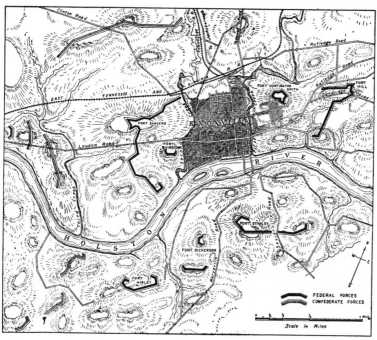

THE SIEGE OF KNOXVILLE, NOVEMBER 17—DECEMBER 4, 1863

cisively. An offensive movement with him inevitably degenerated into a siege.

Jenkins thought of assaulting the enemy's works in front of him but pronounced the attempt to be impracticable. On November 22, McLaws considered that he had pushed his lines near enough to the Union works for an attack and was ordered to make it at night. But McLaws failed to do so, alleging that his officers preferred a daylight assault.

On November 18, Longstreet sent a dispatch from his headquarters, "Four Miles from Knoxville," stating that he had driven the enemy into his fortifications around the town and had made various plans to attack him but had not done so. In fact, the real Longstreet, the Longstreet averse to attack, preferring the defensive, was showing itself. Always, when he was just about to attack a fort, something went wrong.

On November 19, Bragg reported to Richmond that Wheeler had dispersed the enemy's cavalry before Knoxville but that he had received no word from Longstreet. The latter, now an independent commander, had no intention of reporting to the hated Bragg. On the same day Bragg telegraphed Johnston that Sherman's army had arrived at Chattanooga.

On November 20, Longstreet wrote Bragg that the Union position at Knoxville was stronger than at Chattanooga. The enemy made no sign of coming out of their defenses and giving battle. The Union force was at least twenty thousand strong. It could not escape, though it was not possible to invest it completely. It seemed to be a question of starvation for the enemy or reinforcement. "Hurry the Virginia troops up to help me to shut up the place."

This shows how blind Longstreet was to the realities of the situation. He had been sent to Knoxville on what was intended as a flying movement—to destroy the enemy there and to return at once to Bragg. Instead, delays and Longstreet's ponderous deliberation had robbed the movement of the element of speed, and now he was actually proposing to starve the enemy out, a process, of course, calling for much time! Meanwhile the Union army, greatly reinforced, was preparing to move out of Chattanooga and attack the wretched Bragg, who had by this time abandoned the hopeless task of hurrying Longstreet.

On November 21, Longstreet informed Bragg: "I am close in under the enemy's works, but cannot bring him to battle, as he has the other side of the river for foraging. I think that my force is hardly strong enough to warrant my taking his works by assault."

On the same day he sent another dispatch: "Can't you spare me another division? It will shorten the work here very much."

On the same day Longstreet received a dispatch from Bragg: "We have rumors of some movements on your left and rear. Scout in that direction and keep me advised, that I may counteract them."

To this Longstreet replied, curiously enough: "The enemy's threat against your left is for the purpose of inducing you to retire. If you fail to do so, he will be obliged to retire himself, or throw a very strong force in your rear. If he does put a force behind you, you can fall upon it and destroy it, and then resume your position. With the present bad roads I doubt if he can put a very large force behind you. If he does, and you let it get well out to your rear, I think it cannot escape you." [9]

Nothing could better illustrate Longstreet's blindness than this message. Knowing the demoralized condition of Bragg's army and the reinforcements to the Union army in Chattanooga, it seems incredible that he should venture such an opinion. When he should have been hurrying back to do his best for the army on Missionary Ridge, he was thinking of nothing but his own movement.

On November 22, Bragg wrote Longstreet that he had sent General Leadbetter to confer with him and that eleven

[9] *O. R.*, ser. I, vol. XXXI, pt. III, pp. 732-33.

thousand troops were moving to join him, but that it would be well if he could finish with Burnside immediately. "From the great strength of the enemy here you will see the importance of the return of Cleburne's force as soon as possible."

From this dispatch it will be seen how little reason Longstreet had to accuse Bragg of not attempting to further his movement. By sending him Cleburne, Bragg detached from his meager army its best unit. In other words, he was running every risk to make the expedition against Knoxville a success. But no one would ever dream of this from reading Longstreet's account.

As a matter of fact, the siege of Knoxville was a folly, as Hardee and other officers saw. There was little chance of taking the place and nothing of importance to be gained by doing so. Meanwhile, the safety of the main Western army was being imperiled to push this futile expedition, so much like the Suffolk expedition of the early part of the year and so similar in its results. Against such generalship Grant and Sherman were destined to have an easy time of it.

On November 23, Longstreet telegraphed Bragg: "I think I can finish here soon, with another division. I hope that you will allow one of the two to come to me."

On the same day Longstreet sent another message stating that the enemy at Knoxville had heard Bragg was reinforcing him and was making a diversion. He urged that the troops be sent at once. On November 25, he telegraphed again, urging Bragg to send the division entire or take it back, as a smaller reinforcement would be of little use.

Longstreet was nerving himself to make an assault on one of the enemy's fortifications in the effort to take the city. It was time that he did something besides complain of lack of coöperation and troops. Knoxville stands in a beautiful mountain country on the right bank of that loveliest of mountain rivers, the Holston, perched on elevated ground a mile and a half in width. It was very strongly fortified for those times. There were two lines of works, and creeks had been dammed to provide wet ditches.

On November 23, Longstreet received a dispatch from Bragg that should have caused him to abandon the siege at once and prepare to return to Chattanooga. The Union army had moved out and attacked Bragg. Another dispatch informed Longstreet that the firing had ceased but that the enemy was still in front.

Longstreet went on with the siege as if Bragg did not exist. On November 25, Leadbetter joined him, and the two made a thorough reconnaissance of the Union position the next day, November 26. It was determined that the point offering the best chance of success was Fort Sanders, which was west of Knoxville and immediately before the town. McLaws's division lay in front of the lines here.

This work had been built by the Confederates and had been known as Fort Loudoun, but it was renamed for the Union General Sanders, who was killed there. It was a four-sided work, with the eastern face open. The south front was half finished, but the western, and exposed, face had been completed. The ditch was twelve feet wide and seven feet deep. The front of the fort was protected by an abatis of cut trees and wire, somewhat resembling the defenses of the World War.

As early as November 23, McLaws was ready to assault but his officers seemed reluctant, asking for a daylight attack instead. On November 25, Longstreet learned that the enemy was throwing cavalry forward as if to attempt to cut him off from Bragg. Something must be done at once.

That something was the assault that he and Leadbetter agreed on.

Leadbetter at first pronounced in favor of Fort Sanders, but later preferred Mabry's Hill, east of Knoxville. After another examination of the ground, he came back to Fort Sanders. Leadbetter admitted that the best policy was to reduce Knoxville by starvation but claimed that the crisis was such that the attack must be made, and immediately. At this time Longstreet knew a battle had been fought at Chattanooga but nothing of its outcome.

On November 28, McLaws was ordered to advance his line in the night and arrange for the assault. The artillery was to open as soon as light showed. After ten minutes' firing the attacking column would advance. The assault was to be made by three of McLaws's brigades. The echelon or progressive formation, tried by the Confederates so often and never with success, was adopted.

The ditch and parapets of the fort were examined with glasses. It was the opinion of the observers that the ditch could be passed without ladders. The assault was ordered to be made with bayonets and without firing a musket. No shouts were to be raised as the column rushed to the assault. Although the order was given for November 28, the attack was put off until November 29, because the weather was so murky as to hide the fort from the Confederate artillery. Longstreet does not seem to have understood that the murky weather that hid the fort from the view of the Confederates would hide the attacking Confederates from the view of the fort. In fact, the weather was just right for such an attempt, but Longstreet, always averse to attacking, was glad enough to find a reason for postponement. He was again delaying, as if he had all the time in the world and as if the fate of the Army of Tennessee was of no particular concern to him.

If Longstreet was serenely indifferent as to Bragg's fate, his officers were not. On November 28, McLaws wrote him:

"It seems to be a conceded fact that there has been a serious engagement between General Bragg's forces and those of the enemy; with what result is not known so far as I have heard. General Bragg may have maintained his position, may have repulsed the enemy, or may have been driven back. . . . If we have been defeated at Chattanooga, our communications must be made with Virginia. We cannot combine again with General Bragg, even if we should be successful in our assault on Knoxville. . . . I present these considerations and with the force they have on my mind, I beg leave to say that I think we had better delay the assault until we hear the result of the battle of Chattanooga."

To this Longstreet replied:

"I am not at all confident that General Bragg has had a serious battle at Chattanooga, but there is a report that he has, and that he has fallen back to Tunnel Hill. Under this report I am entirely convinced that our only safety is in making the assault upon the enemy's position to-morrow at daylight." [10]

Longstreet, after conferring at length with Leadbetter, had changed his mind and now intended to make the attack at dawn of November 29 instead of in the early morning of that day. After dark on November 28, he decided on the dawn attack, though many batteries had been so arranged as to bear on the fort. The advance was to be a surprise. The signal guns would be fired just before dawn, and the infantry would rush the fort.

[10] *O. R.*, ser. I, vol. XXXI, pt. I, pp. 491-94.

About 10:00 P. M. the Confederate picket line advanced on both sides of Fort Sanders. Some prisoners were taken as well as the enemy's picket pits. The Confederate skirmishers were now close to the fort and the shock troops formed behind them, but in the darkness far behind them.

When the sky lighted in the early morning, three guns gave the signal for the assault. A brief but hot artillery fire followed and the sharpshooters opened on the fort. Then the columns advanced. Owing to the darkness, they had not been formed close to the fort but several hundred yards behind.

The attackers ran into an entanglement of telegraph wires in the abatis that delayed them considerably. Two columns had been formed to attack from two sides, but they had come too close in the darkness and now converged. The ditch was found to be deep, the bank of the escarpment slippery and hard to climb. Some of the attackers succeeded in scaling the parapet and getting into the fort but were all killed or captured. The garrison, a mere handful, showed the most conspicuous gallantry in repelling an assault by overpowering numbers.

Other troops were coming up and the attack would have been resumed, probably with success, but at this moment Longstreet suspended it. A staff officer had just arrived with a telegram from President Davis announcing Bragg's defeat at Missionary Ridge on November 25 and ordering Longstreet to join him at Dalton. Then, at last and reluctantly, Longstreet abandoned the hope of accomplishing anything by attacking Knoxville and set to work to extricate his command from the dangerous position in which it had been placed by the defeat and retreat of the Army of Tennessee.

On the morning of November 29, after learning positively of Bragg's defeat, Longstreet wrote to General Ransom suggesting that the latter join him, "that we may draw all the force from Chattanooga that we can, and in that way relieve the pressure upon General Bragg. . . . Our forces here must capture the army at Knoxville, or force the enemy to relieve it by a strong detachment from the main force." [11]

Bragg's dispatch directed Longstreet to retire into Virginia if he found the road to Dalton blocked. Longstreet wrote to General Vance, commanding another detachment, urging the latter to join him. "The enemy has probably discomforted General Bragg somewhat, and I desire to get as strong a force here as possible, that we may in some way relieve him."

On this same November 29, Longstreet wrote to Leadbetter that he would make arrangements to retreat to Virginia. He would operate in the vicinity of Knoxville so as to draw forces from Chattanooga. "I may be able to do as much for him here as by joining him at this late day, and possibly divert the enemy from his purpose more than I should by going to Dalton."

This was rather fatuous. Probably Longstreet could have joined Bragg at Dalton. He had no desire to do so; he had sought to leave Bragg before calamity had overtaken the latter; now that Bragg was beaten and retreating, he had no wish whatever to go back to him. Longstreet was at last at the head of his own army, small as it was, and he was dreaming of doing great things. It did not suit his purpose to become involved in the new catastrophes that might befall the unhappy Army of Tennessee. He had renounced that army forever.

Meanwhile Richmond had wired Bragg relieving him of command and appointing Hardee in his place. The latter

[11] *O. R.,* ser. I, vol. XXXI, pt. III, pp. 758-59.

had a modesty, a knowledge of his limitations that would have been priceless if possessed by Longstreet. Hardee declined the command on the ground of his inability to lead an army, but accepted pending a successor.

It was on November 30 that Longstreet received a telegram from Richmond informing him that Bragg had fallen back to Dalton and leaving the former free to join him or to return to Virginia.

On December 2, Longstreet wrote to Bragg stating that he still hoped to capture the garrison at Knoxville or force the enemy to relieve it. "I shall hope that you will prevent any succor from Chattanooga." It seems almost incredible that Longstreet should ask poor beaten and discredited Bragg to prevent the triumphant enemy from sending relieving troops from Chattanooga, but it so is written. Again he called on Ransom to join him, desiring to build up that independent army of his.

At this juncture Lee ventured to write a letter of advice to Davis on affairs in Tennessee, and Davis in return telegraphed Lee on December 5, asking him if he could go to Dalton. Lee declined, feeling that he was too badly needed in Virginia.

The authorities were almost in despair. The autumn offensive, for which they had held such high hopes, had failed utterly. The Army of Tennessee was not only beaten but disgraced. Surely somebody was needed at Dalton. Wheeler had sent Longstreet word that he would protect the latter while moving to Dalton, but Longstreet had decided that he was cut off from the Army of Tennessee. Bragg was out, Hardee was only temporary. The question was who would succeed to the command and what should be done. It was Longstreet's supreme hour of opportunity. If he had moved quickly to join Bragg as soon as he heard of the latter's difficulty, he would have been on hand when Bragg was relieved and would have been the natural successor. But Longstreet paid no attention whatever to the news from Bragg until the fact was forced on him that the latter had been routed.

Longstreet had gone West hoping to become Bragg's successor, but he did not wish to succeed him under such circumstances. He was shying off from trouble and imagining he was saving himself from discredit. On the contrary, the authorities had taken his measure and no longer considered him as an army commander. He had been tried and found exceedingly wanting.

By December 6, Longstreet had abandoned the vain dream of capturing Knoxville or preventing its relief and was beginning to fall back toward Virginia. On December 7, he telegraphed President Davis: "If my command can be more usefully employed in some other part of the country, please order the transportation for it."

Yes, Longstreet preferred to be somewhere else. He had no stomach for facing Grant and Grant's formidable army with a far inferior force.

It cannot be said that he accomplished much good for the cause in Tennessee, in spite of having had a large hand in winning the great battle of Chickamauga. He, together with Hill, had so augmented the discontent prevailing in Bragg's army that the army had been ruined and the head of it relegated to chief-of-staff duties in Richmond. Out of the strained situation in Tennessee had developed two political factions in the Confederacy: one including Joseph E. Johnston, Longstreet, and the other opponents of the administration; the other, the administrative faction, which counted among its adherents Bragg and Hood, the latter of whom had given up his allegiance to his former corps commander,

Longstreet, and was now a corps commander himself under Johnston and perhaps already regarded as the latter's potential successor.

Congress, on February 17, 1864, passed resolutions of thanks to Longstreet and his troops, "the commanding general ever displaying great ability, skill and prudence in command, and the officers and men the most heroic bravery, fortitude and energy in every duty they have been called upon to perform."

Perhaps this consoled Longstreet. Perhaps.

CHAPTER XVI

DISILLUSIONMENT

LONGSTREET did not immediately give up the siege of Knoxville because of Bragg's defeat, though it is hard to say what he expected to accomplish under the circumstances. On December 1 a courier from Grant to Burnside was captured bearing a dispatch that revealed the Union plans. Three columns were moving to the relief of Knoxville. It became evident that the Confederates could not remain much longer in that vicinity, though Longstreet lingered for several days. The unhappy Bragg had ordered his cavalry to return to him, and he surely needed it, but Longstreet retained it for a time, unwilling to relinquish any arm of his force.

In this dilemma, for it was a serious situation, Longstreet decided to move around Knoxville and up the Holston River in the effort to form a junction with a force alleged to be coming to join him from Cumberland Gap. The trains were put in motion on December 3, and on December 4 the army began its march along the west side of the Holston. Blain's Crossroads was reached on December 5 and on December 6, Rutledge, where Longstreet remained for two days foraging for food. He halted again at Rogersville, on December 9, where he parted company with Wheeler's cavalry, which made its way to Bragg in Georgia. The army was almost without food except corn, which had to be ground in the few mills to be found.

The Confederate authorities had now to decide what was to be done with Bragg's army and Longstreet's detachment.

To Longstreet's suggestion that Lee be sent to Dalton to attempt to bring order out of chaos and hope out of despair, Lee returned to Davis the following answer on December 7:

"I have had the honor to receive your dispatch, inquiring whether I could go to Dalton. I can if desired, but of the expediency of the measure you can judge better than I can. Unless it is intended that I should take permanent command, I can see no good that will result, even if in that event any could be accomplished. I also fear that I would not receive cordial coöperation, and I think it necessary if I am withdrawn from here that a commander for this army be sent to it. General Ewell's condition, I fear, is too feeble to undergo the fatigue and labor incident to the position. I hope Your Excellency will not suppose that I am offering any obstacles to any measure you may think necessary. I only seek to give you the opportunity to form your opinion after a full consideration of the subject. I have not that confidence either in my strength or ability as would lead me of my own option to undertake the command in question."

Finding Lee thus reluctant, Davis did not press him. It must ever remain a matter of regret that he did not go to Tennessee in September instead of Longstreet, but the latter did not suggest Lee's going until he himself had gone and failed. Lee, with his ability and with the confidence he inspired in all but a few of the highest officers, might have won a victory at Chattanooga of far-reaching consequences. As it was, the discredited Bragg could make nothing of the victory when won, partly because of his own faults and partly because of the disaffection of the officers and men. While the campaign of Chattanooga was being won and lost, Lee was doing nothing of consequence in Virginia and might have been spared. Now that the Army of Tennessee was ruined, there was little chance for him to do anything at Dalton. The government should have used its best soldier when opportunity knocked; to send him to repair irreparable damage was to ask too much, and Davis seems to have felt this on reading Lee's letter. Eventually the despairing step was taken of putting Johnston at the head of the Army of Tennessee, with wild schemes of reinforcing that army to such an extent as to enable it to assume the offensive in the spring. Bragg, called to Richmond as a sort of head of staff, formulated these plans with a mind full of rancor because of his own failure. In reality, Davis's disastrous policy extended to the point where the man who had failed was made mentor and director of his successor. Nothing but disaster could have resulted from such folly, but Davis was determined he would show the country his unabated confidence in Bragg, even if Bragg might no longer command an army.

On December 8, Longstreet sent a dispatch from his whereabouts near Bean's Station, to which place he was being followed by Union cavalry, stating that he had been forced to abandon the siege of Knoxville but that he was trying to strike the Union column coming from Cumberland Gap or some of the other Union forces in the vicinity. He could not expect to accomplish much unless railroad transportation were provided. As it was, his transportation was so limited that he could scarcely haul wheat and corn to the mills for grinding. It was a poor prospect after the glowing hopes with which he had gone West.

Longstreet telegraphed for instructions on December 9, and received a rather tart answer from Cooper that no instructions could be sent him until the authorities knew more of the situation. Longstreet answered, on December 13, that the enemy forces in East Tennessee numbered twenty-seven thousand men and that he himself had twenty thousand since

Ransom had joined him. Although in great need of shoes and clothing, he did not wish to move East, as he considered his position a good one from which to strike the Unionists if they sought to invade Georgia. He thought that sufficient supplies could be found to subsist his army in East Tennessee for the winter.

Near Bean's Station, on December 14, Longstreet made an attempt to strike the enemy following him, and a sharp skirmish took place in which several hundred men were killed or wounded. But beyond capturing seventy wagons laden with supplies Longstreet accomplished nothing.

Hardee, still at the head of the Army of Tennessee, suggested an offensive into Tennessee and Kentucky as the best defensive, at the same time urging a concentration of all available forces in that army. The idea of a forward movement instead of retreat was welcome to Davis and he endorsed it; Bragg was charged with seeing the movement made. On December 17, Johnston was specifically ordered to take command of the Army of Tennessee, and he found this offensive campaign an inheritance from his short-time predecessor, Hardee. That the government was still living in a fool's paradise is evident from a dispatch of Davis to Johnston on December 23 in which the President said:

"The reports concerning the battle of Missionary Ridge show that our loss in killed and wounded was not great, and that the reverse sustained is not attributable to any general demoralization or reluctance to encounter the opposing army. . . . In a letter written to me soon after the battle, General Bragg expressed his unshaken confidence in the courage and morale of the troops."

What thoughts are fathered by wishes! Davis, in his longing for success, was catching at such straws as the beaten general's confidence in the morale of an army that had fled from its foes. In fact, Missionary Ridge was the most ominous of all the events of the war, because there for the first time a Southern army had refused to face the enemy. And yet Davis was dreaming that its morale was unimpaired! Surely little could be looked for but the downfall of the cause.

Longstreet had carefully set the stage for the action near Bean's Station. He had the Union force almost enclosed in a gap in the mountains, but not quite. Longstreet says:

"Thus the troops at the Gap got out during the night, some running over the huge oaks and heavy wood tangles along the crest, by torchlight, to their comrades, some going west by easier ways. So when I sent up in the morning, looking for their doleful surrender, my men found only empty camp kettles, mess-pans, tents and a few abandoned guns, and twelve prisoners, while the Yankees were, no doubt, sitting around their camp fires enjoying the joke with their comrades they had rejoined." [1]

Burnside at Knoxville had been succeeded in command by Foster. Longstreet began to concentrate to attack the new commander, who for his part received reinforcements and advanced as if to offer battle. The Unionists, however, fell back to Blain's Crossroads, where they took position and awaited Longstreet. But the latter was in no mood to attack; the offensive was ever distasteful to him. Believing that Foster had twenty thousand men and himself less than twenty thousand, he did not think the game worth the candle.

And now the inclement season in the mountains put an end to effective military operations. The Confederate troops who remained with the colors were, by this time, seasoned

[1] *M. to A.*, p. 513.

veterans able to bear almost any degree of hardship. Incredible as it may seem, the only food supply at times was parched corn, of which there was enough, and the men were in excellent health. But the troops had no overcoats and their lack of clothing and shoes was the hardship they found most difficult to bear.

Longstreet now proceeded to cross the Holston River, in order to reach the railroad, not far away. By December 20, the troops were on the east side of the river, and Longstreet's headquarters were at Russellville on Christmas Day of 1863.

The troops were quartered in one of the most beautiful regions of the United States, the country of the French Broad. Little touched by the war, in it the hungry, ragged, and shaggy Confederates found abundance of food. "Our wagons," says Longstreet, "immediately on entering the fields were loaded to overflowing. Pumpkins were on the ground in places like apples under a tree. Cattle, sheep, and swine, poultry, vegetables, maple sugar, honey were all abundant for the immediate wants of the troops." But he added, "With all the plentitude of provisions and many things which seemed at the time luxuries, we were not quite happy. Tattered blankets, garments and shoes (the latter going—many gone) opened ways, on all sides, for piercing winter blasts. . . . For shoes we were obliged to resort to the raw hides of beef cattle as temporary protection from the frozen ground. Then we began to find soldiers who could tan the hides of our beeves, some who could make shoes, some who could make shoe-pegs, some who could make shoe lasts, so that it came about that the hides passed rapidly from the beeves to the feet of the soldiers in the form of comfortable shoes. Then came the opening of the railroad, and lo and behold! a shipment of three thousand shoes." [2]

Rest for the infantry but incessant activity for the cavalry, which under W. E. Jones and Martin was constantly skirmishing with the Union cavalry of General Sturgis. On January 3, 1864, Jones gained a brilliant little victory, capturing four hundred prisoners and a number of wagons.

Intense cold put an end to all activity for a time, for on New Year's day of 1864 Longstreet noted that the thermometer dropped below zero, and it remained in that vicinity for two weeks.

And now Longstreet had time to consider the situation and to learn how his stock had fallen. Sent West in the hope that he would prove to be the genius the government was looking for to redeem the losses of 1863 and to clear the way for victory, he had failed and had utterly lost the confidence of the authorities, who were sore over his contemptuous treatment of Bragg and largely blamed him for the unfortunate division of the army that had paved the way for the débâcle of Missionary Ridge. Absent from that field, Longstreet had heard the news of Bragg's disaster with a complacency that vanished the moment he found that he, too, was blamed. The lively Mrs. James Chesnut noted in her diary what a failure Longstreet was when detached from Lee. The country thought the same—that Longstreet was a capable subordinate under a good general but quite incompetent to manage independent operations, something he had always itched to do.

Another full general was appointed by Congress and Longstreet, who seems to have expected the place, was passed over in favor of Kirby Smith, the trans-Mississippi commander. Smith, whose grade had been below Long-

[2] *M. to A.,* p. 521.

street's, was thus elevated over him. Longstreet bitterly commented on this:

"A soldier's honor is his all, and of that they [the authorities] would rob him and degrade him in the eyes of his troops. The cause had passed beyond hope, except from miraculous interposition. The occasion seemed to enforce resignation, but that would have been unsoldierly conduct. Dispassionate judgment suggested, as the proper rounding of the soldier's life, to stay and go down with faithful comrades of long and arduous service." [3]

Longstreet was finding the usual solace for failure in taking action against his subordinates; like Bragg, his non-successes were always due to others' faults. In the whole course of his narrative it is difficult to find an instance in which Longstreet accepts the blame for anything. He is always sagacious, right; the other fellow loses campaigns and battles because he does not follow Longstreet's directions. Thus it is, chapter after chapter. But now, in spite of his self-complacency and self-approval, it was borne in upon him that the country considered him a failure as an army commander. As a corps general in Lee's army, not he but Lee had carried the burden of responsibility; but when Longstreet marched off to Knoxville he put himself in a position where he could not, plausibly, blame anybody else for the entire lack of success. He had made a dull and useless campaign, and one that had cost the Confederacy perhaps its last chance of victory; and he could convince nobody—hardly even himself—that failure was due to Bragg or somebody or something else. He now discovered, what he does not seem to have understood before, that the commander of an army is praised for success and blamed

[3] *M. to A.,* p. 525.

for failure. He felt it was unjust because his opportunity had been small.

Some time before, Longstreet had preferred charges against a brigadier, J. B. Robertson, for the failure of the night attack in Lookout Valley on October 28. Robertson was relieved of his command but restored to it by Bragg. However, Hood was interested in the prosecution of Robertson, who was ordered to Bristol to await a court-martial.

That was only the beginning. On December 17, Major General Lafayette McLaws, a noted officer, was relieved of duty and ordered to Augusta, Georgia. McLaws naturally asked what was the cause of his suspension from duty and received a very vague answer:

"You have exhibited a want of confidence in the efforts and plans which the commanding general has thought proper to adopt, and he is apprehensive that this feeling will extend more or less to the troops under your command. Under these circumstances the commanding general has felt that the interest of the public service would be advanced by your separation from him, and as he could not himself leave, he decided upon the issue of the order which you have received." [4]

This is a classic illustration of the exquisite quality of human inconsistency. Bragg might have applied those words "want of confidence in the efforts and plans which the commanding general has thought proper to adopt" with the utmost literalness to Longstreet; and, much more, he might have charged Longstreet with active efforts to subvert his authority and bring about his removal, something with which the unfortunate McLaws, victim of Longstreet's ire, could not be blamed. As for McLaws, it would have been singular if so intelligent an officer had felt any confidence in the

[4] *M. to A.,* p. 519.

blundering movement by which nearly one half of the army was detached at a critical moment and sent off on a wild-goose chase.

The accusations against McLaws went much further than a mere charge of lack of confidence in the commanding officer. He was charged with neglect of duty on November 28 in not placing his sharpshooters where they could harass Fort Sanders effectively: that on November 29, when the assault was made by McLaws's troops, they were not properly instructed and organized for the assault. And that in the assault of November 29, he made his attack at a point where the ditch was impassable.

A court-martial convened at Richmond, on May 4, 1864, to try the culprit. Of the first two charges he was found not guilty but was found guilty of the third charge, that of failing to provide means to cross the ditch, and was suspended from his command for sixty days. The court had met in February, 1864, but its proceedings were irregular, as Adjutant General Cooper pointed out. The finding of the court on the third count was not sustained by the evidence. Witnesses attested that the ditch where it was entered by the Confederates was not more than four and a half feet deep and, therefore, passable. The sentence of the court was disapproved and McLaws was immediately returned to duty.[5]

Thus ended in failure Longstreet's effort to find compensation for his chagrin or to put the onus for defeat on another. Longstreet's comment on President Davis's action is curious enough:

"The President disapproved the proceedings, passing reprimand upon the court and the commanding general, and ordered the officer to be restored to duty, which was very

[5] O. R., ser. I, vol. XXXI, pt. I, p. 505.

gratifying to me, who could have taken several reprimands to relieve a personal friend of embarrassing position. General McLaws was a classmate, and had been a warm personal friend from childhood. I had no desire to put charges against him, and should have failed to do so even under the directions of the authorities. I am happy to say that our personal relations are as close and interesting as they have ever been." [6]

One may well think that Longstreet's conception of friendship was peculiar and one will certainly challenge the statement that he had no desire to make charges against McLaws. If Longstreet had not desired it, the charges would hardly have been made by subordinate officers. All the evidence goes to show that he approved and even inspired the proceedings against McLaws, apparently with the desire to find a scapegoat for the failure at Knoxville, about which he had grown sensitive as he became aware of the country-wide criticism of it. In other words, Longstreet had done precisely what he had condemned Bragg for doing.

There was still another victim of Longstreet's wrath. Brigadier General E. M. Law, an officer of good record, had come under the ban and was the object of a still more serious charge. This accusation was that Law, in December, 1863, had obtained leave of absence from Longstreet on the pretext that he intended resigning from the infantry and seeking service in the cavalry, but that his real design was to obtain a transfer of his brigade from Longstreet's command to some other quarter. This charge was not entertained by the Richmond authorities and then Longstreet went on to make a second accusation against Law, that he had asked for a leave of absence to take his resignation to Richmond but had clandestinely destroyed the document in-

[6] *M. to A.,* p. 548.

stead of delivering it. Lee himself was so much under Longstreet's influence that, when the matters against Law were submitted to him, he stated, "I examined the charges against General Law and find them of a very grave character." He recommended an investigation.

Davis wisely refused to entertain an accusation of so vague and peculiar a character against an officer of good repute. He said truly enough: "If General Law has misbehaved at Lookout Mountain or elsewhere in the face of the enemy, charges should have been preferred, not injurious statements made in a letter to prejudice his case in a different transaction. General Longstreet has seriously offended against good order and military discipline in rearresting an officer who had been released by the War Department without any new offense having been alleged." [7]

On April 27, Longstreet replied to Lee's letter informing him that Davis had declined to entertain charges against Law and ordered him returned to duty. He declared that in his opinion the failures at Lookout Mountain on October 28 and at Campbell's Station on November 16 were due to "a want of conduct upon the part of Brigadier-General Law. . . . If my efforts to maintain discipline, spirit, and zeal in the discharge of official duty are to be set aside by the return of General Law and his restoration to duty without trial, it cannot be well for me to remain in command. . . . It is necessary, therefore, that General Law should be brought to trial upon the charges that have been preferred against him, or that I be relieved from duty in the Confederate States service. I have ordered the rearrest of General Law upon his return." [8]

The matter became so serious that the Richmond authori-

[7] O. R., ser. I, vol. XXXI, pt. I, p. 474.
[8] Ibid., p. 475.

ties thought of transferring Longstreet to another point, but Lee, who had been rejoined by Longstreet, objected. The result was that Law was retired from active service, a victim apparently of Longstreet's resentment at his efforts to be sent elsewhere. Longstreet was now experiencing the bitterness that Bragg had tasted of having officers seek other service. An examination of the evidence leads irresistibly to that conclusion, for Longstreet did not dare to go so far as to make representations to a court-martial that Law had misbehaved in the field. But Law had committed the error of distrusting and disliking Longstreet, and that was too much for the latter to endure.

These proceedings discredited Longstreet with the Richmond authorities, who were acute enough to understand the real motive behind them. It had probably much to do with the conclusion Davis had come to that Longstreet was of no value as an independent commander; he may have thought that Longstreet, if given time enough, would put every subordinate under arrest. For the harassed government to have to listen to vague and unimportant charges against soldiers of standing was too much.

It thus followed that Longstreet's recommendations fell on deaf ears. They were many but all equally futile. In mid-January, the Union army in East Tennessee advanced against him. He prepared to anticipate the enemy by moving to Dandridge, a town on the French Broad thirty miles from Knoxville. Martin, pushing boldly ahead with his cavalry, had a skirmish with the Union cavalry and drove them back. Longstreet prepared a turning movement that he hoped would catch the Unionists, and almost succeeded, but just in time Granger, commanding the Union force, retired. A rain changed the roads into seas of mud and made pursuit useless. Thus Longstreet lost another opportunity of accomplishing something. Of late all of his operations had been of that nature—well-devised encircling movements that failed at the last moment for some want of combination.

In writing of this adventure Longstreet reveals his naïve vanity, which was catching at any crumb of comfort:

"While yet on the streets of Dandridge, giving directions for such pursuit as we could make, a lady came out upon the sidewalk and invited us into her parlors. When the orders for pursuit were given, I dismounted, and with some members of my staff walked in. After the compliments of the season were passed, we were asked to be seated, and she told something of General Granger during the night before. She had never heard a person swear about another as General Granger did about me. Some of the officers proposed to stop and make a battle, but General Granger swore and said it 'was no use to stop and fight Longstreet. You can't whip him. It don't make any difference whether he has one man or a hundred thousand.' Presently she brought out a flask that General Granger had forgotten, and thought that I should have it. It had about two refreshing inches left in it. Though not left with compliments, it was accepted." [9]

On January 21, Longstreet prepared to move toward Knoxville, in which direction the cavalry had scouted, picking up wagons and a few stragglers from Granger's command. That brought him again to the attention of Grant, who said to Thomas, "I want Longstreet routed and pursued beyond the limits of the state of Tennessee." Foster was ordered to use his cavalry in a raid from Cumberland Gap in Longstreet's rear. On January 26, Longstreet learned that the Union cavalry had moved up the French Broad above Dandridge, and Martin was sent to get in their rear and scatter them. However, in a severe engagement on Jan-

[9] *M. to A.,* p. 529.

uary 27, Martin was defeated with the loss of two hundred prisoners and guns.

While Armstrong's cavalry was holding a part of the Union force, B. R. Johnson's division crossed the river. Armstrong was fighting desperately when Johnson's infantry came to his rescue, but the Union cavalry retired at the approach of the Confederate infantry. Still worried by Longstreet's presence in Tennessee, Grant proposed several raids for the purpose of getting rid of him. In response, Foster called for ten thousand more troops and a ponton bridge to cross the Holston River at Strawberry Plains.

Meanwhile Longstreet was preparing to cross the river at the same place, ordering Jenkins ahead to prepare the way. Grant was thinking of sending Thomas to East Tennessee with a considerable force. He dispatched Schofield on February 11:

"I deem it of the utmost importance to drive Longstreet out immediately, so as to furlough the balance of our veterans, and to prepare for a spring campaign of our own choosing, instead of permitting the enemy to dictate it for us. Thomas is ordered to start ten thousand men, besides the remainder of Granger's corps, at once. He will take no artillery." [10]

Grant, however, soon changed his mind, probably on learning something of the size of Longstreet's command. Consultations with Schofield and Foster led him to this change, as he reported to Halleck. He added, "No danger whatever to be apprehended in East Tennessee."

Under the circumstances Grant was right, but he might well have been mistaken if the Confederate authorities had taken a different view of the situation. Meanwhile Longstreet was trying to do something. Jenkins laid the ponton

[10] *M. to A.*, p. 535.

bridge over the Holston at Strawberry Plains, and Longstreet asked for ten thousand additional troops. Lee approved, proposing to send Pickett's division to him.

As a matter of fact, Longstreet was in a position of strategic importance, as he points out in his book. A Confederate force in East Tennessee might have been a thorn in the flesh to the Unionists in several ways—first, in threatening Sherman from the flank or rear in his invasion of Georgia, and secondly as menacing the Union forces left in Tennessee as soon as Sherman should move down into Georgia. It is probable that Davis would have seen the situation in this light and would have given Longstreet the reinforcement asked for, if the fire of his resentment had not burned high against the commander of the First Corps. Bragg, back in Richmond, had had abundant opportunity to complain of Longstreet's lack of loyalty and practical insubordination; and Longstreet had made himself the object of official dislike by preferring charges of a rather frivolous nature against several officers. The Richmond authorities had come to the conclusion that he could accomplish nothing as an independent commander; the question that presented itself to their minds was whether he should be ordered to join Johnston in Georgia or be sent back to Lee in Virginia.

Davis decided the issue quickly and sharply. On February 19, a telegram from Richmond notified Longstreet that he could not have the reinforcement asked for and at the same time directed him to send Martin's cavalry to Johnston. Longstreet replied that the loss of the cavalry would force him to abandon his projected movement against Knoxville and to fall back to Virginia.

Longstreet began his definite movement toward the East on February 22. He was not disturbed, as the Union cavalry had suffered from the severe weather and was in no condition to pursue energetically. Behind Bull's Gap the army went into camp, extending from the Holston River on the right to the Nolichucky River on the left. Here they remained, doing well for the time and circumstances, for those veterans were so tough and hard, so strong and healthy, that weather or privation had little effect on them. Ragged, shaggy, bearded like the pard, Longstreet's veterans lived cheerfully, if not merrily, through the remaining weeks of that winter.

That Longstreet was not in favor at Richmond is evident from a letter written to McLaws by Bragg, who was Davis's confidential adviser:

"This matter has been carried so far that self-defense may require you to attack, and I can assure you the evidence in my possession is ample to convict of disobedience of orders, neglect of duty, and want of cordial coöperation and support, which resulted in all the disasters after Chickamauga. This matter is worthy of your consideration. General Law has seen me on the subject, as far as his command is concerned. General Benning, I learn, is equally sore, and under the ban of authority because he prefers his country to a faction." [11]

Meanwhile Longstreet had received from Richmond the plan prepared for a campaign by the Army of Tennessee in the spring. This army, commanded by Johnston, was to advance into Tennessee and be joined by Longstreet. It was to break the Union communications and find an opportunity of fighting a battle at an advantage. The plan was impracticable under the circumstances, as the greater part of Tennessee was held by Union forces and as much subsistence and transportation would be needed for an advance through East Tennessee. Such a movement, too, would leave Georgia unguarded from invasion. Johnston received the plan without

[11] *O. R.*, ser. I, vol. LII, pt. II, pp. 633-34. March 4, 1864.

enthusiasm, and Longstreet wrote to him, on March 5, 1864, that it looked uninviting to himself. He called Johnston's attention to the possibility of the enemy's getting in the rear and cutting the army off from its base, which would necessitate dispersal in the mountains.

On March 7, Davis wrote Longstreet that Martin's cavalry had been ordered to Johnston because the latter was badly in need of horse and because Longstreet had more of that arm than he could find subsistence for. He answered, also, a letter of Longstreet's of February 22 in which the latter had proposed to mount his entire command and invade Kentucky. With only mounted troops Longstreet thought he could maintain himself until Johnston joined him.[12] Davis answered that he did not know where to procure the horses and besides it would lead to a wide separation of the Confederate forces. He proposed instead for Longstreet to unite with Johnston at Maryville and strike one of the enemy's units. He added:

"It is needless to point out to you . . . the importance— I may say the necessity—of our taking the initiative." [13]

On March 21, Bragg wired Johnston that the latter had not indicated his acceptance of the plan for a forward movement into Tennessee and Kentucky.

On March 16, 1864, Longstreet had communicated his own plan to the President in a long letter. He reverts to his idea of mounting his whole command and moving into Kentucky, maintaining that many of the men were able to mount themselves. By uniting with Johnston at Maryville, he would force the enemy to concentrate at Nashville for battle. Longstreet, however, was afraid that the two forces could not unite in time, as they were about two hundred

---

[12] *Ibid.*, vol. XXXII, pt. II, p. 791.
[13] *Ibid.*, vol. LII, pt. II, p. 635.

miles apart. Both commands would have to carry everything in the way of subsistence and ammunition. The enemy would be in a position to attack one or the other of the bodies before they could unite. Longstreet then advanced the proposal to concentrate at Johnston's position troops from Mississippi and his own force. But the best possible move would be to concentrate an army at Abingdon, Virginia, by moving Beauregard from South Carolina and joining him there with Longstreet's force. The Confederates could advance into Kentucky if united. The armies of Johnston and Beauregard should be able to unite without difficulty.

On the same day Longstreet wrote to Lee stating his proposal to the President and adding that he feared his views would not be favored by Davis and Bragg. He reasserted his confidence in his plan, declaring, "It can be made an entire success. Your influence with the President, and your prestige as a great leader, will enable you to cause its adoption and successful execution. You can remain with your present army until the head of our column reaches Cumberland Mountains. [From this last statement it would seem that Longstreet expected Lee to take command of the united force, though he says nothing of this in his letter to Davis.] . . . My great hope is in you, and I know that this is the feeling of the army, and I believe it to be of the country.

"You complain of my excess of confidence, but I think that it is based upon good judgment and a proper appreciation of our difficulties. I have entire confidence if our affairs are properly managed, but I have none if they are not well managed." [14]

On March 28, Lee answered Longstreet, stating that either of the plans would do if it could be carried out. "You and Johnston can alone judge of their feasibility. If one or

[14] *O. R.*, ser. I, vol. XXXII, pt. III, pp. 641-42.

the other can be executed, it should be commenced at once. If not, we shall be obliged to conform to their plans and concentrate wherever they are going to attack us."

On March 4, Longstreet had suggested to Lee that the latter join him, leaving enough troops in Virginia to hold Richmond until Johnston's army could reach there.

On March 5, Longstreet wrote to Johnston stating that he had received from the President a proposal for the junction of the two forces with a view of moving into Middle Tennessee on the enemy's communications. Two routes are suggested, one passing south of Knoxville and the Holston River, the other passing Knoxville on the north. On the former course he would have to cross six rivers. The other course would throw him near Knoxville, the enemy's stronghold, and he would have to cross two broad rivers. But Johnston's difficulties seemed to him to be greater than his own.

Johnston replied on March 13 that the President's plan seemed impracticable to him. In the first place, the enemy could prevent the proposed junction at Madisonville. In the second place, it would be necessary to have ten days' food and forage for the army in moving from Madisonville into Middle Tennessee. He declared that the only sound plan for an offensive was to beat the enemy in Georgia and then follow him into Tennessee.

Longstreet wrote to Beauregard proposing the joint movement into Kentucky, but on March 15 stated that he had altered his plan, suggesting now a junction at Pound Gap and a march on Louisville. The united forces could hold Kentucky long enough to force the enemy to withdraw from Georgia and Tennessee. A commentary on his prophetic powers is this paragraph:

"We are all equally interested in the successful issue of

this year's operations, as by success we shall surely win a speedy and happy termination of the war. If, on the other hand, we are unfortunate we shall almost as surely have a continuance of the war for the next four years."

On March 16, Longstreet wrote to Johnston:

"The President and General Bragg seem bent on a campaign into Middle Tennessee. They may adopt my proposition, however, and move Beauregard and myself into Kentucky by Pound Gap. I think it the strongest effort that has been attempted during the war and have confidence in its resulting in a speedy peace.

"General Lee came down to assist me in having it adopted, but we do not know yet what will be done. All agree in the idea that we should take the initiative. If I were with you I am satisfied that we could work out great results, but it would be by a slower and much more tedious and difficult process." [15]

This idea of a concentration of forces for a campaign in Kentucky and Tennessee was a good one, but it came too late. It will be seen from Longstreet's letter that Lee went to Richmond to urge the adoption of Longstreet's plan, but, if so, he was unsuccessful. It was not likely that any ideas of Longstreet would be accepted by the government as long as Bragg, bitter at the treatment he had suffered at Longstreet's hands, was the President's confidential adviser.

Davis and Bragg had set their minds on Johnston's making a forward movement into Middle Tennessee, a maneuver much too daring and too risky for that embodiment of caution. On February 27, 1864, Johnston wrote Bragg that the President and Secretary of War Seddon had given him the impression that it was intended for him to make a forward movement in the spring. In that case much

[15] *O. R.,* ser. I, vol. XXXII, pt. III, p. 637.

would be needed in the way of preparation: more troops, transportation, supplies and forage, pontons and a thousand additional horses. It would be necessary to include Longstreet in the movement as well as troops from Beauregard's and Polk's departments.[16]

Johnston was absolutely right in this: he could not hope to move into Tennessee, in the face of Sherman's powerful army, without more troops and, particularly, without more equipment and supplies than he had. In any event the play would have been in the nature of a forlorn hope, but it would have been madness under the existing conditions. The authorities, however, did not take this view of the situation, particularly Bragg, the chief of staff, who believed or professed to believe that the Army of Tennessee was in good condition for offensive operations.

Meanwhile Longstreet, at Greeneville, Tennessee, uncertain as to his destination but exceedingly fertile in plans that the War Department hardly considered, was getting into a pickle for want of supplies. On March 19, he appealed to Richmond, stating that his force was in danger of starving and would soon be helpless if not relieved. A few days later he informed the authorities that the sending of Martin's horse to Georgia had reduced his cavalry to such an extent that he would be forced to fall back to the line of the Holston River.

On March 25, President Davis replied to Longstreet's suggestions for the coming campaign. To send troops from South Carolina and to give Johnston reinforcements from Alabama and the West would expose the principal cities of the South to capture. He continued to hope that Longstreet would make a junction with Johnston at Maryville, Tennessee.

[16] *Ibid.*, pt. II, pp. 808-9.

Notwithstanding this snub, Longstreet continued to urge his campaign in Kentucky. He could go to Dalton but he would have to travel a thousand miles to get there. He recommended Kershaw to take command of McLaws's division, and Lee effected this. Longstreet added, "I regret that I am in no condition now for any kind of operations. We are living on very short rations, particularly of forage." On April 2, he wired Davis that he would be able to move to Maryville as soon as he had sufficient provisions.

On the same day Longstreet received a severe rebuke from Davis. He had sought to exchange Field for Buckner but had failed. Cooper wrote him:

"The advice you have asked as to 'the distinguished services rendered by this officer and the high recommendations of his commanding generals which have induced the Government to make this unusual promotion and assignment' (I quote your own words) is considered highly insubordinate and demands rebuke. It is also a reflection upon a gallant and meritorious officer, who has been severely wounded in battle in the cause of the Confederate States, and is deemed unbecoming the high position and dignity of the officer who thus makes the reflection." [17]

It is evident that Longstreet was anything but in the good graces of the authorities, who were in a position to point out and refute his impractical propositions. For Longstreet to ask for thousands of horses from the government, and then to have to admit that he could not feed those he had, was to expose himself to ridicule. His proposal to mount his whole army and ride into Kentucky was unfortunate, as it no doubt had something to do with the blindness of the authorities to the advantages of having a force in the mountains of Tennessee. The Georgia campaign of 1864 might

[17] O. R., ser. I, vol. XXXII, pt. III, p. 738.

have been materially affected if Longstreet, properly prepared, could have emerged on Sherman's rear and attacked his communications. In fact, this seems to have been the one genuine strategic movement open to the Confederates in the spring of 1864.

The authorities, however, thought otherwise; Bragg had filled Davis with the idea of the practicability of a forward movement into Tennessee, even in the face of Sherman's army. Thinking it quite possible that Johnston could conduct such a campaign, Davis and Bragg became impatient when the new commander of the Army of Tennessee made all kinds of objections—objections that were sound enough but that the Richmond authorities regarded as mere subterfuges used to avoid decisive action.

It was at this juncture, on April 13, that John B. Hood, now minus a leg but a corps commander in the Army of Tennessee, began what was, in effect, an intrigue looking to the removal of Johnston from the command of the army. He wrote Bragg from Dalton, where the army still remained:

"I received your letter and am sorry to inform you that I have done all in my power to induce General Johnston to accept the proposition you made to move forward. He will not consent, as he desires the troops to be sent here and it is left to him as to what use should be made of them.

"I regret this exceedingly, as my heart was fixed upon our going to the front and regaining Tennessee and Kentucky. . . .

"When we are to be in a better condition to drive the enemy from our country I am not able to comprehend. To regain Tennessee would be of more value to us than a half dozen victories in Virginia. . . .

"I still hope we shall yet go forward; it is for the President and yourself to decide. I well know you have to grapple with many difficulties, as the President has done from the beginning of the war. He has directed us thus far, and in him I have unbounded confidence." [18]

Johnston wished to take the offensive if he had sufficient means, but he was resolved not to do it with the army he then had. He sent an adjutant general, B. S. Ewell, to Richmond to present his case to the authorities. Ewell represented his chief well enough except that he was, in the presence of the President, too confident of Johnston's ability to take the offensive under certain circumstances. The question was put to Johnston whether he could assume the offensive if given fifteen thousand more troops, but the cautious general would not be thus cornered. In the end, he did not go forward, for the very good reason that it was impossible; all that was in his power was to stand on the defensive against Sherman. Precisely the same situation presented itself in Virginia, where Lee was reduced to the defensive against Grant. The one move of possible consequences, an attack in force on Sherman's communications, was not tried until months later, when it was too late.

By this time all of Longstreet's schemes had come to naught. To tell the truth there was little of merit in them, for Longstreet had small idea of the line of demarcation between the possible and impossible. To some extent his proposals were governed by his desire to play an important part in the coming campaign; it had not yet penetrated his head that he had been weighed and found wanting, that his campaign against Knoxville was a model of futility. He imagined that the authorities were prejudiced against him. One of them, Bragg, had every reason to hate him and hated

[18] *O. R.*, ser. I, vol. XXXII, pt. III, p. 781.

him, for Bragg laid the blame of Missionary Ridge at his door, as he had cause to do.

It thus followed that Longstreet's career as an independent commander came to an end in this April, 1864. He was ordered back to Lee, who wanted him and regarded him with affection and confidence. Perhaps Longstreet was not averse to going. It was under Lee that he had gained worldwide fame; as the head of an army, he had reaped nothing but the criticism he had poured out on others. Dissatisfied, criticizing everybody now—except his usual object of criticism, Lee [19]—at loggerheads with the authorities, who would not follow his brilliant suggestions, he went back with his troops to the Army of Northern Virginia, then near Orange, Virginia. He took with him only about ten thousand men. Battle and sickness and desertion had claimed a heavy toll of his force, but those who remained were of the best, men refined in the furnace of adversity and hardship and found to be true gold.

[19] It is fair to add that Fremantle states that Longstreet liked to hear Lee praised.

CHAPTER XVII

AT THE CREST IN THE WILDERNESS

LONGSTREET returned to Lee in April, 1864. The commander greeted his First Corps with a review that General Alexander graphically describes.

"It is now over forty years, but in imagination I can see to-day the large square gate posts, without gate or fence, for troops had been everywhere in that vicinity, marking where a country road led out of a tall oak wood upon an open knoll in front of the centre of our long double lines. And as the well-remembered figure of Lee upon Traveller, at the head of his staff, rides between the posts and comes out upon the ground, the bugle sounds a signal, the guns thunder out a salute, Lee reins up Traveller and bares his good gray head and looks at us, and we give the 'rebel yell' and shout and cry and wave our flags and look at him once more." [1]

Spring was coming in the year 1864, but it brought little hope to the hard-pressed Confederacy. Tennessee was now definitely lost, and the two main Western armies confronted each other in Georgia. In Virginia the Army of Northern Virginia and the Army of the Potomac looked at each other from the opposite sides of the Rapidan River. Grant, now commander in chief of all the Union armies, had left Sherman to attend to Johnston in Georgia and had himself come to direct the Army of the Potomac, which was still nominally commanded by Meade. Grant's success at Missionary

[1] *Military Memoirs of a Confederate*, p. 493.

Ridge had made him rather deprecatory of the prowess of
Lee, whose prestige as a commander had fallen with his
defeat at Gettysburg. With an admirably equipped army of
one hundred and twenty thousand men facing the poorly-
fed and worse-clothed Confederate army of sixty thousand
men, Grant felt confident of the result—entirely too confident, as events showed. As a matter of fact, he came nearer
to total defeat than any other Union commander who had
opposed Lee.

The Confederates were, for the first time, wholly on
the defensive, since their dwindling numbers and resources
made it quite impossible for them to take the offensive in
any terrain. Nevertheless, Davis and Bragg in Richmond
had not forgiven Johnston for not attempting the impossible and already regarded him as a failure. Bragg's feeling
was due, in large part, to a perfectly human resentment
at being superseded in command by the popular and trusted
Johnston.

The stage was thus set for disaster in the West, but in
the East the Confederates were stronger to the extent that
Longstreet's roving propensities had been cured. At last he
was beginning to realize that he was not a great general and
that his fame and prestige were mainly due to the fact that
he had served under Lee. He was no longer trying to escape
from his chief to other fields.

Yet he was still advising Lee in his professional, slightly
condescending fashion, for he did not even now believe that
Lee was really a great general, but only fortunate or popular. Still he thought better of Lee than did D. H. Hill, who
frankly criticized the Confederate commander all through
the campaign of 1864—Hill, that curious, hard-fighting,
censorious, literary soldier who found faults in everybody.

On returning to the Army of Northern Virginia, Longstreet says, "I took the earliest opportunity to suggest that the preliminaries of the campaign should be carefully confined to strategic manœuvre until we could show better generalship . . . that we should first show that the power of battle is in generalship more than in the number of soldiers, which, properly illustrated, would make the weaker numbers of the contention the stronger force." [2]

Lee seems to have listened to the lectures on strategy with his usual humility and lack of irritation. The Confederate commander had learned the supreme lesson of self-control even more completely than had Washington and it was not for him to show annoyance at Longstreet's patronage, now that Georgia's governor was so disaffected to the cause as to be keeping out of the Western army thousands of badly-needed men. Suppose he should order home the Georgia troops in Lee's army—that would mean the speedy end of the Confederacy. So Lee continued to endure, as he had so long, instruction in strategy by a lieutenant who had done nothing whatever in that field himself when given the opportunity.

Longstreet's idea of generalship had not changed; it was always that of maneuvering the enemy into a position where he would have to attack at every disadvantage. That was in reality almost Longstreet's sole conception of generalship. To be attacked in a strong position, as at Fredericksburg, and to repulse the enemy, leaving the field covered with the fallen. To do that again and again until the war should be won. But how could any war be won in that way?

Lee, with an insight into an adversary's plans greater perhaps than that of any other general in history, by the first of May knew just about what Grant was going to do. On May 2, 1864, he stood with a group of officers at the

2 *M. to A.,* p. 551.

signal station on Clark's Mountain, looking through his
field-glasses at the camps of the Union army north of the
Rapidan. Lowering his glasses, he expressed the opinion that
the Union army would cross the river at Ely's or Germanna
fords. By the evening of May 4, the Unionists were crossing at both places named.

Lee's headquarters were near the village of Orange.
Ewell's corps was along the Rapidan River above Mine Run
and Hill's on the left of Ewell and higher up the river.
Longstreet's corps was in the vicinity of Gordonsville; part
of it was at Mechanicsville south of that town. In this disposition of his forces Lee made the mistake that possibly
prevented his winning the greatest victory of the war. Ewell
and Hill were where he could bring them quickly to oppose
the Union movement, but Longstreet was farther away, and
Longstreet was the slowest marcher in his army. Lee should
have taken the precaution to bring Longstreet to Orange,
where the self-willed subordinate would have been under
his eye. With the odds against him, it was imperative that
the army should respond to his will like a well-oiled
machine.

Grant had decided not to make a frontal attack on Lee's
lines, which had daunted Meade in December, 1863. They
were indeed formidable, though in attacking them Grant
could have used his artillery with effect. By the course he
took he rendered his artillery of no service, and artillery
was precisely the arm in which the Union army was in-
contestably superior to the Confederate. Not that Grant
counted on losing the services of his ordnance; he expected
to and hoped to use it with telling effect, but Lee prevented
him. It was Grant's plan to swing around Lee's right wing
and force the latter to fight in the open field away from
entrenchments, for at the beginning of the operations of

1864 neither army expected to fight behind hastily-raised fieldworks; that was the development of the next few days.

What Grant feared was that Lee would oppose his crossing of the Rapidan River at Germanna ford, where the larger part of his force passed over the stream. But in opposing such a crossing Lee's troops would have come under the fire of the numerous and well-appointed Union guns; and, moreover, if Lee had been able to prevent a crossing at Germanna he could not have guarded the upper fords at the same time. Thwarted at Germanna, Grant could have passed around Lee's left instead of his right; with his great superiority of force, he could not have been prevented from crossing the river somewhere.

All the same, when Grant's troops passed the stream without opposition, the Union commander heaved a sigh of relief; his rather derogatory opinion of Lee's generalship was strengthened by Lee's letting him get over a stream where resistance would have been awkward to say the least. It now became the opinion of the Union leaders that Lee was falling back to the North Anna River to make his stand there. There is so much to say for this latter course that it may have been Lee's wisest choice, and yet he came so near to winning a decisive victory in the Wilderness that most students think his decision was a stroke of genius. For Lee decided to let the Union army cross the river unimpeded and then to assail it in the jungle known as the Wilderness, through which it must pass to get around his right. In the dense underbrush of that tangled forest, penetrated only by narrow wood roads, the dreaded Union artillery would have little scope for action and the odds against the Southerners would be reduced; in fact, in the thickets the odds would be nearly even, provided the whole Confederate army was just where Lee desired it to be. He did manage to handle Ewell's and Hill's corps to marvelous effect, but Longstreet was out of hand and this limited the success of his brilliant strategy.

The Army of the Potomac began to cross the Rapidan River about midnight of May 3 on pontons laid at three fords, Ely's, Germanna, and Culpeper Mine. Hancock's Second Corps crossed at Ely's, the easternmost of the fords; Warren's Fifth Corps, followed by Sedgwick's Sixth Corps, crossed at Germanna, the westernmost ford. The sixty-five miles of wagon trains accompanying the army took until midday of May 5 in crossing at Culpeper Mine ford and Germanna ford. In order to get around Lee, Grant had to move southward; and the highways running north and south were bisected by two parallel east and west roads. It was Lee's simple but excellent plan to move his army down these parallel east-west roads and strike the Union army as it was moving southward. Strung out on narrow wood roads, the Unionists might be taken at a disadvantage and could not, certainly, use their artillery effectively.

Because the dense thickets limited army movements in large measures to these few roads, the battle of the Wilderness is perhaps the easiest of all the engagements of the Civil War to understand. It was fought mainly on the two east-west roads, the Orange turnpike and the Orange plank road, and the main intersecting highway, the Brock road. The Confederates pushed down the two Orange roads from the west and the Unionists resisted along the line of the Brock road.

Lee, learning early in the morning of May 4, that the Union army was crossing the Rapidan, put Ewell's corps in motion on the east-west road nearest the Rapidan River, known as the Orange turnpike, and two divisions of Hill's corps on the parallel highway, the Orange plank road.

If Lee knew what the enemy was about, Longstreet did not. As late as 10:30 A. M. on May 4, he wrote Lee that he feared the enemy was trying to draw the Confederates toward Fredericksburg, but that the latter should stay away from that place because their flanks and rear would be open to an attack from West Point, many miles distant.[3]

On May 4, Lee sent Longstreet an order to move east on the Orange plank road behind Hill. This order reached Longstreet not later than 10:30 A. M.

At 11:00 A. M., Longstreet ordered Field to prepare to move at once to Richard's Shop at the junction of the old Fredericksburg and Lawyer's [Doctor's] roads southeast of Verdiersville, which is on the Orange turnpike. The best route would probably be by Brock's Bridge and the junction of the Marquis and old Fredericksburg roads. He would try to send Field guides, but the latter should seek guides in addition.

This choice of routes was unfortunate. Longstreet would have done better to move to Orange Courthouse and there take the Orange plank road behind Hill, who would have been out of the way long before the former could have reached the road. As it was, Longstreet made a circular march by way of Brock's Bridge, with the result that he did not get into the battle of May 5 at all and only into that of May 6 when the outnumbered Confederates were being driven back. It must be admitted that Lee himself was partly to blame for the result. Knowing Longstreet's willful nature and deliberateness, no matter how perilous the crisis might be, he should have given his lieutenant the most definite instructions and sent him guides.

Longstreet himself says: "We were ordered forward by the plank road to Parker's Store; the order was received

[3] *O. R.*, ser. I, vol. XXXVI, pt. II, p. 947.

after one o'clock [May 4], and sent out for information of the commanders, who were ordered to prepare and march. But I asked for and received authority to march by a shorter route that would at the same time relieve the Plank road of pressure of troops and trains. . . . By the same despatch I asked and subsequently obtained leave to go on to the Brock road, where we could look for and hope to intercept the enemy's march, and cause him to develop plans before he could get out of the Wilderness. We marched at four o'clock by the Lawyer's [Doctor's] road. Our chief quarter-master, Colonel Taylor, whose home was between Orange Court-house and the Wilderness, had been ordered to se-cure the services of the most competent guide to be found. We halted at Brock's Bridge for rest, and there Colonel Taylor brought up our guide, James Robinson. . . . The march was resumed, and continued with swinging step, with occasional rests, until we reached Richard's Shop, at five P. M. of the 5th. . . .

"The distance of the march was twenty-eight miles. Soon after my arrival at the shops, Colonel Venable, of general head-quarters staff, came with orders for a change of direc-tion of the column through the wood to unite with the troops of the Third Corps on the Plank road." [4]

Thus we find Longstreet moving in leisurely fashion in an arc while the other two corps of the army were engaged in a desperate conflict. He underestimates the length of his route. He states that he did not receive the order to march until 1:00 P. M. of May 4, but his order to Field to move to Richard's Shop is dated 11:00 A. M.; and it seems highly probable that the note he wrote to Lee and dated 10:30 A. M., cautioning the general against being drawn down to Fredericksburg, was in response to Lee's order to move.

[4] *M. to A.,* pp. 556-57.

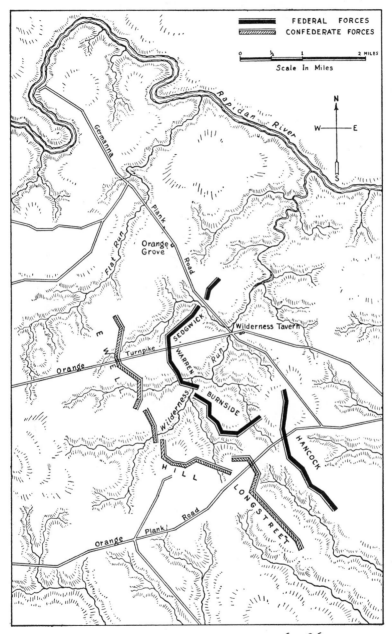

BATTLE OF THE WILDERNESS, MAY 6, 1864

Either this is true or Longstreet sent orders to Field in advance of his instructions from Lee, which is improbable. It would appear that Longstreet received his instructions in the forenoon of May 4 and moved with such deliberateness that he covered only twenty-eight miles by 5:00 P. M. of May 5. He was always a slow marcher. Considering the exigencies of the occasion, this shows a disregard for the welfare of the army almost incredible, if true. Longstreet usually took his time and would hurry for no crisis, however great, but it really appears that he did better marching than ordinarily on this occasion. We find him, at nightfall of May 5, miles from the battlefield, where the Confederates have been engaged for nearly a day, and in such need of direction that a staff officer is sent to guide him across country to the Plank road, which he should have followed in the first place and would doubtless have followed but for his habit of improving on his directions and orders. He had no intention of obeying orders without changes.

Meanwhile Ewell and Hill had been fighting furiously, and Lee was waiting with strained patience for the appearance of his wandering First Corps. The cause of the Confederacy may have been definitely lost by this Maytime, but if so, Lee's men did not know it. All accounts indicate that the hairy and ragged veterans of Lee's army were never in better spirits or more confident of the result than when they moved along the two parallel east-west roads through the dense forest known as the Wilderness. Laughing and joking in the face of the death that had grown familiar to them, they came at last into contact with the columns of bluecoats moving southward in the effort to swing around Lee.

Some time in the morning of May 5, Ewell's troops on the Orange turnpike saw the Union troops crossing the road from the direction of Germanna ford, where they had passed the river. Ewell, forming line of battle across the turnpike, sent word to Lee, who was with Hill on the Plank road. Ewell was told to keep step with Hill's troops, only a mile or so away on the Plank road, whose progress could be noted by the sound of firing. He was cautioned not to bring on a general engagement until Longstreet had come up. By this time Longstreet should have been on the Orange plank road not far behind Hill if he had followed Lee's original instructions instead of obtaining permission to make a wandering march to the east. Longstreet was, in fact, nearly twenty-four hours away.

Ewell, in the immediate presence of the enemy, could not prevent the battle from beginning. The leading brigade, some time earlier, had fallen on the Union vedettes and driven them in upon the main body, thereby discovering its line of march. The Union force here was Warren's Fifth Corps. Warren, finding the Confederates on his flank, formed line of battle and drove them up the road toward Orange for a mile or more. Then Ewell, throwing in the rest of his corps, halted the advance of the Unionists and finally drove them back. By this time, mid-afternoon, the fighting had developed into a battle involving two corps, Warren's and Ewell's. On the Confederate side, Johnson's division held the turnpike, with Rodes's division on the right and Early's in reserve.

Ewell held his own easily against Warren, but now Sedgwick's corps, coming from the Rapidan, joined Warren on the right. Early was sent by Ewell to hold him off. A terrible conflict followed in the woods between the turnpike and the river. In the dense thickets the swaying lines could see only a few yards in front; and the troops on both sides, pouring their volleys into the smoke-screened bushes before them, died unseeing and unseen. In this frightful struggle artillery was useless and cavalry helpless. Thus Lee had so reduced the odds against him that Ewell, with one corps, repulsed two Union corps until nightfall, maintaining himself against every effort to drive him.

At the same time Hill was advancing down the Orange plank road to the east, and, if Longstreet had been behind him, the Army of the Potomac would have been in a critical position, strung out on several roads and with miles between some of the units. But with only two small corps, Lee could not gain the victory his skill and boldness deserved.

While Ewell was fighting on the turnpike, Hill struck the Union skirmishers on the Orange plank road near Parker's Store on the outskirts of the Wilderness. Driving them in, Hill's men followed them to the junction of the Germanna ford road and the Brock road, where the Union line of battle was posted so as to cover the junction. Here Getty's division of the Sixth Corps came into sharp conflict with Heth's division leading Hill's column. Hancock's corps, moving on Spotsylvania Courthouse by way of Chancellorsville, was recalled and ordered to attack Hill. Hancock lost some time in throwing up breastworks on the Brock road and then moved in line of battle up the Orange plank road and assailed Hill.

Here the struggle was, if anything, more desperate than on the turnpike. In the smoke-enveloped trees and bushes nothing could be seen but the flashes of the guns on either side, but trees and bushes were torn to pieces by the hail of lead that left thousands of dead and wounded men on the ground. There have been few sterner tests of a soldier's metal than this horrible combat in the Virginia jungle. Night found Hill holding off Hancock's corps on the Plank road just as Ewell was maintaining his ground against Warren and Sedgwick on the turnpike. The Union losses were the larger, and the morale of the Southerners had risen with the fighting. Lee was holding his own against the greater part of the far larger Union army with only two of his three corps.

He had waited anxiously all the afternoon for Longstreet, who, if present, could have been thrown on Hancock's left flank with disastrous results for Hancock. With Hancock crushed, Warren and Sedgwick on the turnpike would have been in a perilous position. Now at nightfall Lee sent a message to Longstreet to march by night so as to reach the battlefield by daylight.

Longstreet waited from 5:00 P. M. on May 5 to 1:00 A. M. on May 6 before he moved, surely a long rest to give men who had marched only twenty-eight miles in a day and a half. (But they had marched more.) If he had moved by 11:00 P. M., as no doubt Lee expected, he would have reached Hill's line by daylight, but again Longstreet would not hurry. No matter what happened, he intended to move with his usual deliberation. He states, in one account, that from Mechanicsville to Parker's Store was thirty-four miles; from Parker's Store to the battlefield, three miles. The actual distance is nearly forty miles. The time used in marching was thirty-six hours, including two nights. Longstreet complains that Lee sent no officer to guide him.

The most heroic fighting of the day had been done by the two divisions of Hill's corps, Heth and Wilcox, which had stood off six divisions of Hancock's corps. Outnumbered three to one, the Confederates had made such good use of the dense cover that they had held their line and inflicted much greater losses than they had suffered.

The men, however, were worn out by the struggle. The lines were disarranged and in places fronted in different directions. Expecting to be relieved by fresh troops at any moment, the division commanders made no effort to rearrange their lines and throw up breastworks. But as they were not relieved, they were caught napping in the early morning of May 6.

Hancock had made his preparations and attacked with great vigor at earliest dawn. Wilcox, south of the Plank road, was enveloped and flanked by overwhelming numbers. The troops, giving way, retired in disorder up the Plank road until they came under the protection of one of their batteries. But the Unionists, tasting victory, were not to be denied. Lee, a little in the rear, was apprised of the turn events had taken by seeing the Plank road filled with a hurrying and disorderly throng of men; on both sides of the road the retreating Confederates stumbled through the bushes and over the fields in their effort to escape the enveloping folds being thrown around them.

Lee had learned in the night that Longstreet would not be up at dawn. Strangely enough, he sent no warning to the commanders of the troops immediately in his front, upon whom the blow would fall if the Unionists attacked. Probably Lee was solicitous for the comfort of the weary soldiers who had fought for long hours against heavy odds, but in this case solicitude was mistaken. He took a chance that the Unionists would not renew their attack at daylight and he surely expected Longstreet early in the morning. In so doing, he ran a risk that brought him perilously close to decisive defeat. Now that the Unionists were charging and defeat stared him in the face, he sent another messenger to hurry up the lagging Longstreet, many hours late.

Lee was never better than in the moment of crisis, when he forgot his theories of tactics and took charge himself. As the rout came streaming up the Plank road, a mass of running, shouting men fleeing from the dense blue lines to be seen through the smoke haze, Lee rode into the thick and sought to rally the fugitives. Around him were the soldiers of McGowan's South Carolina brigade, a notably good command.

"My God, General McGowan," he cried, "is this splendid brigade of yours running like a flock of sheep?"

McGowan was quick to explain. "General, these men are not whipped. They only want a place to form, and they will fight as well as ever they did."

But there was no place there for a broken command to reform, as the Union line of battle on the road and far to the left and right of it swept confidently forward, believing the day to be won. Lee's right wing was on the verge of being rolled up; never in all the course of the war had the peril been as great. Wilcox came up to Lee, anxious and asking for orders.

"Longstreet must be here," Lee answered. "Go bring him up."

Wilcox rode into the field behind, and at this moment the twelve guns of Poague's battery opened on the advancing Unionists with canister. Hill was there with the guns and directed the fire. The effect was to check the advance of the Unionists, who had no artillery at hand. Still the check was momentary, as a few guns could not hold back such an overwhelming infantry force.

At that moment Fortune, which had frowned on them before, now began to favor the sore-beset Southerners. The officers around Lee saw approaching from the rear, through the smoke and the crowds of stragglers and fugitives, a compact column of fours moving swiftly and composedly forward. At the moment of extreme crisis, the dramatic climax, like a veritable *deus et machina*, Longstreet had arrived.

His tardiness had exposed Lee to the utmost peril, but he had come at last. In perfect order, with ranks closed and no stragglers, these veterans came on at a trot and almost instantly began to deploy in the field to the south of the road, to meet the Union onset.

To the troops in the road, Lee more excited than he had ever been known to be, called out, "Who are you, my boys?"

"Texas boys," they called back.

Lee took off his hat and waved it as he realized that his best troops were on the firing line.

"Hurrah for Texas!" he shouted. "Hurrah for Texas!"

As the Texans deployed, Lee rode forward among them. It was then they discerned his purpose to lead them in the charge. Excited by the emergency and filled with the ardor of battle, he had forgotten for the moment that he was the commander of the army and remembered only that he was a soldier and that the enemy was in front.

The soldiers knew his place if he did not. They instantly realized the awful peril he would be in if he rode into the charge on his conspicuous white horse.

"Go back, General Lee," they called. He continued to ride ahead. Then they crowded around him, calling out, "We won't go on unless you go back!" A sergeant seized his bridle rein but Lee was not to be stopped. At that moment his staff officer, Venable, came up and cried that Longstreet was at hand. That brought Lee back to the realities of the moment. Turning, he rode to where Longstreet sat his horse surrounded by his staff officers.

Longstreet, utterly unperturbed as he always was in extreme danger, had already formed his line of battle, Kershaw on the right of the Plank road, Field on the left. Through his line of battle the rear stragglers of Wilcox's and Heth's broken divisions made their way, as the ranks opened to let them pass. Then Longstreet's line of battle quickly advanced on the oncoming Unionists.

Field's troops, north of the road, were in the thickets that marked the southernmost end of the Wilderness. As Hancock's men came onward through the pines unaware of what was prepared for them, Gregg's Texas brigade, the remnant of Hood's, the finest body of troops America has ever seen, threw itself on the bluecoats with terrific force. There was a crash, and then the Wilderness was filled with the roll of musketry as blue and gray fired into each other's faces. In ten minutes half of Gregg's brigade lay dead or wounded, but the Unionists had halted and were wavering. Then the supporting brigade came up, and Field's division swept resistlessly forward. The Unionists, disordered by their hasty advance through the pines and broken by the terrible volleys poured into them, were retreating in turn. What half an hour before had seemed a Union victory now, through Longstreet's arrival, began to look like defeat. It was one of the great moments of American history.

The Southerners were driving the foe. The line of battle swept forward to a row of log breastworks thrown up by the Unionists the day before and, like a resistless wave surging over a sea wall, halted a moment and then swept forward over the logs, driving the Unionists before them. The bluecoats rallied and reclaimed the earthworks, only to be driven out again. The Confederate line of battle pushed onward and carried a second line of breastworks, to be driven back in turn by the hurrying Union supports. And so for two hours the battle moved forward and backward, as one side pushed up and then the other; but on the whole fortune continued to favor the Confederates. In that terrible infantry duel the fire of the Confederates proved the deadlier and while the ground was strewn with their killed and wounded, the Unionists were fighting with decreasing determination. Their losses were very heavy, especially of officers. They had suffered that reversal of morale that always befalls troops who are driven back after a great initial success.

Longstreet, cool as ever and thoroughly aroused from his sullen apathy by the fire of battle, was fully alive and eager to take advantage of any opportunity. It was the great hour of his life. His supreme quality was his ability to size up a situation, in the midst of the most appalling noise and confusion and the most evident peril, with as complete detachment as if in a library reading of a battle. Uttermost danger could do nothing more than quicken slightly the pulse that never beat rapidly; it had no effect on those iron nerves. While the Union commanders were thinking only of checking the Confederate advance, Longstreet was studying the ground in the effort to find an opportunity to attack at an advantage.

Lee had intended to strike the left flank of the Union army and had directed Longstreet's march with that purpose in view. If Longstreet had come up in the late afternoon of the day before, Hancock would have been in extreme peril. Now with Heth and Wilcox disabled, the Union danger was less but it was still great. Lee was not with Longstreet now; he was attempting to form a junction between the widely divided corps of Hill and Ewell.

It was suggested to Longstreet that it might be possible to get on the Union flank and roll it up. Longstreet instantly responded, sending the chief engineer of the army, M. L. Smith, to see if a way could be found leading around the Union position. Smith, a good officer, moving southward through the bushes, presently came on the roadbed of an unfinished railroad (now the Virginia Central) which, un-occupied, led directly past the Union flank. It was a wonderful opportunity.

It was 10:00 A. M. when Smith returned and reported. Longstreet without hesitation ordered his adjutant general, Moxley Sorrel, to take three brigades down the railroad bed and hurl them on the Union flank, which Smith had discovered extended a little beyond the Plank road. In other words, the Union flank was "in the air," and Longstreet seized the opportunity to attack it. Lee was told of the proposed movement but made no objection; it was his habit to let Longstreet·fight his battle.

About 11:00 A. M., Longstreet threw his brigades on the railroad bed against the flank of the unsuspecting Unionists. A terrific roar of musketry apprised Lee that the Confederates were now on the offensive. The sound, approaching rapidly, apprised him even before the reports came in that the movement was a complete success. The Unionists, fought out in the morning and thrown back with heavy losses, were in no position to resist a flank attack. Seldom had a movement in the war been more successful than this assault of Longstreet's, which was much like his advance through the gap in the Union line at Chickamauga. "The signs of demoralization and even panic among the troops of Hancock's left wing, who had been hurled back by Mahone's flank attack, were too plain to be mistaken by the Confederates, who believed that Chancellorsville was about to be repeated," says General Law, who was there.

At this moment Jenkins's brigade was moved forward on the Plank road, supported by Kershaw's division, while the flanking force was to come into position on the right. But the adjustment was not made. The flanking force was in line of battle south of the road and almost parallel with it, so that the two forces were now at right angles to each other.

Just then Longstreet and Kershaw rode with Jenkins to the head of the latter's brigade as it moved forward along the Plank road. The thick forest made it difficult to recognize objects at any distance. As Longstreet and his companions rode down this road, a few shots rang out on the north side. Mahone's line of battle on the south side of the road and parallel to it, dimly discerning figures on the road and taking them for the enemy, suddenly poured a volley into the head of Jenkins's approaching column.

Both Longstreet and Jenkins, in front, were struck down. Jenkins, mortally wounded, died in a few hours. Longstreet was terribly hurt and utterly incapacitated.

Jenkins's troops raised their muskets to return the fire, when Kershaw cried out, "They are friends!" and saved a holocaust.

The damage, however, was done. Longstreet says: "At the moment that Jenkins fell I received a severe shock from a minie ball passing through my throat and right shoulder. The blow lifted me from the saddle, and my right arm dropped to my side, but I settled back to my seat and started to ride on, when in a minute the flow of blood admonished me that my work for the day was done. As I turned to ride back, members of my staff, seeing me about to fall, dismounted and lifted me to the ground." [5]

Longstreet ordered Field, the senior officer there, to push the enemy. But Field was perplexed by the fact that a column was moving on the Plank road while a line of battle was stretched out south of the road and almost at right angles to the column. Just then, R. H. Anderson, Field's senior, came up, and a little later Lee himself, who had been

[5] *M. to A.,* p. 564.

informed of Longstreet's misfortune. Longstreet says, "The plans, orders and opportunity were explained to him, but the woods concealed everything except the lines of troops alongside the road. General Lee did not care to handle the troops in broken lines, and ordered formation in a general line for parallel battle."

What Lee did, and what Field says was necessary to do, was to arrange the two perpendicular lines so as to make them parallel. In doing so the Confederates consumed several hours, as it was difficult to move troops in the dense forest. When they did go forward again, Hancock's men had recovered from their surprise and built log breastworks the Confederates could not take. Repulsed with severe loss, the latter finally fell back, and the battle of the Wilderness on that front came to an end in occasional firing.

Here it would seem Lee erred, because he did not fully realize the nature of the case; he had not seen the fleeing bluecoats exhibiting unmistakable signs of rout. If the troops that had done the flanking had been pushed forward at once, without loss of time, while the column on the Plank road was held back and formed in line, it is possible that the Confederates might have won a great advantage. At all events, it would seem to have been a mistake to consume several hours in reorganizing the line and then making an attack on a restored and prepared enemy; in war, time is everything, especially when panic is in the air, as it was at that moment.

On the left wing Ewell had a chance to win a decided advantage, as the right wing of the Union army was also in the air, that is, resting on no natural defense. But by this time Ewell was worn out with the struggle and, besides, he was under the influence of Early, who refused to credit the intelligence that the Confederates could outflank the foe.

Late in the day, almost at twilight, Gordon, who urged the movement, did go forward and found the Union right wing in the air, but as evening was falling it was too late to accomplish anything. The Confederates lost two opportunities, on each wing, to win a decided victory.

Thus it was that night fell on May 6, 1864, with Grant having missed by the narrowest chance, and great good luck, a severe defeat. He had miscalculated and had been outfought. The Confederates, instead of retreating, had attacked him in the forest and, instead of being beaten as he thought would certainly happen if they could be caught away from their fortifications, had driven the Unionists back at every point and almost routed them. But by midnight the Unionists had so fortified the Brock road, which they held, with log breastworks and earthen, that Grant invited another attack by the Confederates.

Through all that terrible night searching parties wandered through the flaming and smoking bushes looking for the dead and wounded, who lay in every hollow, in thickets and behind logs. The casualties on both sides had been very heavy, but the Confederate infantry had upheld its reputation, and by far the greater number of still or writhing figures wore the blue. Lee's army was confident and in good spirits, while the Union morale had suffered. It was in that hour that Grant made the great decision of his life. Hooker had retreated across the river a year before, though he had not been so badly mauled as Grant was on this occasion. Grant, though two of his corps had been decimated and almost stampeded and though he did not know what surprises Lee might have for him on the morrow, determined to stand his ground. He decided, indeed, to go on doing what he had started to do, that is, to move around Lee's right and intervene between him and Richmond.

Lee, reading Grant's mind, also raced eastward, with the result that the latter found him in position at Spotsylvania Courthouse, when the Union troops came up. There followed battles even bloodier and more terrible than the Wilderness, battles in which Grant's losses exceeded anything ever known before in America—losses the exact extent of which was never known, for they were, naturally enough, minimized.

The whole Confederate responsibility now rested on Lee's shoulders. Longstreet was gone, badly wounded; Stuart was dead, mortally wounded in opposing Sheridan's cavalry near Richmond; Ewell was in such health as to be unable to continue in the field; Hill alone remained of the high command, and Hill was the least able of the corps commanders.

Longstreet was succeeded by R. H. Anderson, no gain for Lee, while Ewell's place was taken by Early, who had really commanded the corps for some time. Stuart's shoes were worthily filled by Wade Hampton, one of the finest soldiers America has ever produced, but Hampton could not find the remounts necessary to keep the cavalry efficient.

Lee's army was going downhill, for thousands of the bravest and best had fallen and their places could not easily be filled. Grant, on the other hand, had replacements of about the same quality as the men who had fallen in the Wilderness and at Spotsylvania. He continued to swing around to the east, still endeavoring to get between Lee and Richmond. Failing in this and suffering a terrible defeat at Cold Harbor, he at length at the middle of June, 1864, passed all the way around Richmond, which he was unable to approach, and established himself at Petersburg, the key to the Confederate capital because the point through which the railways supplying it passed. Here the war stalemated from late June, 1864, until April, 1865.

Longstreet missed the awful struggle of Spotsylvania, the race eastward, the slaughter of Cold Harbor, the establishment of the lines at Petersburg. He was lying on a bed of pain, spitting blood and fighting for his life. As he was borne to the rear after being wounded, the soldiers said to each other, "He is dead, and they are telling us he is only wounded." Hearing this, Longstreet had the presence of mind and courage to raise his hat, which lay across his face, whereat the relieved troops burst into cheers.[6]

Longstreet himself attributes his wounding to his own impatience. Seeing the opportunity and fearing that Lee would change his plan, he rode forward to needless exposure and so suffered his wound. It was characteristic of the recklessness of the Confederate generals; both Jackson and Longstreet were victims of a temerity that is out of place in high commanding officers, a temerity that robbed the South of two chances to win decisive victory and lost it the services of two of its foremost soldiers.

That Longstreet, when wounded, seems to have been on the point of complete success is indicated by the evidence of the Unionists themselves. Hancock said to Longstreet years afterward, "You rolled me up like a wet blanket, and it was some hours before I could reorganize for battle."[7]

[6] *M. to A.*, p. 566.
[7] *Ibid.*, p. 568.

CHAPTER XVIII

RETURN TO ARMS

FROM the battlefield Longstreet was conveyed to the home of a friend, Erasmus Taylor, at Meadow Farm near Orange Courthouse. Here he was cared for for some days while his wound was examined and treated. The injury in the throat would have killed a man of less vigor, but Longstreet was a viking, a physical being of the strongest texture, able to endure almost any hurt and recover. From Orange he went by train to Lynchburg, where he was cared for by a relative, Mrs. Caroline Garland, widow of General Samuel Garland, killed at South Mountain. When able to ride in a carriage, Longstreet was taken to the home of Colonel John D. Alexander at Campbell Courthouse. But this place was in the line of Hunter's raiders, and Longstreet went to Augusta, Georgia, where he stayed with kinsmen, the Sibleys, and later to Union Point.

He was just able to sit up when news came that Joseph E. Johnston, commanding the Army of Tennessee, had been superseded by John B. Hood. That was on July 17, 1864. Longstreet was asked to take command of the corps vacated by Hood's elevation, but was obliged to answer that he was unable to serve.

In this part of his book he falls into the most curious errors. Johnston was relieved on July 17. Longstreet states, "Later came sadder news from Virginia announcing the fall of our Cavalier, J. E. B. Stuart. The most famous American rider fell mortally wounded on the 18th of May." Stuart was wounded on May 11, while Longstreet was still prostrate from his injury, and more than two months before the superseding of Johnston by Hood. This is a good illustration of the imperfect nature of Longstreet's memoirs, which can be accepted only with the greatest caution.

About October 1, 1864, Longstreet was able to ride horseback once more, and his recovery speedily followed. Some days later he left his wife and family and took the train for Richmond, eager to get in harness again, for Longstreet loved war, that is, when it was conducted according to his ideas of what war should be.

He found Lee depressed by the perplexities of the situation. "The general," he says, "seemed worn by past labors, besides suffering at seasons from severe sciatica." But Lee was rejoiced to see Longstreet, who was far better than Anderson and Hill and whom he trusted to a much greater degree. From "Randolph's House," near Richmond, Longstreet wrote, on October 18, 1864, to Lee's assistant adjutant general, W. H. Taylor, asking for an assignment. "If I can be of service in any position, I prefer to go on duty." If there was nothing for him east of the Mississippi he would cheerfully go to the west side. West of the Mississippi the Confederate commanders had little to do, and perhaps it was for this reason that Longstreet was not averse to service there. Besides, he was not yet able to use his wounded arm and thus felt somewhat incapacitated still. Longstreet was given the command of the part of the long Confederate line on the north side of the James River and the part south of the river as far as Swift Creek, not far from Petersburg, the left side of the Confederate position and the less deeply menaced.

The Confederates on the north side of the James River were glad of Longstreet's return, for things had not been going well in that sector. On September 29, 1864, the Unionists had made a surprise attack on Fort Harrison, a point in the Confederate main line not far from Chaffin's Bluff on the river. Sweeping suddenly up to the high earthen embankment, the bluecoats had scaled the slope and routed or captured the handful of defenders. But in attempting to widen the break in the line by capturing Fort Gilmer, to the north of Fort Harrison, the Unionists had been repulsed with loss. Lee, disturbed by this sinister episode, had the next day, September 30, made strenuous attempts to retake Fort Harrison but had failed with severe loss. The men did not fight with the old spirit and, were, besides, exposed to a sweeping artillery fire when charging over the cleared space between the lines. After that Lee contented himself with throwing up a new line of earthworks confronting Fort Harrison, which remained in Union hands without further inconveniencing the Confederates. The ground in front of Fort Harrison was planted with subterra shells, set off by concussion; the enemy made no attempt to test the efficiency of the torpedoes.

Longstreet's command consisted of Ewell's Local Defense troops, Hoke's division, Field's division, and Gary's brigade of cavalry, as well as Pickett's division on the south side of the James River. Ewell's home guards held the trenches from the river to Fort Gilmer; Hoke, those between the Newmarket and Darbytown roads; and Field, from the Darbytown road to the Charles City road. Gary picketed White Oak Swamp, the fords of which had been obstructed.

Longstreet felt sure that the enemy, with their superior force, would try to pass around his left flank, which was anything but secure because it did not extend to the Williamsburg road. When, on October 25, he heard that large bodies of Unionists had crossed to the north side of the river, he directed Field to place a regiment across the Charles City road and otherwise disposed his scanty force so as to cover his long line. On the morning of October 27, masses of the enemy were seen in motion.

What was happening was that Grant designed an assault on the Petersburg lines, and General Benjamin Butler was assigned the task of making a demonstration north of the James to cover the real attack. Part of the Eighteenth Corps, under Weitzel, was to advance to the Williamsburg road beyond White Oak Swamp and part of the Tenth Corps under Terry to move upon the Charles City road and the Darbytown road.

It was Longstreet's merit that he saw through the design. While primarily attempting a demonstration, the Unionists were prepared to make a real effort to turn the Confederate left flank if conditions proved favorable. Seeing by the long-continued skirmishing near the Charles City road that the real attack would not be made there, Longstreet argued that the Unionists would try to cross White Oak Swamp and occupy the old works on the Williamsburg and Nine-Mile roads. He then rapidly pushed his troops northward along the line of works, leaving only skirmishers in them.

Field's men were just crossing the Williamsburg road when Weitzel's skirmishers were seen advancing, followed by the line of battle. The Union force, with the spray of skirmishers in front, moved over the open ground on both sides of the Williamsburg road at 3:30 P. M. But to the surprise of the Unionists, instead of meeting only the desultory shots of pickets, they were greeted with a burst of musketry mixed with canister from guns. They succeeded in approaching the trenches held by the Confederates, but there they broke and fell back, with considerable loss. A body coming upon Gary's cavalry on the Nine-Mile road was likewise defeated.

After nightfall Weitzel withdrew his force through the rain and darkness. It was one of the most brilliant affairs ever conducted by Longstreet and illustrates the fact that he was a master of defensive tactics. The Unionists lost more than a thousand men, while the Confederate casualties do not seem to have been above a hundred. This had the further effect of ending all serious designs of the Unionists on the Confederate line north of the James. It was too vigilantly held.[1]

Longstreet's line ran now as follows: Pickett from the Appomattox to the James River; Hoke from the James River to Field; Field from Hoke to Gary; Gary at White Oak Swamp; northwest of Richmond, Ewell's Local Defense troops.

There followed some weeks of quiet along the lines, broken only by sharpshooting, which was nothing like as intense in Longstreet's sector as south of the James. On the south side the enemy was moving late in November, and Lee telegraphed Longstreet for troops. The latter had Hoke and Field get ready to move. Longstreet thought that Grant was making for Burkeville, a railroad junction some distance south of Richmond, and that he would weaken his force north of the James River for the movement. Therefore Longstreet argued that it would be better to leave all his troops intact on the north side, so that he might assail the weakened Unionists there and bag them. Then his entire force could be moved to the south side of the river for an attack on the Unionists there.[2] But if the Confederates

---

[1] *O. R.*, ser. I, vol. XLII, pt. I, p. 871.
[2] *O. R.*, ser. I, vol. XLII, pt. III, p. 1223.

attacked on the south side before doing anything on the north side, Lee should employ a corps. However, Longstreet preferred to attack the Unionists on both sides of the river at the same time.

On November 24, Longstreet declared that he could not send any troops to the south side because reports indicated the presence of the Tenth Corps in his front and also possibly that of the Sixth Corps. He intended to have the roads leading from White Oak Swamp to the Williamsburg road broken up with plows in order to prevent the enemy from moving cannon. He suggested that this method of breaking up the roads be used to hamper Sherman's march through the South. Again he told Lee that everything depended on Grant's purpose. If the Union general was moving on Burkeville, Lee should try to turn his left flank; if he intended to attack the Southside Railroad, it would be best to act defensively on the south side and offensively on the north side. At this time Longstreet had an itch to try his luck in an attack on the Union lines before him, which he thought he could take if partly denuded of troops.

On December 7, a scout informed Lee that the enemy were shifting troops from the north side to the south side of the James River, and Pickett confirmed the report. This seemed to give Longstreet an opening, and Lee called his attention to it. Longstreet, however, was not eager. He told Lee he would himself attack or send troops to the south side, as Lee might prefer. If Lee could wait a day or two, he would make a reconnaissance in force that should enable him to size up the situation.[3]

On December 11, Longstreet advanced to Newmarket Heights, finding the enemy fortified, though not in heavy force. He made no attack beyond driving in the pickets.

[3] O. R., ser. I, vol. XLII, pt. III, p. 1260.

Late in December, Lee asked Longstreet for troops to send to Gordonsville. Longstreet answered that he would dispatch Field if Pickett were sent to relieve the former. He needed one good division to hold the lines north of the James, but could use Local Defense troops for the rest. Two brigades were ordered to Gordonsville, but Longstreet asked if artillery and cavalry would be sent in proportion; otherwise, the infantry would do little good. The total force thus detached was thirty-three hundred men.

Local Defense troops were called home by the government, with Lee protesting that he did not know where to find men to hold his extreme left, very thinly guarded. Longstreet confirmed this by informing Lee that his force was so small he could hold the line only as far as the Williamsburg road, which meant that the northwest area of Richmond was practically undefended. In fact, Lee's left was in the air, even though the enemy did not choose to attack in that sector. In other words, between Ewell's Local Defense troops, holding the western approach to Richmond, and Longstreet, occupying the eastern face of the line north of the James River, there was a considerable hiatus. Between the Williamsburg road and the Nine-Mile road, a varying distance of from one to two miles, there was no defense whatever, and Longstreet had to be prepared at all times to throw troops into the gap when the enemy should move to occupy it. But his victory over the Unionists, on October 27, had so dampened their ardor that they were unenterprising on the north side for some time.

Lee was apprehensive that Ewell's line, facing west, would be broken and hoped that Longstreet could detach troops to strengthen it. Longstreet, however, thought that his own line would be well secured if it was as strongly held as Ewell's. If Ewell's force should be withdrawn and replaced by his own, he would have nothing with which to meet a flanking move, always to be apprehended.[4]

Lee felt that Longstreet might do something against the enemy in front of his lines, but the latter demurred. It was true, he admitted on December 30, that a portion of the opposing force had been withdrawn but he was faced by parts of the Twenty-fourth and Twenty-fifth Corps as well as the Eighth. The trouble with attacking the enemy was that they could reinforce readily unless Lee kept them occupied on the south side of the river.

The first days of 1865 passed without excitement. The cold and the bad roads made the Unionists inactive. Lee communicated to Longstreet a plan for consolidating regiments, for many commands in the army had become so small as to be over-officered and ineffective. Longstreet agreed that a reorganization would help, but he wished simply to consolidate existing regiments rather than to make new ones out of fragments as Lee suggested.

Desertion had become so rife as almost to threaten the army's existence. In Anderson's brigade, the government informed Longstreet, it appeared that a number of men had signed an agreement to leave when paid off. This rumor was probably untrue, Cooper added, and was caused by the fact that the men had not been paid for many months and were dissatisfied. Worthless as Confederate money was, it bought something.

Men were few, so few that someone complained to the government that there was a gap of about five hundred yards, opposite Fort Harrison, left entirely without defenders by the withdrawal of Local Defense troops.[5]

In January Lee's army was weakened by the detachment

---

[4] *O. R.*, ser. I, vol. XLII, pt. III, p. 1343.
[5] *O. R.*, ser. I, vol. XLII, pt. III, p. 000; *ibid.*, vol. XLVI, pt. II, p. 1169.

of Hoke (five thousand men) to Wilmington and Wade Hampton to South Carolina. These withdrawals were fatal, particularly that of Hampton, who could not be replaced. After his going Confederate cavalry operations were not what they had been.

In the winter the Confederates were disposed as follows: Hill, from the extreme right at Hatcher's Run to Fort Gregg; Gordon and Anderson, from Fort Gregg to the Appomattox; Longstreet, from the Appomattox to the Confederate left at White Oak Swamp. The defenses on the right were greatly strengthened.

On February 1, 1865, Longstreet informed Lee that matters on his line were much as they had been for some time. The engineers were busy constructing a road in the rear of the defenses for the movement of artillery. The troops had been working on the line of defenses between the Williamsburg and Nine-Mile roads, but it was only half-finished for lack of labor; he needed Negro workmen. His line could be turned in a day's march, and, with his insufficient force, such a turning move would be hard to stop. He asked for Pickett and more artillery in order to prevent it. He needed cavalry still more, as the Unionists had seven regiments of cavalry on the north side against his two very small ones. He was not strong enough to do anything more than stand on the defensive. If he attacked and captured a portion of the enemy's line, he could not hold it for want of men.[6]

The next day Longstreet had the assurance to write Lee suggesting that Johnston be reappointed to the command of the Army of Tennessee, now an almost non-existent fragment. He thought that Johnston might be able to restore it. "I have served under General Johnston," he added, "and as far as I am capable of judging, I am satisfied that

[6] *O. R.*, ser. I, vol. XLVI, pt. II, p. 1188.

he is one of our ablest and best generals." He added that Johnston had not been successful, partly because he had not been supported by the government.

This opinion of Longstreet's was possibly an echo from the controversy of the previous year, in which he had found himself in opposition to Bragg and Davis and, therefore, in sympathy with Johnston. Lee does not appear to have answered the letter, but he took Longstreet's advice and appointed Johnston, in which appointment the government concurred. Lee had just been made commander in chief of all the armies, but he hesitated to use his authority, so deeply rooted was his deference to the government.

On February 4, Longstreet told Lee he could hardly detach troops for service on the south side, as he did not have men enough to hold the line of the Chickahominy River against a determined attack. He thought Grant would attack Richmond from the north, which movement seemed indicated by the crossing of Union troops in considerable force from the south side of the river.

On February 9, Lee asked Longstreet's advice on a technical matter on the south side. He thought the picket posts near Elliott's salient were so constructed that the enemy could rush them from their own picket posts. Would Longstreet examine the line and see if the picket posts could be remodeled so as to prevent such a happening? [7] Longstreet answered that he had never seen a picket line that could not be taken. In fact, the picket line was commanded by fire from the parapets and bombproofs in the rear. He was himself thinking of playing the same trick on the enemy that the Confederate engineers apprehended and of attacking the Union picket line.

On February 14, Longstreet made a suggestion that might

[7] *Ibid.*, p. 1227.

have seemed improper and even insubordinate but for the circumstances. The spring would see the enemy in motion and it would be difficult to meet them. Food was necessary and could not be obtained as before; the way to get it, and other necessities, was to seize the gold and use it to buy provisions. Gold would soon bring plenty of supplies. If there was no law for impressing gold, it should be taken without law.[8]

Lee answered that the gold would buy provisions, but where was it to be found? It was not in the treasury or in the banks. Then he sketched the whole threatening situation and expressed a desire to see Longstreet, though he could not leave his post. Longstreet answered that the gold could be obtained by sending officers to the vaults where it was stored, and Longstreet was right. There was still a good deal of gold in Richmond—unused while the nation perished. But Lee was not the man who could bring himself to acting unscrupulously in any emergency. He would do all that he could for the cause—legitimately; he would do nothing more. Longstreet was not so scrupulous, and Longstreet was right if the cause was still to be fought for.

At the last of February, Longstreet came into contact with the Union General Ord and discussed with him the situation and the hope of peace. On the last day of the month he again saw Ord. Longstreet suggested a military convention to arrange terms of peace, as he informed Lee on March 1. Ord told him that Grant had authority to treat with Lee, if Lee had authority, and proposed that Lee should indicate his desire to confer with him. Longstreet suggested that the proposed meeting take place on the north side of the river, no doubt hoping to be present. Nothing, however, came of the plan, as Grant declined to meet Lee

[8] *Ibid.*, p. 1233.

in such a manner after Lee had complied with Longstreet's suggestion and expressed a wish to discuss peace terms. The war had to be fought out to the bitter end.

On March 5, Longstreet suggested to Lee that Sheridan was coming to Richmond to reinforce Grant, which was a fact. It seemed best to await the enemy, unless they were making for Lynchburg, when the Confederates might take the field against them. Again Longstreet urged the seizure of gold, averring that there were abundant supplies to be bought in North Carolina—for gold. But Lee would have none of this brigandage. On March 10, Longstreet repeated his oft-repeated demand for the rest of Pickett's division, declaring that deserters had come in with the information that Thomas had arrived in his front and that there were thirty thousand Unionists in camp on the Williamsburg road. He still thought the main attack would be made north of the James, and perhaps that sector was actually considered by Grant.

In the middle of the month Longstreet was directed to send troops against Sheridan, reported to be moving to Hanover Courthouse. He prepared to send Pickett and three batteries against him. Corse's brigade moved out north from Richmond. Longstreet accompanied it.

Longstreet, on March 14, moved out the Telegraph road to its junction with the "Ashland Road," probably the Mountain road. At that point he waited for Fitz Lee's cavalry, directed to join him. On the morning of March 15, Longstreet sent a dispatch to Ewell stating that he was still waiting for the cavalry, without which it would be useless to move against cavalry. Wild reports came to Richmond of Sheridan's movements, but Longstreet could not obtain any definite information about them. Sheridan seemed to be at Ashland, and Longstreet again asked Ewell for

Fitz Lee's cavalry. And then Pickett requested the Confederate cavalry, the whereabouts of which could not be learned. The infantry was waiting just beyond the Chickahominy River. Early stuck to the opinion that Sheridan was about to attack Richmond on the north side and from the Shenandoah Valley, so informing Secretary of War Breckinridge.

But Sheridan did not come that way and so Longstreet did not fight him. It is interesting to speculate on the different course events might have taken if Sheridan and Longstreet had clashed outside of Richmond. It is possible that Sheridan would have been so crippled that he would not have won the victory at Five Forks, on April 1, which broke Lee's lines. In other words, the war might have lasted a while longer. The Unionists did not wish to attack Longstreet's defenses. They declared that the works were perfect.

On March 18, the Unionists drove in Longstreet's cavalry pickets on the Williamsburg road, to cover the passage of troops over the Chickahominy, as he thought. He at once prepared to attack, having just returned from the projected movement against Sheridan. But nothing came of it.

On March 20, Longstreet urged Lee to make preparations to prevent a raid on the Danville Railroad. As the enemy had done nothing north of the James, he reasoned they would attempt something against Lee's supply lines, now reduced to the Southside Railroad and the Richmond and Danville. To stave off the raid Longstreet suggested that dismounted cavalry be put in the trenches, thereby relieving infantry for field service. The suggestion does not seem to have been adopted. But Lee was now satisfied that Grant was preparing for offensive operations along his whole line and directed Longstreet to be ready to move with such forces as could be taken from the trenches to any point that might be attacked. At the same time, Lee called on Davis to request Virginia to furnish Negroes as soldiers.

Longstreet shipped Pickett's division to Lee on March 25, but he reported movements on the Pamunkey and the presence of the enemy on the Richmond and Fredericksburg Railroad; also there were troop movements across the river. On the same day (March 25) Longstreet informed Lee that scouts reported Sheridan's force as crossing the lower Chickahominy. He desired to meet any advance of the enemy on the Williamsburg road, but Pickett's departure to the right wing forced him to remain within his lines. On the same day Longstreet complained that Georgia troops were being solicited to leave the army in order to join the home army in their state.

On March 27, Longstreet suggested that a cavalry force be sent with Pickett to watch Sheridan's movements; he thought that infantry and cavalry together would do better than cavalry alone. In fact, the cavalry at this time was somewhat demoralized by the wretched condition of the horses, which were almost starving.[9]

On March 29, Longstreet had suggestions to make in regard to the fleet in the James River, which he thought should be used to obstruct the enemy's advance up the river. A battery of heavy guns (rifled field guns) would be better against gunboats than any other kind of ordnance. On the same day he informed Lee that if Field's division were removed, as was suggested, Local Defense troops would have to be put in its place. Called on to make suggestions for officers for the new Negro troops, Longstreet suggested some names but did not think much of the project. He declared that men were trying to get out of service under the pretense of raising Negro companies.

[9] O. R., ser. I, vol. XLVI, pt. II, p. 1357.

On the fatal day, April 1, when Lee's lines were broken, Longstreet reported that only Negro troops were in the Union defenses on the north side of the river. Demonstrations and the difficulty of getting through the picket lines had prevented Longstreet's scouts from securing accurate information of the movement of troops from the north side to the south side preceding Sheridan's attack on Lee's extreme right.

But now Lee was calling for troops to stem the tide; Longstreet replied that he would send them as soon as he had transportation, and would try to have troops in Petersburg that day. Field's division was at once ordered to leave; if it had been sent before it might have accomplished something. Lee had sent not only for Field's division but for Longstreet to accompany it. While Longstreet prepared to move with the bulk of his force, he asked Ewell to occupy his old lines with Local Defense troops in order to prevent the enemy from breaking through. At that time he did not know the extent of the disaster at Five Forks.

At 10:40 P. M. Lee wired Secretary of War Breckinridge that the enemy had broken his lines and that he would begin to withdraw from the James River. The only chance of concentrating troops was near the Danville railroad. On the morning of April 2, Lee informed Davis that it was absolutely necessary to abandon his position that night. The troops would move to Amelia Courthouse. Preparations were made at once for withdrawal from Petersburg.

Longstreet's and Hill's corps were to cross the Appomattox at Battersea Factory and take the river road north of the Appomattox. Other troops would move on other routes.

CHAPTER XIX

THE FINAL PHASE

THE Confederate lines about Richmond and Petersburg, forty miles in length, were finally broken at Five Forks on the extreme right by Sheridan, using both infantry and cavalry skillfully. The Confederates, poorly handled, made a stout resistance but, taken in the flank by much larger numbers, were routed and scattered. Pickett's division, moved from Longstreet's sector to the extreme right, was involved in this defeat, which tarnished its ancient glory. It would appear from certain evidence that Lee never forgave Pickett.

It was unfortunate for the Confederates that Longstreet did not command on this field. With all his faults, Longstreet was able, far abler than the rather dull and humdrum Pickett. Longstreet, on such a field, would have weighed the chances carefully and, finding the game going against him irrevocably, would have withdrawn without material loss. Lee himself was somewhat to blame for the disaster, for Pickett was left in an isolated position without support. If Lee intended to fight to save the railroad behind his extreme right, he might as well have taken greater chances and drawn more troops from his left. As it was, Longstreet was sitting comfortably behind his works while the Confederate right was being broken. If Longstreet and another brigade had been at Five Forks, the story might have been different.

It would only have postponed the inevitable a little longer. Lee, faced with the necessity of making use of Long-·

334

street in this emergency, sent him a message on the same day giving him the choice of attacking north of the James or sending more of his men to the south side. Longstreet at once prepared to forward Field, his best command, to Petersburg, but before this could be done the news arrived that Lee was preparing to retreat from the city he had defended so long and so obstinately.

"General Lee orders that your division be sent to Petersburg at once," Adjutant General Latrobe dispatched Field. In a later dispatch he added, "It is important beyond measure that no time be lost." This was late on April 1 and after Lee knew of the disaster at Five Forks. It was his one chance of retrieving the situation, to save the railroad from the enemy's clutches. Longstreet was to accompany the troops, for Lee was determined to have the benefit of his counsel and efforts.

Longstreet, hurrying for once, reached Lee's headquarters at the Turnbull house about 4:00 A. M. of April 2. Field's division was on the railroad coming to Petersburg. Longstreet says of his experience on the way to Lee:

"The darkness of night still covered us when we crossed over James River by the pontoon bridge, but before long land and water batteries lifted their bombs over their lazy curves, screaming shells came through the freighted night to light our ride, and signal sky-rockets gave momentary illumination." [1] Longstreet had an impulse to stop and aid the embattled Mahone but his orders were imperative and he hastened on to Lee. He knew that Weitzel, north of the James, was making ready to storm the defenses he had just left but he had to abandon them. These were described by the entering Unionists as perfect.

The Union batteries were in full fire on the Confederate

[1] *M. to A.*, p. 603.

trenches when Longstreet, crossing the Appomattox, rode through the streets of Petersburg and out to the west to Lee's headquarters. When passing the railroad station, Longstreet paused to learn that none of Field's troops had yet arrived. Leaving orders for the detachments to move as soon as they got off the trains, he hurried on.

Longstreet reached headquarters before dawn. Staff officers were restlessly roaming about but Lee was still stretched on his weary couch, though awake. When informed that Longstreet had come, Lee called his lieutenant to his bed and gave orders for him to march to the support of the routed troops near Five Forks. As usual, he did not blame Pickett or Fitz Lee, in command at Five Forks, but complained of the large numbers of the enemy and of the repeating carbines of the cavalry, which made them far superior to the Southern horsemen. He was weary, disturbed by the pains of his "rheumatic ailment," as Longstreet calls it.

Longstreet was not destined to rally the troops on the extreme right. While Lee was still talking to him, officers came in to report the breaking of the lines in front of headquarters. That line, like the one-horse shay, was now giving way everywhere and could not be held for any length of time. Going to the front door with Longstreet, Lee saw the Union skirmishers approaching and appealed to his lieutenant to arrest their movement. Longstreet could only answer that none of his troops had yet arrived from Richmond. Then staff officers rode off to find other troops, somewhat delaying the Union advance. A. P. Hill, informed of the breaking of the lines and seeking his troops, ran into the enemy skirmishers and was killed.

Now that Hill was killed (which Lee quickly learned), the commander sent orders for Heth to take command of the Third Corps. But Heth was cut off from Lee by the enemy's advance and could not come. Lee then put the Third Corps under Longstreet, who thus had the major portions of two corps under him. The situation was most critical, but the Confederates on some sectors were holding out with grim fortitude. Mahone, especially, not only held his own but repulsed attacks with loss.

The Unionists had selected the front between Forts Fisher and Welch for the assault of April 2. Marcus Wright and the Sixth Corps carried the works, which were thinly held. On reaching Hatcher's Run, the Sixth Corps turned toward Petersburg. The Twenty-fourth Corps under Gibbon passed the Sixth Corps. The Confederate works near Fort Stedman were carried by General Parke, who massed Hartranft's division on the right of Fort Sedgwick and Potter's on the left. At 4:30 the attacking party went forward; the pioneers cut away the abatis and the Southern works were taken. But a rear line held out, and Parke recoiled from it. The position captured was near the Jerusalem plank road; Gordon made several efforts to retake it.

The main line of Confederate works on the Appomattox west of Petersburg ran along the bank of Old Town Creek. On the opposite side of the creek about a thousand yards distant were Forts Gregg and Whitworth. Field, of Longstreet, Gordon, and part of Wilcox were put in the main Confederate line.

Longstreet, consulting with Lee as to what to do in the emergency, just such a situation as brought out the best in him, saw Benning's brigade coming from the direction of Petersburg. The brigade was six hundred strong, and Longstreet asked for two hundred of the men. Taking these, he posted them behind a canal and stretched out the remainder of the brigade in a skirmish line confronting the Union skirmish line, which was in front of the masses of the Union line of battle now coming on. At that moment, Lee sent a message to Richmond stating that he would have to retreat from Petersburg. This dispatch reached Davis while he was in church.

Two earthworks, Fort Gregg and Fort Whitworth, remained for the Unionists to take before they could call the Confederate position their own. Field's troops had come up by this time, and Longstreet stretched them out in the face of the enemy and ordered them to entrench.

The Unionists now pressed forward in a wave in this sector, forcing Lee and his staff back to the inner line. Lee left amidst whizzing rifle balls and exploding shells. The Turnbull house, his headquarters, was soon blazing. It was important to hold Fort Gregg, one of the key positions, until nightfall. About five hundred men of Wilcox's division were assigned to this fort and ordered to hold it to the last.

These heroes held back the Unionists by a most Spartan defense, using rifles and field guns and, at length, bayonets. Masses of the enemy swarmed up the parapet of the fort, on which six Union flags were at one time planted. At length Fort Gregg was surrounded and stormed from all sides. When the victors entered it, they found a large part of the little garrison dead or wounded.

Fort Gregg thus fell only after a desperate defense in which about half of the tiny garrison were killed or wounded. To the right beyond Fort Gregg no Confederate line remained. The Southern troops on the extreme right, attacked by masses of the enemy, had been forced back and away; the Unionists were between them and Lee. Still the Confederates immediately in front of Petersburg were resisting vigorously. It was now Lee's sole purpose to hold the town until night, when he would be able to withdraw his forces under cover of darkness. Fort Whitworth was captured after a short resistance, as Wilcox sought to withdraw the garrison intact, but a large part of it was captured.

If a general assault had been made on the Confederates at this time, it is possible that Appomattox would have been anticipated by a week, but the Union troops were not sufficiently concentrated for such an effort and Lee was enabled to hold out until nightfall. Gordon's and Mahone's commands were keeping the enemy at bay; Gordon, with incomparable audacity, was actually thinking of taking the offensive in turn. Lee sent him word to remain simply on the defensive. Nearly everywhere the Confederates were face to face with ruin and death. Some guns, brought up the day before from the James River lines, were being served near Lee with cool effect.[2]

Just before the attack on Fort Gregg, Benning's brigade, the advance of Field's division, had been strung out in a skirmish line between Fort Baldwin and the Appomattox River. But the men were few, and when the rest of Field came up, Longstreet had only the thinnest of lines. He kept sending to Lee for reinforcements until Lee's patience gave out and he returned the answer that he had no more men. But Longstreet skillfully availed himself of his handful, taking up a short line near the river and throwing up fieldworks.

It was now early afternoon, and the Confederate commands in front of Petersburg were still holding out and would evidently be able to hold out until nightfall. The Union forces were considerably disarrayed by the broken ground and their casualties and had lost much of their original impulse. Now that the first surprise was over, the

2 Freeman, *op. cit.*, IV, 50.

Confederates were cool and determined. Used to desperate situations, the men were not at all demoralized. The high command might have given up hope of success but the army had not. Lee was able quietly to arrange for the evacuation that must take place that night. Grant was also preparing for it, preferring to surround Lee in the open country to storming the last defenses held by such desperate men.

The retreat was complicated by the fact that the Union army completely held the roads south of the Appomattox. Lee was thus forced to retreat north of the river for some miles and then cross to the south side, an operation necessitating two crossings by the force in Petersburg. The troops north of the James would have to cross that river and later the Appomattox. The troops cut off by the breaking of the lines on April 1 and 2, Anderson's and Pickett's commands, had to retreat along the south bank of the Appomattox until they came into contact with Lee's main force.

Soon after dark the retreat began. Field's division, and Heth's and Wilcox's following, crossed the Appomattox, and the Second Corps after them. They destroyed the bridge. The Local Defense troops from Chaffin's Bluff, on the north side of the James River, crossed that river and joined in the retreat. The sailors and marines on the south side of the river came along; Kershaw crossed the James at Richmond, as did Ewell's Local Defense troops. Mahone had gone on ahead to cover the movement of the troops from the north side of the James.

Lee now actually had in hand a larger force than for some short time past, but it was made up of divers elements, containing many home guards and sailors, anything but an effective army for field service. Longstreet made a good march through roads heavy with mud, reaching Goode's Bridge on the Appomattox sixteen miles from Petersburg, on April 3.

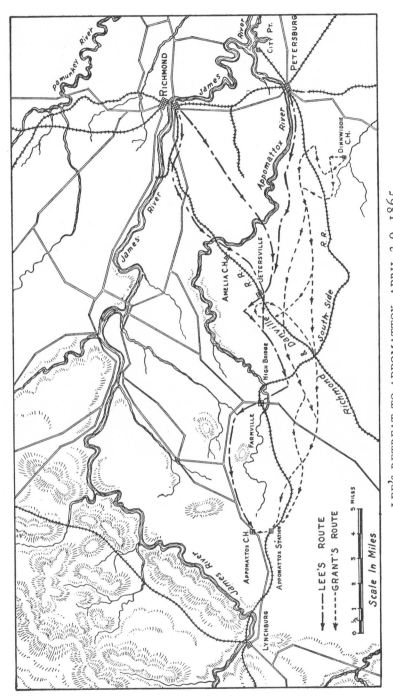

LEE'S RETREAT TO APPOMATTOX, APRIL 3–9, 1865

——— LEE'S ROUTE

------- GRANT'S ROUTE

Scale In Miles

Field and Wilcox at once crossed the river to cover the passage of other troops. On April 4, Mahone crossed, and a part of Heth's division on the south side of the river came up. Finally Longstreet reached Amelia Courthouse, Lee's first objective, with the Union cavalry hovering around but hesitating to attack infantry. There Longstreet put Field, Heth, and Wilcox in line of battle, hoping to strike the pursuing enemy, but there was nothing at hand but cavalry. The main column of Sheridan's force was hastening to Jetersville, south of Amelia, to cut Lee off from the direct route to Danville. The Confederate troops might have pressed on and passed Jetersville before Sheridan came up in force, but the provisions Lee expected to find at Amelia were not there and the men had to forage for supplies. It appears that in the hurry of the retreat specific orders for the sending of supplies to Amelia had not been given, probably an omission on the part of Lee's staff.

Longstreet and Gordon had been ordered to cross the Appomattox at Bevill's Bridge, the one highest up, but the approaches to that bridge were found to be covered by high water; and they crossed at Goode's Bridge, lower down, which was overtaxed by the passing troops. Here was the first important delay. It was followed by the halt for securing food at Amelia.

Lee rode with Longstreet's advance into Amelia. On April 4, the army concentrated there. Wilcox's division arrived at 1:00 p. m. Some of Heth's came up. Gordon was near by. Mahone was at Goode's Bridge waiting for Ewell. Anderson and the cavalry were a few miles away.

At nightfall the Union cavalry withdrew, and Longstreet took his men out of line of battle. The rear of Lee's army, Ewell's troops from Richmond, was coming up; his forces were in hand. And but for the lack of supplies, the situation might not have seemed hopeless. As it was, there was no lack of supplies—millions of rations at Danville—but these provisions had not come up; the men were starving. Moreover, the thousand wagons of the army, hauled by feeble cattle, were stretched out over miles of road and would certainly hold back the army unless it could move along the line of the railroad to Danville.

On the morning of April 5, Longstreet started southward toward Jetersville behind a force of cavalry. Other troops followed. By this time Ewell had come, but his wagon train carrying rations was captured, a great loss to the army.

Lee accompanied Longstreet. Seven miles from Amelia they came upon the enemy in position. The commander, after carefully surveying the Unionists, concluded that they were too strong to attack. This meant that the route southward was blocked. And indeed Sheridan was at Jetersville just beyond and had entrenched across the road, closing the way.

Lee had now only one course open to him: to pass on to Lynchburg, where he could obtain supplies and whence he might be able to move southward to Danville, his objective. At Danville he would be on the North Carolina line and near Johnston's army. But with hungry troops and starved horses, he would have to leave the main route, the railway, and cut across by narrow and almost impassable country ways.

"No orders came," Longstreet says, "the afternoon was passing, further delays seemed perilous. I drew the command off and filed to the right to cross Flat Creek to march for Farmville. The other infantry and trains and artillery followed and kept the march until a late hour, halting for a short rest before daylight." [3] But already the Union cav-

---

[3] *M. to A.*, p. 610.

alry was ahead of the Confederates. They had attacked the wagon trains, destroying a number of wagons and tying up traffic on the narrow road. Some of the wagons had to be sent on the road the troops were taking to Amelia Springs. This night march of April 5-6, 1865, resulted in the Confederates' making a little distance but not enough to get away from the pursuing enemy. At Flat Creek near Amelia Springs the troops were held by the breaking of a bridge.

Lee's situation was now almost hopeless. But still he continued to hope against hope. He was making for Farmville, his immediate objective. Longstreet was in front, and Lee went with him, unfortunately, instead of remaining in the rear. Behind Longstreet came, in order, Anderson, Ewell, and Gordon. Gordon, having the best command, was given the post of honor and danger.

Knowing that Lee must move either to Danville or Lynchburg, Grant had given directions with the view of intercepting his march in either direction. Sheridan, with his cavalry and the Fifth Corps, was to move westward near the Appomattox River, so as to strike the Richmond and Danville Railroad. Meade, with the Second and Sixth corps, was to follow Sheridan in the direction of Amelia Courthouse. Ord, with the Twenty-fourth Corps, followed by the Ninth Corps, was to move along the Southside Railroad to Burke's Junction (now Burkeville). The pursuit of Lee began early on April 3.

In the afternoon of April 4, Sheridan learned that Lee was at Amelia Courthouse, eight miles northeast of Jetersville, and sent word to Meade and Grant, meanwhile entrenching with the Fifth Corps near Jetersville. Meade, on receiving Sheridan's message, ordered the Second and Sixth corps to Jetersville. Both arrived in the course of April 5.

Lee was not concentrated at Amelia until April 5. Finding his way blocked, he turned west for Farmville. About sunset the head of Lee's column, Longstreet, reached Amelia Springs. On the morning of April 5, Sheridan sent a cavalry force to Painesville, five miles north of Amelia Springs, to learn if the Confederates were moving in that direction. There the Union cavalry found a wagon train. It drove off the cavalry escort and burned the wagons.

The Confederates continued their march through the night of April 5-6. The head of Longstreet's column reached Rice about 6:00 A. M. on April 6. Lee joined him; Longstreet waited for the rest of the army. Ewell, far to the rear, was at Amelia Springs about 8:00 A. M. Fitz Lee's cavalry joined Longstreet at Rice in the morning.

Meade planned to attack Lee in the morning of April 6, with the Second, Fifth, and Sixth corps, and Sheridan's cavalry. Accordingly, he directed the march of the troops on Amelia. In the night of April 5, Ord reached Burkeville after a wonderful march. He was directed by Grant to destroy High Bridge and other bridges over the Appomattox in Lee's front, in order to arrest the Confederate movement. Before dawn of April 6, Ord sent a small force of infantry and cavalry to burn the bridges at Farmville.

On the morning of April 6, the Unionists advancing on Amelia learned that a Confederate column was moving westward, near Flat Creek. Humphreys at once prepared to attack the column.

The Unionists also discovered that wagon trains were moving in a northwest direction near Deatonsville. In the forenoon they discovered two infantry columns, some miles away, moving rapidly. Realizing that Lee had passed across the front of the Union army at night, Meade at once changed the direction of his columns. The Second Corps moved on

Deatonsville, the Fifth on the right of the Second, the
Sixth on the left of the Second.

April 6 was now well advanced. The army, lacking food
and utterly weary, was marching slowly and straggling
badly. Half of Ewell's Local Defense troops had fallen out
of the line of march; other commands had lost many men.
Demoralization had set in from lack of food, for soldiers
can face all other sufferings better than empty bellies.

Lee rode on with a small escort to Rice, about twelve
miles from Amelia Springs and not far from Farmville. It
was a station on the Southside Railroad and so of some
importance. Longstreet arrived before long after an excellent march, considering the state of the roads and the weakness of the hungry men. Hearing that Union cavalry had
passed up the road toward Farmville, Longstreet seized
what cavalry was available and sent them in pursuit, in the
effort to prevent the destruction of the bridge over the
Appomattox at Farmville, essential to the safety of the
army.

Following Longstreet, Wilcox's division, and then Heth's
and Mahone's had come up. But Anderson, who should have
been next, did not arrive. Presently came word that Union
cavalry had attacked the wagon trains. It was evident that
the rear of the army was in danger, and Lee sent Mahone
back to aid it.

What had happened was that at Little Sailor's Creek, near
the Appomattox River, Anderson and Ewell had taken one
road and Gordon another. Anderson and Ewell, following
the left-hand road, crossed the little stream and found themselves almost surrounded by Union infantry and cavalry.
They had delayed in the effort to save the wagon trains and
had been caught. Forming on a hillside overlooking Little
Sailor's Creek, the Confederates struck the Unionists in a

body and scattered them in a magnificent charge. But on the other side of the creek the Unionists had artillery in position, while the Confederates did not have a single gun. Surrounded on three sides and overwhelmed by artillery and rifle fire, Anderson's and Ewell's men, after heavy losses in killed and wounded, were obliged to surrender. It was one of the worst disasters, if not the worst, ever suffered by Lee's army. Ewell, Kershaw, G. W. C. Lee, the General's son, and thousands of men fell into the enemy's hands. Meanwhile Gordon, who had taken the right-hand road, had also been assailed, but he beat off the enemy's attacks and joined Lee with his command intact. If Lee had learned of the situation at Sailor's Creek earlier, he might have sent back his troops at Rice and caught a large Union force between two fires. It does not appear, however, that he knew of the disaster until the affair was practically over. (Mahone's account that Lee was near the battlefield, quoted by Freeman, seems impossible, in view of the fact that a large Union force occupied the gap between Lee's main force and the rear guard. Lee did ride toward the fight, however.)

With more than a third of his army lost at Sailor's Creek, because of the efforts of the rear guard to protect a wagon train hourly growing more useless, Lee's position was now past hope. His remaining force, losing men every hour, was too small to be of any effect whatever, for he had not more than twenty thousand men of all arms. But he had no intention of giving up as long as any avenue of escape remained.

Lee now rode back to Rice from his jaunt toward Sailor's Creek. No fighting was going on there. Longstreet's troops were waiting orders, and with them fragments of other commands. Gordon was still fighting but was to come up later. His own casualties were large; Lee's total loss that day was about eight thousand men. Only six divisions remained, all but two of them very small.

From the enemy's viewpoint it had been a wonderful day. The Second Corps had crossed Flat Creek and begun to skirmish with Gordon's men, a fight that was kept up for fourteen miles. The line of battle followed the skirmishers through a broken country and over bad roads with wonderful celerity; there was no letup in the chase.

Anderson halted three miles west of Deatonsville, where the road forks, one road crossing Little Sailor's Creek directly and going on to Rice, the other turning abruptly to the right and crossing the main creek below.

Crook, the cavalryman, attempted to cut off the wagon trains at the road junction but was driven off by Anderson, who had stopped to protect the wagons. Ewell, coming up at this moment, took part in a second repulse of Crook. When Gordon's column reached the fork, Anderson and Ewell crossed the creek and formed line of battle on the high ground just beyond it.

Crook and Merritt crossed the creek. Gordon took the road to the right. Humphreys, on arriving at the fork about 4:30 P. M., saw the Confederates drawn up beyond the creek. Knowing that Sheridan's cavalry was between the Confederates and Rice, Humphreys continued in pursuit of Gordon, turning to the right. The running contest with Gordon continued for three miles farther, the road being strewn with military equipment of all sorts. Near Perkinson's Mill on Sailor's Creek the sharp action already described took place in the late afternoon, in which the main trains of Lee's army and several hundred prisoners were taken. Gordon formed line of battle beyond the creek and held back the Unionists for a time, then continued on his way.

Returning to Rice about sundown, Lee ordered Longstreet to move to Farmville and thence to Lynchburg. Field, Heth, and Wilcox set out on the road, followed by the wagon trains; the cavalry followed in Longstreet's rear. Mahone and Gordon were to cross the Appomattox at High Bridge.

"I heard nothing of the affair at Sailor's Creek," says Longstreet, "nor from General Lee until next morning . . . we marched and crossed the Appomattox at Farmville without loss. . . . We crossed early in the morning [April 7] and received two days' rations—the first regular issue since we left Richmond—halted our wagons, made fires, got out cooking utensils, and were just ready to prepare a good breakfast." Then Lee, coming up, informed Longstreet that the bridges over the Appomattox had been fired before the cavalry had crossed and that part of the command was cut off; he ordered the troops to hurry onward.[4] There was something of a panic as troops and wagoners hurriedly packed up to march. Lee himself led the column, which hastened on. "I thought it better to let them pass me," says Longstreet, "and to quiet their apprehensions a little, rode at a walk."[5]

The Union cavalry was now riding almost into the Confederate column. By some blunder the bridges over the river had not been burned, as Lee ordered, and the enemy came on unimpeded. Lee was excited, declaring that part of his cavalry had been cut off and lost, but Longstreet sought to reassure him by telling him that the horse would find fords and cross.

Lee rode with Longstreet's troops to a point several miles north of Farmville, the coal pits. The weary chief looked on and saw his men win their last victory, for the Union

[4] *M. to A.*, p. 616.
[5] *Ibid.*, p. 617.

cavalry was completely routed by the Southern riders, with heavy loss. This success temporarily rallied Lee's flagging spirits and he spoke hopefully. Near Cumberland Church, three miles from Farmville, Mahone drew up his command in line of battle to protect the passage of the wagon trains, while Gordon moved through the woods to convoy them. In the afternoon the Union infantry, coming up, attacked Mahone, whose left flank was unprotected. With the aid of troops sent back by Longstreet and Gordon, Mahone defeated the attempt, taking prisoners.

At nightfall Lee went to a cottage near Cumberland Church to spend the night and was joined by Longstreet. There the commander received a note from Grant demanding his surrender.[6] Longstreet was sitting beside Lee when the note arrived. Lee, after reading it, handed it to Longstreet without a word. Longstreet, read it in turn and said, "Not yet." But Lee, without showing his answer to Longstreet, sent it off; in it he asked Grant to state his terms.[7]

In fact, Lee was not yet ready to give up, for there remained a ray of hope. At eleven o'clock Gordon moved on again, without regard to the weariness of men and beasts. Longstreet followed at twelve. At 1:00 A. M. the wagon train started off.

Lee was now making for Appomattox station on the railway in order to secure food for his starving men. From Appomattox he planned to go to Lynchburg, where he could cross the broad James River. Once south of the James, he would have a fair chance of escape with the remnant of his force.

This day, April 8, wore away almost without incident. The annoying attacks of the Union cavalry had entirely

<hr />

[6] Freeman, op. cit., IV, 103.
[7] M. to A., p. 619.

ceased; indeed, the enemy cavalry had received such a lesson the day before that they were cautious, and, more than this, they were now seeking to get ahead of Lee and cut him off from Lynchburg. Through the mud the weary but still not-despairing troops plodded on.

"We passed abandoned wagons in flames," says Long-street, "and limbers and caissons of artillery burning some-times in the middle of the road. One of my battery com-manders reported his horses too weak to haul his guns. He was ordered to bury the guns and cover their burial-places with old leaves and brushwood. Many weary soldiers were picked up, and many came to the column from the wood-land, some with, many without, arms—all asking for food."

The night of April 7, the artillerist Pendleton had held a little council of war with other officers, at which the de-cision was made to advise Lee to surrender. In the morning of April 8, Pendleton, coming to Longstreet, informed him of the proceedings of the council and asked him to bear the message to Lee.

"Much surprised," Longstreet says, "I turned and asked if he did not know that the Articles of War provided that officers or soldiers who asked commanding officers to sur-render should be shot, and said, 'If General Lee doesn't know when to surrender until I tell him, he will never know.'"

Pendleton was thus rebuffed by Longstreet, who, how-ever, probably knew that something was in the wind. The former then went on to Lee and delivered the message himself. But the commander was not yet ready to surrender and he declined Pendleton's recommendation with most con-siderate courtesy. Lee had not entirely abandoned the hope of escape, though his hope was slight. He felt it his duty

to fight on until no way of escape remained. Then would
come the time to give up.

On this day, April 8, Grant stated his terms of surrender.
Lee, though not accepting them, agreed to meet him at a
certain point on the Richmond road at ten o'clock the next
morning. Though Lee did not know it at the time, all hope
was gone because on April 8 Sheridan's cavalry had seized
four train-loads of supplies for Lee at Appomattox station.
Thus if Lee had been able to pass the cordon now fast encircling him, he would have been without food for his men;
and soldiers cannot live without food, whatever may be the
case with other human beings.

About dark Gordon's column had halted a mile from
Appomattox Courthouse. In front were wagons and artillery; behind was Longstreet, five or six miles from the
courthouse. Lee and Longstreet, with staff officers, made
their camp in the woods. There were no tents and no provisions. As the spring night air was chilly, some one lighted
a fire, about which Lee and the officers sat on the ground.[8]

About nine o'clock the sound of artillery firing came to
the weary group—this time, most ominously, *from the front.*
It meant that the army was practically surrounded. The
horizon all around reflected the glow of the Union camp-
fires. Lee, perfectly calm in this last crisis, sent summons
to his lieutenants to attend a council of war. Presently Fitz
Lee and Gordon came up, and with these and Longstreet,
already at hand, Lee began his final council.

Lee stood by the fire. Longstreet sat on a log; Gordon
and Fitz Lee, weary, stretched out on the ground. Lee explained the situation as he knew it and asked for opinions.
The others were still prepared to fight. If there was nothing but cavalry in front, the infantry could drive it off; if

[8] Freeman, *op. cit.,* IV, 114.

the Union infantry stood across the line of march, nothing remained but surrender. So the officers prepared to work out the last battle orders for the Army of Northern Virginia.

The troops were to advance at 1:00 A. M. Fitz Lee would lead the way and drive the enemy from his front, covering the wagons. Gordon was to follow and break the Union containing force. Longstreet would hold the rear and repel attacks from that direction. The army was to move to Campbell Courthouse instead of to Lynchburg.

Longstreet prepared to go to sleep. "General Lee," he says, "made his headquarters near the rear-guard, and spread his couch about a hundred feet from the saddle and blanket that were my pillow and spread for the night. If he had a more comfortable bed than mine I do not know, but I think not." [9] It is likely that sleep did not visit Lee's eyes that night. On the other hand, it is probable that Longstreet, tired by the day's ride, slept well. With those steel nerves of his, no contingency upset him greatly.

Shortly after midnight the troops began to move forward to their stations. "It was five o'clock when the advance commands moved, four hours after the time ordered," Longstreet states. But before that time Lee rode ahead, and soon the guns announced the beginning of the movement. What was left of the army was stretched out on a single road in a column about four miles long; there were not more than eight thousand men in the line of battle, though a swarm of stragglers was at hand.

The attack opened at five o'clock. The artillery was blazing and, with its roar, was mixed the rattle of musketry. But the battle stood still; it was evident that the Confederates were not driving the foe. Presently a staff officer came to Lee to explain the situation. Gordon, passing through

[9] *M. to A.*, p. 623.

Appomattox village, had driven off a force of Unionists, only to find a heavier line immediately in the front. The enemy, infantry and cavalry, was endeavoring to surround Gordon and cut him off. A staff officer made his way from Lee to Gordon and asked the state of affairs.

"Tell General Lee," Gordon answered, "I have fought my corps to a frazzle, and I fear I can do nothing unless I am heavily supported by Longstreet's corps." Lee listened as the aide reported Gordon's words. Longstreet was arrayed to hold off the clustering enemy on the rear; he could not spare a man.

"Then," Lee said, "there is nothing left me but to go and see General Grant, and I would rather die a thousand deaths." [10] For a short time he was almost overcome by emotion, rebellious against fate. Presently he sent for Longstreet. The lieutenant joined him.

"He was dressed in a suit of new uniform," Longstreet says, "sword and sash, handsomely embroidered belt, boots, and a pair of gold spurs. At first approach his compact figure appeared as a man in the flush vigor of forty summers, but as I drew near, the handsome apparel and brave bearing failed to conceal his profound depression. He stood near the embers of some burned rails, received me with graceful salutation." [11]

In a few words Lee outlined the situation as it stood at the moment and asked Longstreet's opinion. "I asked," Longstreet says, "if the bloody sacrifice of his army could help the cause in other quarters." Lee said he thought not. "Then," said Longstreet, "your situation speaks for itself."

Mahone, called up next, gave the same opinion, that it was time to see Grant about surrender. Longstreet, appealed

[10] *M. to A.*, p. 624, quoting A. L. Long, *Memoirs of Robert E. Lee.*
[11] *M. to A.*, p. 624.

to by Mahone, supported his opinion. Lee then mounted his horse and rode off to meet Grant, while a lively skirmish was going on. For hostilities were continuing, the Unionists preparing to attack, the Confederates ready to repel them. Longstreet indeed formed line of battle, placing batteries to support the infantry. Thus the Army of Northern Virginia was drawn up for the last time.

While the line was forming word was brought to Longstreet that a break had been found in the Union cordon. Hoping against hope, he called for a courier to catch Lee and tell him of the chance of escape. The rider was off like the wind and presently caught Lee, but it was too late; Lee had sent a note asking for an interview with the Union commander.

A Confederate officer now rode forward to the Union line to ask for a truce for the conference of the two commanders. Custer, the cavalryman, demanded to know the officer's authority and was referred to Longstreet. He then asked to be taken to Longstreet and presently rode up, his yellow hair flowing over his shoulders.

"In the name of General Sheridan I demand the unconditional surrender of the army," he said to Longstreet.[12] The latter replied that he did not command the Southern army and that Custer was within the Confederate lines in disrespect to Grant as well as to himself. Custer, moderating his tone, remarked that further bloodshed would be deplorable.

"As you are now more reasonable," Longstreet answered, "I will say that General Lee has gone to meet General Grant, and it is for them to determine the future of the armies."

Custer rode away. Before long Lee came back, awaiting

[12] *M. to A.*, p. 627.

a reply to his note. He told Longstreet of his fear that Grant would demand harsh terms. Longstreet, who knew Grant well, attempted to console him by saying that the terms would be fair. But Lee was not assured and kept up a desultory conversation with his lieutenant until an officer approached with the return note. Lee still spoke of humiliating terms, and Longstreet advised him to break off negotiations and tell Grant to do his worst. Lee, riding off to meet the Union commander, seemed to Longstreet to be cheered by the prospect of another fight. But the terms Grant offered were generous enough; the surrender followed.

The Unionists did not immediately grant the truce asked and advanced in line of battle. Lee rode back to join Longstreet, who had prepared for attack if attack should come. He remained near Longstreet until about eleven o'clock, while everything looked like another battle. Just then a Union officer appeared bearing a note from Meade agreeing to an informal truce on that sector and suggesting that Lee send a duplicate of his letter to Grant. Lee then dispatched another note. At that moment his army was almost surrounded and was in danger of annihilation, if the truce granted separately by Sheridan, Ord, and Meade along different parts of the Union front should be broken. Lee was now anxious to consummate the surrender and thereby save the lives of his faithful followers. Then came his conversation with Longstreet (as given before). Grant's answer to this final note arranged for the conference and Lee rode off to it. The two commanders, meeting in the McLean house at Appomattox, agreed on the terms while Longstreet waited in considerable suspense.

After what seemed an interminable time to the anxious soldiers, who knew that surrender was in the air, Lee was

seen riding slowly back. "From force of habit," says Longstreet, "a burst of salutations greeted him, but quieted as
suddenly as they arose. The road was packed by standing
troops as he approached, the men with hats off, heads and
hearts bowed down. As he passed they raised their heads
and looked upon him with swimming eyes. Those who could
find voice said good-by, those who could not speak, and were
near, passed their hands gently over the sides of Traveller.
He rode with his hat off, and had sufficient control to fix
his eyes on a line between the ears of Traveller and look
neither to right nor left."

Almost immediately a practical question arose. The army
had with it United States money, and the chief ordnance
officer asked Lee what was to be done with it. Lee sent for
Longstreet's opinion. The latter could not see the utility of
turning over to the enemy money badly needed by the Southern soldiers and advised Lee to use it to pay them. Three
hundred dollars was brought as his share to Longstreet, who
took a hundred dollars and asked to have the rest distributed
among the men of Field's division.

Longstreet, appointed by Lee as one of the three Confederate commissioners to arrange the details of the surrender, entered the McLean house. There he came upon
Grant, who arose, shook hands with him and offered a cigar,
which, Longstreet adds, "was gratefully received." It was a
moment when sedatives were helpful.

The commissioners paroled 28,356 men, who included
not only the army as it then was but thousands of stragglers
that had come up before or that came up later. Longstreet's
own command was the only large unit; it comprised 14,833
men, consisting of the remains of the First and Third corps.

On the night of April 9, Longstreet camped in the woods,
with Lee near by. Longstreet, though he wrote of the sur-

render philosophically enough in later years, was bitter at the time. He declared he had felt for months that the Confederate cause was hopeless and that if he ever fought again he would be sure that it was necessary.[13]

In after years he was fully reconciled to the event. But at the moment he, perhaps, had some feeling of the fatefulness of the lost cause. For few more fateful causes have ever been lost. It was the beginning of the end of the immemorial stand for constitutional liberty, destined to die the earth over. From Appomattox, faintly and veiled by the years but still an incarnating reality, arose the specter of the Totalitarian State, now stretching its shadow across the world.

[13] Freeman, *op. cit.*, IV, 159.

CHAPTER XX

IN HIS HABIT AS HE LIVED

Nothing is more difficult than to get what may be called a representative likeness of a historical character. We can see him as he was at one time or another, but we find it hard indeed to fix the image of the man at the height of his powers, at the time when we wish to crystallize him in memory.

Since Longstreet lived to a good old age, he remains for most of us a shaggy-whiskered old man, benevolent and mild in appearance. That he was not so in his prime goes without saying. Then he was a typical soldier of a nation that owned few razors and little soap, a nation that did no shaving.

A contemporary account of about 1865 is interesting:

"The personal appearance of General Longstreet was not engaging; it was decidedly sombre; his bluish grey eye was intelligent—but cold; a very heavy brown beard was allowed to grow untrimmed; he seldom spoke unnecessarily; his weather-stained clothes, splashed boots and heavy black felt hat gave a certain fierceness of aspect to the man. His temper was high and combative, and he was quick to imagine slights to his importance."

All the pictures we get of Longstreet emphasize the massiveness of the man, his powerful physical constitution, his enjoyment of the material things of life. His career as a soldier is pretty well known. His spiritual side has been little studied and remains to be analyzed.

James Longstreet, like many other Confederate soldiers,

really died on April 9, 1865. They all lived, of course, in a way, as the Greeks pictured the dead as living in Tartarus, but for all great things the lives of most of them were over. It is pathetic to think of them: Davis, president of an insurance company that failed; Beauregard and Early, officials of a lottery; R. H. Anderson and others half starving in petty offices. And so it goes, the dethroned heroes making some kind of unheroic living in the drabbest circumstances. Only Lee refused to be anything but great; the ruin of the cause did not keep him from looking ahead, striving with all his might for accomplishment. The others—how they must have envied the honored graves of Jackson and Stuart!

Longstreet was not given to introspection, misgivings. It was fortunate for him that he could think of the mistakes of others, never of his own. He was destined to suffer much in the nearly forty years of life that remained to him after Appomattox. But there were no internal qualms, no searchings of the heart. He was the victim of persecution always, never the sufferer of punishment. And, perhaps, that was why he was able to live on until the machinery of his splendid body broke down.

Seldom has a man more completely illustrated his character than did Longstreet by his deeds and words—more by his deeds than by his words. Longstreet had given little thought to the art of war; he was no reader of books like Jackson, the student. His idea of the theory of war was, as it might be expressed, casually picked up. He had heard, perhaps, of Turenne; he could hardly have read of the great French strategist, for Longstreet did not read books. Anyway, he had heard that campaigns were to be won by strategy, by maneuvering rather than by battle. This was his obsession, particularly at Gettysburg, where he irked Lee in the great crisis by suggesting hardly possible evolutions.

Again, at the beginning of 1864, he was lecturing Lee on maneuvering rather than on fighting.

How he did lecture Lee, like a professor condescending to a schoolboy! He was always full of suggestions, running over with them. He was never at loss for the proper thing to do in any given situation. If his offerings sometimes seemed futile and amateurish to others, Lee never received them with anything but grave courtesy. There is something in that great humility of Lee that almost makes the tears come—the hero, bearing the burden of the cause on his shoulders, the strategist whose genius almost turned the tide and cheated fate—as he listens with full consideration to the egotistical Longstreet telling him the best course to follow under all circumstances.

That seems strange, but what is stranger is that Longstreet to a certain extent imposed that powerful and trenchant will of his on Lee; it must have been the influence that a self-confident, self-assertive man has over the humble soul, over the man who feels his limitations and his ignorance. Certainly, at the Second Manassas, he forced Jackson to fight for life and prevented the full carrying out of Confederate plans. Longstreet, in Maryland, made abortive Lee's attempt to hold the passes of South Mountain and thereby committed the Confederates to battle at Sharpsburg. There his influence with Lee failed for the time, for Lee, in the immediate presence of the enemy and with his fighting blood up, would not let Longstreet ease him out of Maryland without a fight. Longstreet handled his troops admirably at Fredericksburg, to fighting at which place Lee was committed by his government. Longstreet, by embarking on the Suffolk Campaign and by refusing to heed Lee's pleas to return in time, forced Lee and Jackson to take desperate risks at Chancellorsville. Longstreet at Gettysburg attempted to argue Lee out of fighting, and, failing in that, fought as a man foredoomed to defeat. Yet it is fair to him to say that the risks Lee took at Gettysburg justified him in remonstrating against the battle. Curiously enough, his conduct at Gettysburg is that for which he is most censured. After Gettysburg, Longstreet succeeded in projecting the plan to reinforce Bragg, thereby reducing Lee to impotence for the autumn of 1863. Longstreet, in Tennessee, won the battle of Chickamauga but was, in considerable degree, responsible for subsequent disasters by fanning the discontent with Bragg and by leaving Bragg at an unfortunate season and then failing to return to him in time, precisely as he had done at Suffolk. Longstreet, in the Wilderness, was a day late, thereby putting Lee in extreme peril; but he acted with such judgment and vigor when he at last arrived that Grant narrowly escaped a disastrous defeat. Wounded, Longstreet was long out of events; when he returned he did all that was possible under the circumstances but had no more opportunities of importance. Such is the story of James Longstreet.

For the psychologist the main interest in the War of Secession revolves about the relations of Lee and Longstreet. The question, in how far did Longstreet influence Lee and Confederate strategy, holds in itself the key to the failure of the South—at least one is fascinated by the implication that the answer to this question would tell the tale.

How far did Longstreet, with that overpowering will of his, influence events? We know that he did influence events but we are not certain as to the degree.

Freeman, in his great book, *R. E. Lee*, has made a revelation of the character of the Southern chieftain. It is a profound study of one of the leading figures in American history. He points out the effect of Longstreet's personality on Lee. It might be well to emphasize the reasons.

In the first place, Longstreet had a most powerful will, one felt by everybody with whom he came into contact. His will was so powerful that it might have made him the leading character of the drama if it had not been counterbalanced by certain deficiencies. Longstreet was not a student of war, not a deep thinker on the subject of war, and when placed in positions demanding knowledge and initiative he failed. Not having studied strategical combinations in all circumstances, he did not know what to do.

The point is that Lee had not studied the art of war deeply, either. What he would have become if he had bent his mind to the task of gaining a comprehensive knowledge of the subject, no one can say.

Lee possessed a powerful mind but he did not like to use it. Or, to put the matter more justly, he did not like to use it out of the line of routine duty. Given some engineering task, he performed it admirably, but he never took the trouble to gain any deep knowledge of strategy and logistics. His leisure was spent in the social converse he passionately loved, for Lee loved talk.

He was certainly no student. How, then, did he manage to show such marvelous strategic insight? How could he read the designs of opponents, whose plans were dark to men of the type of Longstreet and even of that of Jackson? The answer is a strange one but true—instinct. Lee had a hereditary instinct for war, handed down to him no doubt by many soldier ancestors, and that instinct was better than the painfully acquired knowledge of Jackson. One sees the two men as they spend their evenings: Jackson, toiling away with his campaigns of Napoleon and his maps; Lee, exchanging gossip with his wife and the neighbors. And yet

Lee was the greater man, the keener inspiration. What Lee had came down to him from generations of fighters; he did not need to study. And yet one wonders what might have happened if he had given himself absolutely to his profession, as Jackson did. Would he have been the greatest soldier of all time? Perhaps.

When war came in 1861 Lee was inexperienced. He had never handled large bodies of men in war and he had much to learn. Especially, he was ignorant of the use of a staff. That knowledge he never did acquire. While McClellan was laboriously hunting through his army for young officers who could draw maps, Lee was not thinking of maps. He never did have maps that were any good except those made by Jackson. Maps interested Jackson. Lee never learned to use staff officers so as to make systematic observations. He did not know how to employ staff officers in guiding and leading troops. And that was one reason, perhaps, why Longstreet so grievously underrated him. Longstreet handled his own staff better than Lee did his; one of his officers, Moxley Sorrel, was the best staff officer in the Confederate service.

Lee was lacking, to a certain extent, in force of expression. That is, he could not impose his will on others in the absolute degree in which masterful men do. Time and again his orders were disobeyed and he did nothing about it. Again, he let others, particularly Longstreet, argue with him after plans had been adopted; he let Longstreet change those plans by argument. He permitted Longstreet to shape events somewhat, because Longstreet was so masterful, so certain of himself, so self-expressive, while he, Lee, was uncertain of himself and always repressed. The result was that events were always turning out differently from Lee's intentions and hopes. Nothing happened that Longstreet did not, in a certain measure, influence. Whether or not that influence

was sufficient to turn the balance against the South is precisely the most fascinating problem in American history.
Probably it was not.

Longstreet was a soldier of great natural talent, but that
talent he never developed by thought. He had much insight
into war and, by flashes, was brilliant, but he had no real
grasp of strategy such as Jackson, for instance, had derived
from his study of Napoleon.

Longstreet was not a great strategist, hardly a competent
one. Both of his independent campaigns, at Suffolk and in
East Tennessee, were inglorious failures in which much time
and many men were lost without any compensating gain.
But in the field of tactics, Longstreet was much abler. He
handled his men well on the battlefield, especially on the
defensive. His troops were better managed than Jackson's
at Fredericksburg. He had a quick eye for the kaleidoscopic
changes of a battlefield and he was never better than amidst
the noise and confusion of a battle, because then his sluggish
nature became vividly alive. His tactics at Sharpsburg,
Chickamauga, and the Wilderness were all that could be
desired. On the other hand, at times he was negligent and
inefficient, handling his troops to poor advantage.

He had the perfect natural equipment for a soldier. In
the first place, he was enormously strong and healthy. He
was seldom sick, no matter how much exposed, and when
desperately wounded, he soon recovered. His nerves were
so wholly iron that he never seems to have known fear, even
in the midst of the most appalling scenes. In fact, Longstreet
was a man of great physical and moral courage. The latter
he showed in the sad years of his life, when he cut himself
off from all his former friends and associates. If there was
anything in heaven or earth that Longstreet feared it is not
known.

He had a marvelous influence over men. Lee and Jackson were both popular with the soldiers who served under them, but it is doubtful if either of them commanded the measure of devotion that was Longstreet's. Hood declared he would follow him in preference to all others. His troops had great confidence in him, affection for "Old Pete," as they called him. This feeling was not due wholly to his reputation and ability as a general. Partly it came from Longstreet's solicitude for his soldiers, for he gave much thought and care to the welfare of his men. It is possible that he would have been a better general if he had not been so solicitous, for Longstreet's preference for the defensive probably arose, in part, from his dislike of losing men, his shrinking from long lists of killed and wounded, which so little affected that superior soldier, Jackson. He had great sympathy for the private soldier.

Longstreet had many great qualities and he figured in some of the most moving scenes in American history, but he was not a great man. Did this failure arise from his own mental limitations? Probably not. Longstreet had a good mind, but he had something else that neutralized his mental qualities to a large degree. He was entirely too confident of his own knowledge, too reluctant to learn. He sat at no man's feet—not even Lee's.

In fact, his book *From Manassas to Appomattox* is filled almost from end to end with criticisms of Lee's generalship. In one place he states that, in his opinion, Lee was not a master of the art of war. One wonders who he thought was a master of the art. Possibly Joseph E. Johnston, whom Longstreet liked better than Lee and who he seems to have thought was, in some ways, a better general. Or Grant, whose success so dazzled Longstreet that he apparently considered him the first soldier of the war.

Longstreet's failure to attain the heights was due, in large part, to just that critical, carping mood of his. He was unable to recognize the great qualities of any military accomplishment—at least of Lee's and Jackson's—and he had a penetrating eye for weaknesses. And when there were no weaknesses, when accomplishment was well-nigh perfect, Longstreet could find flaws. In this vein is his criticism of Lee's operations at Chancellorsville, in which, in his longing to censure, he betrays himself into the most untenable opinions, such as the one that Lee should have remained behind his trenches at Fredericksburg after Hooker had crossed the Rappahannock and was practically across his communications. Thus does the critic reveal his own limitations.

Longstreet had many of the faculties that go to make a great commander, along with many weaknesses, and yet he was not a great commander, not much more really than an average corps general. That this was so indicates a cardinal fault, some sin strong enough to neutralize the virtues.

That sin in Longstreet was overweening ambition. He was beside himself with the thirst and hunger for fame and high position. The passion goaded him always, giving him no rest. Always he sought to push himself forward, not over-careful as to the means; ever he was discontented at being under Lee, thinking himself to be the better man, seeing in his mind's eye movements that would demonstrate the superiority. That itching of his colored all his generalship. It led him late in 1862 to advocate a detachment of troops from Lee's army for the West, since such a move might give him the chance to command an army elsewhere. It prevented his obeying orders in April, 1863, and returning home to Lee on the eve of the battle of Chancellorsville, because he was loath to give up that independent command, with which, when conferred on him, he could do nothing.

It goaded him to suggest the detachment of his corps to go to Tennessee in September, 1863; he thought the movement proper strategy, which it may or may not have been. That is beside the question. The main reason Longstreet advocated the move was that he desired to leave Lee and command his own army. It brought him to the madness of concurring in his separation from Bragg when Grant was coming to Chattanooga to take command of the Army of the Tennessee. If he left Bragg he would have that precious independent command, the chance to win glory for himself and not for a superior.

Longstreet's career is one of those that point a moral and adorn a tale. The moral is that a man will rise to greater heights by forgetting himself than by fending for himself. Jackson rose to supreme heights for the reason that he was always thinking of the cause, never of himself. *Contra,* Longstreet always thought first of himself, secondarily of the cause.

It was only when he forgot himself under some great compulsion, temporarily lost sight of his interest and his glory, that he attained the summit, and for all too brief a moment. Amidst the bellowing and flaming woods of Chickamauga, in the confusion and carnage of that awful field, Longstreet forgot himself, aroused for once out of his somber self-absorption. Then he acted vigorously, surely, splendidly, doing much to win a battle that, by all the rules, the Confederates had no right to expect to gain. Again, in the jungle of the Wilderness, in that hour of crisis, with the Union army recoiling from the blazing line of gray, Longstreet seized the opportunity with superb promptness and poise and almost won an advantage that might have been decisive. But those moments were rare. Mostly, he was absorbed in sullen calculations to find some way to advance himself, to gain the position of eminence he always thought was his due.

Longstreet never lived in the thin air of the great elevations like Lee and Jackson, those souls we cannot entirely understand because they were so lofty. Longstreet was of the earth earthy and, in his ambition and self-seeking, akin to the most of us and so understandable by the most of us. He was a man among men as Lee and Jackson were not. Lee's officers were never quite comfortable with him; they always stood in a certain dread of his gentle reproofs for some natural way of living. But Longstreet had the bad habits that endear men to men. He smoked and drank and cursed like usual men. One does not find a record of his ever having been drunk, but he liked whiskey and he is unhypocritical enough to acknowledge it. He does not say he took a drink because he was tired or sick but because he liked it, and we respect him for his manly candor.

Longstreet was rather silent and sullen, perhaps because he was somewhat deaf. He had a good many friends but was not very companionable. In early life he seems to have taken little interest in religion, in that respect being unlike Lee and Jackson, who were forever going to church or talking about religion or writing about it. Longstreet in his dispatches never ascribes victory to God, though he may have done so in his heart. At least there is no demonstration. Only once in his book does he indulge in cant and that is a magnificent piece of cant—so magnificent that one sees that to Longstreet cant did not come naturally. That one time he censures Lee for forgetting God in his self-confidence and Jackson for seeking (in Longstreet's opinion) newspaper notoriety—something, by the way, that Longstreet dearly loved.

He was not ashamed to admit his lack of piety in his years

of vigor. He tells the story of an old family servant, Daniel, who once long after the war visited him when in a town in Mississippi and who asked him,

" 'Marse Jim, do you belong to any church?'

" 'Oh, yes,' I said, 'I try to be a good Christian.'

"He laughed loud and long, and said:

" 'Something must have scared you mighty bad, to change you so from what you was when I had to care for you.' " [1]

In his last years he seems to have been something of a churchman, no doubt a sad and ominous change in the eyes of those who had known him in his rather godless prime.

Of Longstreet it may be said as much almost as of any man in history that, if he could have forgotten himself, he would have risen to great heights. But he never forgot himself—or very rarely—and so only a few times he reached the summits where the lofty dwell. He remains in history merely as the noted commander of a corps in Lee's army.

[1] *M. to A.*, p. 638.

CHAPTER XXI

LONGSTREET PAYS THE PIPER

In April, 1865, James Longstreet found himself out of employment for the first time since leaving the military college. If the Confederacy had succeeded he would have had a high place in the army of the new nation, but as it had perished the question of making a living presented itself. This was a terrible problem to the hundreds of higher officers of the Confederate army, thrown on a cold, cold world without money and without any other trade, in many cases, than the profession of arms.

Longstreet, however, was of a rather cheerful nature, even if he was not particularly conversational. Perhaps to him less than to any other member of the high command was the fall of the Confederacy an inexplicable tragedy, for Longstreet was little interested in politics and had no particular political principles. He had fought on the Southern side for the sole and sufficient reason that he was a Southerner. If he had been Northern-born, he would have fought just as ardently on the Northern side.

He was, too, of a nature that believes in success. He seems to have had a subconscious idea that the North was right because it won the war. He thought that the South had had a good chance to win, a chance which was thrown away by the blunders of the Richmond administration and the errors of Lee. From the end of the war to the end of his, life he appears to have considered Grant the great general of the war, the supreme figure of the struggle. Since the war was over and its secession issue forever settled, Longstreet believed in forgetting it as far as possible. He turned his face to the future, just as Lee did, but with a very different perspective.

For some time Longstreet must have been in a quandary as to ways and means. He was a soldier, nothing else. He was not adapted to law, knowing nothing about it and being somewhat deaf. Medicine was likewise out of his ken. It would have been ridiculous for him to go to teaching as so many Confederate officers did; one cannot visualize Longstreet as a professor in a boys' academy or a girls' seminary. Preaching, to which many Confederates turned in the hour of need, was likewise entirely out of Longstreet's alley. What was there left? Farming and business. He might have done well at farming; perhaps he made the mistake of his life in not tilling the soil as an occupation. But farming in the South in 1865, with hosts of idle and impudent Negroes standing around and believing that emancipation meant release from the curse of Adam, must have seemed a desperate affair. Longstreet decided on business.

How well he did in business it is a little difficult to say. In January, 1866, after receiving pardon from the United States government, he went into business in New Orleans with William, Miller, and Edward Owen, brothers, as a cotton broker. He says he speedily found "fair prosperity." However, before the year 1866 was out he accepted a position as president of an insurance company with a salary of $5,000, besides continuing in the cotton business.

So far he had done well. What became of his insurance company later does not appear; no doubt, it failed like the one with which Jefferson Davis was connected. At all events, Longstreet did not long go on with it.

He attributes his subsequent disasters to speaking his mind

on the subject of politics. Speaking one's mind on politics is always a ticklish business, but speaking one's mind on politics in the South in the hectic year 1867 was sometimes a matter of life and death.

The state of Louisiana in the grip of the Reconstruction, with a colored majority in the electorate, was in a desperate condition, and the people of New Orleans were in no frame of mind for dispassionate discussions of the rights of man. They could not bring themselves to acquiesce in the colossal folly of Congress in putting the Negro race in power in the Far South. When Longstreet was called on, with other Confederate generals, to give his opinion, he was so unwise as to counsel submission. In a letter of June 3, 1867, he wrote:

"It is fair to assume that the strongest laws are those established by the sword. The ideas that divided political parties before the war—upon the rights of the States—were thoroughly discussed by our wisest statesmen, and eventually appealed to the arbitrament of the sword. The decision was in favor of the North, so that her construction becomes the law, and should be so accepted."

In other words, Longstreet was willing to be reconstructed while the great majority of the white citizens of Louisiana were bitterly opposed to it. And that was to lead to the tragedy of his life. The point is that he appears to have been perfectly sincere.

Longstreet's mental processes were rather simple, as in the case of so many soldiers. He did not in the least realize that a war does not end with the termination of hostilities. The War between the States continued until 1898, and was only ended by the Spanish-American War. The World War is still being vigorously waged. Longstreet as one of the leading figures of the War of Secession, as a member of the Southern high command, could not go over to the North,

even in a degree, without being considered as a traitor to
the cause, which was all the dearer to the Southern people
for being lost. Such considerations were beyond his mental
horizon.

The letter to the newspaper ruined Longstreet. He says:
"The day after the announcement old comrades passed me
on the streets without speaking. Business began to grow dull.
General Hood (the only one of my old comrades who occa-
sionally visited me) thought that he could save the insurance business, and in a few weeks I found myself at
leisure." [1]

For the next year and a half Longstreet must have had a
struggle with poverty. Then his necessities were relieved,
but in such way as to damn him deeper. In 1869, President
Grant, with whom Longstreet had been intimate in early
years and who seems always to have cherished a friendly
feeling for him, gave him the place of surveyor of customs
in New Orleans. Longstreet held this place from 1869 to
1873, and a terrible place it was.

It carried with it, or in Longstreet's opinion it carried with
it, the necessity of becoming a Republican—"Black Republican," as the name was shudderingly repeated in the homes
of New Orleans. To the people of the South, Longstreet
seemed a deserter, a kind of traitor. The pathetic thing is
that he could not understand this state of mind at all, did
not recognize the fact that the holding of a high command
in the Confederate army imposed any post-bellum obliga-
tions on him. He never understood this to the day of his
death.

As a result of holding federal office in New Orleans,
Longstreet was brought into politics in a most appalling
period. The misery of Louisiana reached its peak in 1873,

[1] *M. to A.*, p. 637.

when the desperate citizens of New Orleans made a determined effort to get rid of the horrible Reconstruction government that cursed the state. It was hardly worth while to hold elections in Louisiana, since they were always given to the faction in power by the returning board, no matter what the returns might be.

In 1873 there were rival state governments in Louisiana, that of John McEnery, fusion candidate elected in 1872, and that of William Pitt Kellogg, Radical Republican, who refused to concede defeat. New Orleans was policed by the Negroes in an organization known as the Metropolitan Police, commanded by one A. S. Badger, under whom was Longstreet as a sort of second in command. These Negro policemen lorded it over New Orleans, making themselves intensely obnoxious to the Caucasians. The latter organized the White League in April, 1874.

The crisis came on September 14, 1874. Davidson B. Penn, in McEnery's absence, assumed the governorship and appointed F. N. Ogden commander of the state forces. This put the latter at the head of a body of armed men determined to end the iniquitous Kellogg government. One of the fiercest street fights in American history took place on that day in New Orleans, in which sixteen members of the White League were killed and forty-five wounded, and eleven of the Metropolitan Police were killed and sixty wounded. Longstreet was on the scene at the time, though it is probable that he did not have much of a hand in the riot. His presence on the side of an armed Negro force engaged in a bloody conflict with white men completed his ruin in the eyes of the Southern people. He was never forgiven for this.

Longstreet was supervisor of internal revenue, 1878; a postmaster, 1879; minister to Turkey, 1880; later United

States marshal; and he held other federal offices, especially that of railroad commissioner. He seems to have amassed a fair competency, but he paid for it the price of ostracism. Also his military reputation, the pride of his life, was bitterly assailed; he found himself blamed for the loss of the battle of Gettysburg and the failure of the Southern cause. And this, naturally, pierced his soul; he suffered agonies and engaged in the bitterest controversies over it.

General W. N. Pendleton began the controversy by charging that Longstreet disobeyed orders in not making his attack on July 2 at dawn as ordered by Lee. Longstreet easily proved that he had received no such order, but the debate was only beginning; it filled the pages of the *Southern Historical Society Papers* for several years.

Longstreet himself gave three versions of the battle of Gettysburg. The first was first published in a Philadelphia newspaper in 1877 and was afterwards included in a volume known as *The Annals of the War*. His second story, written in 1884 and first published in *The Century Magazine*, was afterwards reprinted in *Battles and Leaders of the Civil War*. His last account, written in 1895, is to be found in *From Manassas to Appomattox*. The three stories vary so much in detail that, as Dr. Freeman has pointed out, they cannot be reconciled.[2]

Longstreet's chief adversary was Jubal A. Early, for whom he cherished the most intense dislike. Early, who regarded Longstreet as a turncoat, returned the sentiment cordially. Others joined in against Longstreet, notably John B. Gordon, who was led by the prevailing feeling to say bitter things. Longstreet, striving to defend his military reputation, made statements about Lee that he must have regretted afterward, things such as men say when their hearts are

---

2 Freeman, *op. cit.*, III, 74 n.

bursting. He did not injure Lee; unhappily, he still further prejudiced the Southern people against him.

However, Longstreet still had friends and admirers. He never altogether lost the sympathy of many of the officers and men of the First Corps, even when he was most unpopular. As the years passed and the Reconstruction receded into the distance, the resentment felt against the noted Confederate general softened. It never entirely died away and still lingers in the legend that Longstreet lost Gettysburg, but it became mixed with admiration for his other deeds and with a sentiment of respect for the massive old man, with the long white side whiskers, declining into weakness from his once heroic strength.

Longstreet first found that the feeling in regard to him had changed in the Confederate Reunion in Richmond in 1896, when he was loudly cheered all along the line of march. The same thing occurred at the Atlanta Reunion in 1898. People were forgetting their animosities and remembering that, after all, Longstreet was the last survivor of the Confederate high command. The others had gone long before.

He became religious in his declining years. In early life he was an Episcopalian, but in New Orleans, in the stress of the Reconstruction, he found himself to be intensely disliked by the members of his church. Consolation for this came in his union with the Roman Catholic Church, which he joined under the ministrations of the noted Confederate poet, Father Ryan. He remained a consistent member of the fold until the end.

The old soldier had a pleasant family life in his last years. His first wife died many years before himself, and he married in old age (1897) Helen Dortsch, who seems to have cared for him tenderly and who survived him. An ardent

partisan of her husband's, Mrs. Longstreet published in
1905 *Lee and Longstreet at High Tide*, a curious jumble of
biographical matter and arguments in defense of his military fame.

Longstreet's final years were like those of most men who
linger too long on this transitory stage, the world. The
wound in his throat continued to give him pain and he lost
the sight of an eye. However, he bore his sufferings manfully, seemingly more concerned with the attacks on him as
a general than with his physical afflictions. In spite of his
handicaps he remained active nearly to the end, undertaking
in his last years a trip to Mexico in which he went over the
battlefields of his youth. He died at Gainesville, Georgia,
January 2, 1904, and was buried in that place. Some Confederate organizations declined to send flowers to the funeral.

INDEX

INDEX

Blackwater River, Longstreet's line, 160, 163; Suffolk campaign, 166
Bonham, M. S., location at Bull Run, 14; action at Bull Run, 21
Boonsboro, Md., Hill and Longstreet at, 118; mentioned, 115, 120
Bradford, Gamaliel, comment on Longstreet, 3
Bragg, Maj.-Gen. Braxton, commissioned as major-general, 25; reputation as commander, 173; uncertainty before Chickamauga, 223; Battle of Chickamauga, 223-238; against Rosecrans, 151, 172, 214, 215; plans for Johnston, 289, 292; blame for Johnston, 296; wire to Johnston, 286; adherent of Davis, 267; removal of rebellious subordinates by Davis, 246; made head of staff, Richmond, 271; demoralized as commander, 216, 217, 222, 242; disaffection of army, 249, 250; subordinates distrustful, 221; round robin of rebellious officers, 243; in Georgia, 269; obstacle to Lee's plans, 289, 290; letter from Hood about Johnston, 292, 293; arrival of Longstreet, 227; Longstreet and Hill sent in aid of, 220, 221; advice of Longstreet asked, 240; conference with Longstreet and others, 250, 251; conference with Longstreet, 254-256, 258-260; on Lookout Mountain with Longstreet, 248; opposition to Longstreet, 241, 293, 294; Longstreet rebellious, 247; disaffection fanned by Longstreet, 362; in Longstreet's plans, 164; Longstreet's departure from, 251; ruined by Longstreet's departure, 252; letter to McLaws explaining removal, 277; letter, 285
Branch, L. O., on Chickahominy, 64, 65
Brandy Station, camp of Lee and Jackson, 96; cavalry action, 175
Brannan, Gen., position at Chickamauga, 224
Breckinridge, John C., at Chickamauga, 231, 232; conference with

Bragg and Longstreet, 250, 251; message from Lee about Five Forks, 333; mentioned, 241
Bristoe Station, campaign mentioned, 247; trains captured, 98; mentioned, 100
Brown, Gov. Joseph, opposition to Davis, 157; state army, 154
Brown's Ferry, 248
Buckner, Maj.-Gen. S. B., to join Bragg, 226; Battle of Chickamauga, 223, 228, 235; advice to Davis about Bragg, 244; removal from Bragg's army, 246; Longstreet's efforts to exchange for Field, 291; mentioned, 241
Buel, C. C., book quoted, 80, 119, 121, 126, 186; book cited, 35, 41, 99, 117, 197
Bull Run. See Manassas, First Battle
Bull's Gap, Longstreet in camp, 285
Burke's Junction, Ord's route, 344
Burkeville, 323; Ord's route, 345
Burnside, Maj.-Gen. A. E., with troops from N. C., 89; dissatisfaction of division generals, 140; overawed by lieutenants, 149; at Fort Monroe, 159; put in command, 139; plans against Lee, 142; courier from Grant captured, 269; crossing at Fredericksburg, 143; plans at Fredericksburg, 144; ruined by Fredericksburg, 150; sent to Kentucky, 163; at Knoxville, 251; resignation of commission, 153; succeeded by Foster, 273
Butler, Gen. Benjamin, demonstration, 34
Butterfield, at Marye's Heights, 148

Campbell Courthouse, in final phase, 353
Carlisle, Penna., 179
Casey, Silas, in peninsular campaign, 34, 35; at Seven Pines, 43, 47
Cashtown, Southern army in, 180, 181; mentioned, 212
Casualties, Brown's Ferry, 248; Chickamauga, unprecedented, 238;